Neoliberalism Revisited

NEOLIBERALISM REVISITED

Economic Restructuring and Mexico's Political Future

edited by

GERARDO OTERO

Simon Fraser University

WestviewPress

A Division of HarperCollins*Publishers*

Portions of Chapters 1 and 12 by Gerardo Otero are from Gerardo Otero, "Mexico's Political Future(s) in a Globalizing Economy," *Canadian Review of Sociology and Anthropology*, 32(3):316–339. Reprinted with permission of the Canadian Sociology and Anthropology Association.

Portions of Chapter 9 by Lynn Stephen are taken from Lynn Stephen, "Women in Mexico's Popular Movements: Survival Strategies Against Ecological and Economic Impoverishment," *Latin American Perspectives*, 19(1):73–96, copyright ©1992 by Sage Publications. Reprinted by permission of Sage Publications, Inc.

Published in 1996 in the United States of America by Westview Press, Inc., 5500 Central Avenue, Boulder, Colorado 80301-2877, and in the United Kingdom by Westview Press, 12 Hid's Copse Road, Cumnor Hill, Oxford OX2 9JJ.

A CIP catalog record of this book is available from the Library of Congress.
Hardcover: ISBN 0-8133-2440-8
Paperback: ISBN 0-8133-2441-6

The paper used in this publication meets the requirements of the American National Standard for Permanence of Paper for Printed Library Materials Z39.48-1984.

10   9   8   7   6   5   4   3   2   1

Contents

Tables

Acknowledgments

The International Development Research Centre (IDRC) in Ottawa and the Inter-American Organization for Higher Education (IOHE) in Quebec provided me with funds toward the editorial costs to produce this book. I am indebted to Paz Buttedahl of IDRC and Penny Houghton of IOHE for their kind support.

The chapters in this book have been revised numerous times, and for this I thank my diligent and patient contributors. In the process several people have offered generous and constructive criticism, particularly Leigh Pyne, University of Wisconsin at Madison, and James Wessman, State University of New York at Albany, who acted as external reviewers of previous versions. Barbara Ellington of Westview Press has used her keenly trained eyes and mind to make useful suggestions for revision. She has been very positive and supportive during this process. I greatly appreciate the critical readings of earlier versions of my introductory and concluding chapters by friends and colleagues, and I exonerate them from remaining limitations: Bill Canak, David Vern Carruthers, Humberto Cartón de Grammont, Marilyn Gates, Gary Gereffi, Gordon Laxer, Ron Newton, Ilán Semo, Peter Singelmann, Judith Teichman, and Francisco Valdés Ugalde.

Several people at Simon Fraser University helped me in many ways. I am particularly grateful to Annita Mahoney, who entered numerous revisions of the manuscript. Students who were my research assistants at various times also gave me valuable aid. In chronological order, I thank Dylan Von Gunten, Marcel Vanderslyus, Kerry Preibisch, Robyn Adamache, Steffanie Scott, Danielle Scott, and Brian Green. My wife, Paty, and our sons, Alex and Rodrigo, have provided me with love and emotional support, and I thus dedicate my efforts to them.

Gerardo Otero

1

Neoliberal Reform and Politics in Mexico: An Overview

Gerardo Otero

Mexican government and civil society face enormous challenges brought about by neoliberal economic restructuring at a time when democratic political transition is simultaneously at the forefront of national and international agendas. After the 1982 debt crisis in Mexico and the introduction of neoliberal reforms, a critical dilemma came to the fore: Would the process of economic restructuring involve a more equitable redistribution of income and thus be compatible with a sustained transition to political democracy? Although it is hard to establish that income redistribution is a prerequisite for a democratic transition, it should be clear that without such economic reform an authoritarian and repressive political regime would be more likely to emerge than a democracy.[1] Part of the dilemma for the Mexican regime is that it confronts nearly insurmountable international pressures to continue neoliberal economic restructuring. These pressures have been exacerbated as the world economy becomes increasingly global.

The implementation of the North American Free Trade Agreement (NAFTA) on 1 January 1994, linking Mexico with Canada and the United States, further strengthens neoliberal ideology and the forces of global capitalism in Mexico. Canada and the United States are both members of the so-called Group of 7, or G7, which also includes Japan, Germany, Italy, France, and the United Kingdom. Leaders of G7 countries meet annually to try to coordinate their macroeconomic policies in order to promote economic growth and stability on a world scale. Furthermore, in March 1994 Mexico accepted membership in the Organization for Economic Development and Cooperation (OECD). OECD is a broader group of twenty-five wealthy nations that promotes economic liberalism. Mexico's new status in the world economy has put it on the same playing field with its northern neighbors.

Yet this does not mean necessarily that the players are of similar stature. The fact that Mexico's social and political organizations are more diverse than those of Canada and the United States was highlighted dramatically by the Indian peasant rebellion in Chiapas led by the Ejército Zapatista de Liberación Nacional (EZLN, or Zapatista National Liberation Army), which erupted on the same day that NAFTA was inaugurated. Although EZLN was a formerly unknown group, its military action put Mexico in the spotlight. It seemed contradictory that in a country that was gaining First World status there could exist the kind of gross social and political inequalities that could bring about a violent uprising.

The Chiapas uprising was but the most radical expression of discontent with growing inequality and lack of democracy in Mexico. The society and polity could not adjust quickly enough to match the swift pace with which radical changes were being introduced in the Mexican economy to get it in tune with the global economy and implement North American economic integration. Such changes involved a major shift in the development model that Mexico had followed since the 1930s of high protectionism, government deficits, and state intervention. In the 1980s the Mexican state moved to introduce a series of measures to open the economy to foreign trade and investment and to reduce the role of the state in the economy substantially by massive privatizations of state firms, cutting most subsidies, and giving a free rein to market forces. Organizations in civil society, however, have increased their demand for social and political changes, which have come at a much slower pace.

This book brings together scholars from anthropology, economics, history, political science, and sociology, all of whom take interdisciplinary approaches in their investigation of the social and political implications of neoliberalism in Mexico. Some chapters emphasize the economic or the political realities of various dimensions of Mexican society, but all connect those realities to wider social processes at the national and international levels.

The notion of "desirable development" is implicit in all of the following chapters. In this concept economic growth is associated not only with equitable distribution of resources in order to raise the standards of living for the majority of the population but also with political democracy (Kincaid and Portes, 1994). Although electoral democracy is a precondition of such a political system, citizen participation in decisionmaking is also an essential ingredient if society is to go beyond an "elite democracy." Finally, in this scheme development also includes the environmental sustainability of economic growth patterns (Lipietz, 1992).

In this chapter, however, I will take a slightly different tack and propose a "bottom-up linkages" approach that focuses on both global and national-level processes and their interrelationships. My argument is that a bottom-up linkages approach can help us both in better understanding the process of development and in providing clues as to how the process may be affected by social action and public policy toward a more desirable form of development. Although the new political economy of the world-system perspective has evolved in the direction of linking global and national processes (McMichael and Myhre, 1990), the emphasis is still disproportionately placed on global issues, as in dependency and earlier world-system theory. The latter, in particular, tends to be fixated on the question of global economic surplus and how it is allocated among zones or countries in the world system, with abstract "capital" as the main determinant of most processes. A more integrative research strategy, with a shorter-term view and more concrete variables, is necessary (Gereffi and Korzeniewicz, 1994). This chapter offers new approaches to understanding the interaction of national and global processes as they affect the political outcomes at the level of the nation-state. Because Mexico is becoming increasingly integrated into the North American economy, it is critical to specify the ways in which integration influences political processes and to identify the social forces that might steer developments in a more desirable direction.

With regard to the global processes, the dominant actors continue to be national governments and suprastate organizations such as the International Monetary Fund (IMF), the World Bank, and the General Agreement on Tariffs and Trade (now renamed the World Trade Organization). But there are increasing signs of emerging cross-border coalitions that could be seeds of a transnational civil society. This was seen most clearly in the struggle against passage of NAFTA, in which labor and environmental groups from the three countries involved joined forces (Thorup, 1991; Carrillo, 1992; Fox, 1992; Carr, Chapter 11, this volume; del Castillo V., Chapter 2, this volume).[2]

Country-level factors, on the other hand, account for the distinctiveness of world capitalism's imprint on the nation-state. The key question is how national specificities and regional diversity work together to affect the ways in which global processes become internalized in societies. In Mexico's case, country-level analysis is made more complex by its vast regional heterogeneity, not only geographical and physical but social, economic, and political as well (Van Young, 1992). To state it simply, one could say that capitalism has developed most intensely and economic integration with North America is most advanced in the western and northern regions, along with the metropolitan area of Mexico City. In contrast, the south and southeast, the most densely populated regions and with the largest proportions of indigenous peoples, still suffer from archaic social and power structures; poverty is pervasive. The fact that neoliberal reform has exacerbated social polarization is in part the result of its sweeping application with little regard for regional diversity.

In order to conceptualize possible futures for Mexico's development, we must understand the overhaul of the world economy in the past three decades and the way in which the United States is confronting its own economic challenges. This analysis is necessary because U.S. choices set limits on the economic and political alternatives available to the Mexican people.

Crisis of Postwar Capitalism in the United States

The central proposition of this section is that current trends toward the globalization of world capitalism result from the crisis of "Fordism" in the United
States. The Fordist regime of capital accumulation, which was strengthened
after World War II, was predicated primarily on the U.S. internal market and
on a balance between mass production and mass consumption (Aglietta, 1979).

Fordism involved a period of stable economic growth and capital accumulation that lasted until the late 1960s in the United States. It was an economic
arrangement that depended on a productivity pact among the welfare state, the
corporate sector, and labor unions in which production and productivity expanded to the benefit of all parties involved (with the exclusion of most
women and minorities). With a balance between expanding mass production
and mass consumption, unemployment remained below 4 percent, and the
gross national product (GNP) grew at a rate of 5 percent annually.

By the late 1960s a crisis of profitability emerged in consequence of an excess
of productive capacity in relation to effective demand. One related aspect was
the slowing rate of growth in the productivity of U.S. workers relative to that
in other advanced capitalist countries, namely Japan and Germany. In response
to this crisis, many U.S. transnational corporations began to relocate their production sites either to the southern, less unionized parts of the United States or
to Third World countries. The goal was lower wage costs in order to restore
profitability.

Such reorganization of production required a free trade regime worldwide,
as companies were scattering several parts of their production processes in various countries, even though their main market target continued to be the
United States. The U.S. government thus began actively to promote the tearing
down of barriers to international trade in order to facilitate the globalization of
the economy. This movement, however, also broke the "virtuous circle" between mass production and mass consumption that had been forged in the
U.S. national economy during Fordist development. The rupture soon included
a significant attack on the welfare state, on unionism, and generally on the income gains that had been attained by U.S. workers. The unionized labor force,
for instance, declined from 30 percent in 1970 to 12 percent in 1994 (*The Economist*, 1994a:20). Such attacks were waged most purposefully by the administrations of Ronald Reagan and George Bush.[3]

Alternatives to U.S. Capitalism

Now that East-West confrontation has subsided, new cleavages in world capitalism—differences among its U.S., German, and Japanese variants—have
emerged. The ways in which crises of profitability and competitiveness are

addressed in each of these variants will have a great influence on the rest of the world. Based on trends of the past two decades, the different approaches in dealing with economic performance may be outlined as follows.

Whereas the U.S. state has followed basically a neoliberal policy with regard to industry and international trade, other advanced capitalist countries, most notably Japan, have established purposeful industrial policies and selective protection of key industries (Kenney and Florida, 1994; Kuttner, 1991). In Japan, the legendary MITI (Ministry of International Trade and Industry) has played a critical role in determining the sectors of the economy in which Japanese private companies would concentrate their energies. Such long-term planning and partnership between state and private firms have resulted in enormous payoffs in terms of economic growth, market leadership, technological innovation, job security for workers, and, not least, redistributive social policies. In contrast, many U.S. firms have been downsizing or closing up shop, subject as they have been to the laissez-faire rules of free market policies. These have caused massive layoffs, which severely disrupt the lives of individuals, families, and entire communities, as well as shifts in consumption and savings patterns at the macroeconomic level. Such an approach to economic restructuring has not helped improve the adversarial industrial relations that came to prevail in the United States over the past two decades (Kochan et al., 1989).

A second major contrast between U.S. and other versions of advanced capitalism, namely those in the northern parts of western Europe, appears in the welfare state policies providing for a social economy. Even Germany, which is one of the most conservative of European states, spends almost half of its GNP through the public sector. It offers its citizens generous support and universal social security (Kuttner, 1991:7). Policies geared toward a social economy do require higher taxation and higher rates of unionization of the workforce as well as greater regulation, but in the end they pay off in the form of more equitable societies.

Third, at the level of the firm, U.S.-based companies have pursued primarily a defensive strategy based on lowering wage costs, whereas German and Japanese firms have pursued an offensive strategy based on technological innovation, increased product quality, and new forms of labor relations. The defensive strategy adopted by the United States has proved to be incompatible with increasing standards of living for large sectors of the population; the opposite is the case for the German and Japanese models. That is, U.S. society has become less equitable in the past two decades, with a larger number of people under the poverty line and declining real wages for unskilled workers.

According to Michael Albert, a French entrepreneur, these differences in capitalisms have resulted in more equitable societies in Europe and Japan, with significantly greater proportions of their populations included in the "middle class" (defined in terms of income). In the United States only 50 percent of its population has an income equal to or higher than the national mean; the figures are 75 percent in Germany, 80 percent in Sweden and Switzerland, and 89 percent in Japan (cited in Castañeda, 1993:519 fn.).

Because the trend toward continentalization of the Americas seems to be irreversible, an important question is to what extent this process will impose the U.S. variant of capitalism on the hemisphere, or whether Mexico and Latin America might be able to pursue a different combination of capitalist traits. If a margin of choice exists, its direction will depend on two critical factors: (1) the extent and character of political transition in Mexico and (2) the extent to which a North American civil society begins to take shape with countervailing organizations from Canada, Mexico, and the United States pushing toward a more equitable form of development and a democratic politics for all North America. Most of this book focuses on the first factor and its economic determinants, but Chapters 11 and 12 address the second. Before I introduce Mexico's political transition, I give a brief account of the country's economic change from import-substitution industrialization to neoliberalism.

From Import Substitution to Neoliberalism

Like most Latin American countries, Mexico is still trying to find its way out of the economic crisis that erupted in the early 1980s when the import-substitution industrialization (ISI) strategy fell apart. The crisis was manifested in a mounting foreign debt that had been contracted as a result of the incapacity of the national economy to keep financing its industrialization process along the path of the ISI strategy. The central features of this strategy included protectionist measures against foreign trade, state subsidies of local production and consumption based on increasing government deficits, the formation of a parastate sector in the economy, and direct foreign investment by transnational corporations. Initially, agriculture played a crucial role in financing the importation of capital goods necessary for industrialization (de Janvry, 1987; Barkin and Suárez 1982; Gates, 1993; Sanderson, 1986; Whiteford and Ferguson, 1991). But once the antiagricultural bias in the ISI model took its toll, foreign indebtedness became the new engine to keep industrialization going. Finally, the discovery of large oil reserves in Mexico allowed the government to contemplate deeper foreign debt. Unfortunately, the oil boom that followed (1978–1981) was too short-lived. But it was long enough for the Mexican economy to become "petrolized"—in 1982, 75 percent of foreign exchange was accounted for by oil revenues.

From 1970 to the early 1980s, Mexico's foreign debt climbed from $3.2 billion to over $100 billion. Mexico was the first Latin American nation to declare a moratorium on payments to service its foreign debt in July 1982. The announcement sent shock waves throughout the world's financial system and manifested a deeper crisis in the ISI strategy itself. Mexico had exhausted agriculture, oil revenues, and indebtedness as means to subsidize a protected industrialization process, and new avenues for economic growth had to be found. Once the crisis became evident, most Latin American governments were pressured by the international financial agencies to adopt neoliberal policies to restructure their countries' economies away from ISI so that they could continue servicing the foreign debt (Canak, 1989; Meller, 1991; Petras and Brill, 1986). Many governments had themselves become convinced that the prior economic strategy was not working well.

The most salient features of the neoliberal economic model that is now being pursued are the reverse of those of its ISI predecessor: an export-oriented industrialization (EOI) strategy promoted by opening the economy to foreign trade, massive withdrawal of public subsidies in most sectors of the economy, privatization of formerly state-owned enterprises, and, not least, a policy of controlling wages downward to attract new waves of foreign investment (partly to offset the effects of previously flown domestic capital). Opening of the economy was initially formalized when Mexico joined the General Agreement on Tariffs and Trade (GATT) in 1986. Before then, as of 1982, all imports required previous government permits and were subject to a top tariff of 100 percent and an average tariff of 27 percent. By 1990 no permits were required for most imports, and the highest tariff was 16 percent with an average of 11 percent (Urías Brambila, 1993:1099). Furthermore, a new law regulating foreign investment was enacted in 1989 to permit 100 percent foreign ownership in most sectors of the economy. Because attracting new foreign capital is a central piece of the neoliberal reform, further deregulation of direct foreign investment was enacted in December 1993 in preparation for the start of NAFTA.

This major overhaul in the economic model has involved extensive social and political changes in Mexican society. Poverty and inequality have grown to such extents that a popular phrase that has come to capture the nature of the 1980s is "the lost decade." On top of this, neoliberalism has created a crisis of its own that exploded 19 December 1994 after the Mexican government was forced to devalue the peso in view of extremely low reserves of foreign exchange. The latter plummeted from about $29 billion in February to less than $7 billion in December 1994 (*The Economist*, 1995a). The U.S. dollar went up from about 3.35 pesos to over 6 pesos in just a few days.

This crisis was precipitated by several factors directly related to the neoliberal reform and the way it has been managed. First is the paradoxical import-intensity of the newly introduced export-led industrialization. Many of the parts and components of Mexico's manufactured exports had to be imported. Because liberalization of imports was so great, the rate of growth of consumer imports was much higher than the corresponding rates for capital and intermediary goods. Imports increased by 238 percent from 1985 to 1992, whereas exports grew only 73 percent in the same period (de Palma, 1995). The ensuing yearly trade deficits could only grow, and for January–November 1994 the deficit stood at $16.85 billion, up 37 percent from the same period in 1993 (*Wall Street Journal*, 1995).

Growing trade deficits led to the second factor triggering the 1995 crisis: They were financed primarily with the influx of portfolio capital into the Mexican stock market, a very volatile form of financing. Of new capital flows into Mexico, six times as much went into speculation in the stock market as direct productive investment in the early 1990s (Bradsher, 1995). Speculative capital could leave the country as soon as it entered. With Mexico's political crisis and an increase in U.S. interest rates, foreign investors felt safer by taking their dollars out of Mexico.

A third factor in the crisis was the government's growing short-term debt, most of it in the hands of foreigners. Of a total debt of about $160 billion, $30 billion was to come due in 1995. Of the latter, more than $16 billion was in the form of dollar-denominated treasury bills, or *tesobonos* (which the government chose to define as internal, not foreign, debt). Furthermore, the Central Bank increased money supply by 20 percent during the electoral year of 1994, a move that built inflationary pressures (*The Economist*, 1995b). All of these factors combined turned into an explosive economic mix leading to the downfall of the peso.

Given the gravity of the crisis and because NAFTA was already in place, the Clinton administration was eager to rescue the peso and thus protect U.S. investors in Mexico. It convinced the International Monetary Fund and other international banks to come up with a rescue package of almost $50 billion to back up Mexico's debt and thus stabilize the peso. The Clinton administration itself committed discretionary funds of $20 billion toward the endeavor but attached costly strings for Mexico's sovereignty. Washington gained veto power over most of Mexico's economic decisions for the ensuing decade (Sanger, 1995).[4]

On the political front, President Ernesto Zedillo approached the crisis by hardening his stance with the EZLN. After repeated overtures to restart the negotiation process that had broken down in June 1994, Zedillo's administration launched an all-out offensive on 9 February 1995 by declaring that the Zapatista leaders were criminals. He ordered the Attorney General's Office, backed by 60,000 soldiers of the federal army already in Chiapas, to implement arrest warrants. Simultaneously, at least sixty people were arrested in various parts of Mexico on charges of being part of the EZLN. Zedillo aides admitted that the crackdown was designed both to calm international investors and to improve Zedillo's image to make him into a "tough guy" (Golden, 1995a). After enormous pressure from Mexican civil society and international groups, however, the Zedillo administration offered an amnesty law and new negotiations to the Zapatistas (Golden, 1995b).[5]

Furthermore, the 1995 crisis was heightened economically with tight austerity measures of a neoliberal kind, as happened after 1982: more cuts in government spending, an increase in the value-added tax from 10 percent to 15 percent, bank interest rates of 60 percent, increases in the prices of goods provided by state firms such as electricity and gasoline of 35 percent to 50 percent, and more privatizations of state companies, including formerly sacrosanct sections of the secondary petrochemical industry (which used to be the exclusive domain of state-owned Pemex). All this was done while maintaining a cap on wage increases at an average of 12 percent. Inflationary pressures were high, and the government expected an economic contraction of at least 2 percent in 1995 (*The Economist,* 1995b). The actual contraction was more than 7 percent.

These trends clearly point in the direction of further social and economic polarization and political hardening. Minimum wages had already lost over 50 percent in real purchasing power during the previous decade, and more losses are now expected.⁶ Over one million workers lost their jobs during the first half of 1995. It thus remains to be seen whether economic restructuring in a neoliberal direction can be compatible with a democratic political transition and social reform in Mexico. A more likely outcome is that the crisis provoked by neoliberalism will ultimately push the political system toward greater hardening or toward such bankruptcy that democratization becomes inevitable. One argument that can be made to support the latter possibility may be taken from Seymour Martin Lipset: "If autocracies fail economically, and/or socially, their lack of legitimacy will facilitate a breakdown" (1994:9). Furthermore, Lipset added, the "breakdown of such a system may require a major catalytic event, a defeat in war, a drastic economic decline, or a break in the unity of the government elite" (1994:9). In contemporary Mexico, economic decline is undeniable, the EZLN has achieved widespread sympathy in Mexican society and internationally, and increasing divisions in the ruling political group led to the 1994 assassinations of two major political figures: Luis Donaldo Colosio, the presidential candidate of the Partido Revolucionario Institucional (PRI), on 23 March, and political reformer José Francisco Ruiz Massieu, the PRI's secretary general, on 28 September. Raúl Salinas, older brother of the former president, is now in jail accused of masterminding Ruiz Massieu's murder, and former President Carlos Salinas himself is in virtual exile in Montreal amid allegations that he was involved in a cover-up of Colosio's assassination.

The only precedent of such an extreme rupture between an outgoing president and his successor in contemporary Mexican history dates to 1934–1935, when President Lázaro Cárdenas forced his predecessor, Plutarco Elías Calles, into exile. It was during and after the Cárdenas administration that most of the current institutions of the Mexican state were built. Could it be that today's economic and political crisis will lead to the configuration of a new political regime in Mexico? In order to understand the significance of the political crisis, a fuller description of Mexico's political system is necessary.

The Mexican State and the Political System

For Latin America, the paradoxical decade of the 1980s was not only a lost decade in economic terms; it was also a time when most countries began to experience a return or a transition to democratic political regimes. Mexico, however, was an exception to this regional trend, in that its political system continues to be dominated by one-party rule established in 1929. But some significant change has been forced upon the state by civil society. The student movement of 1968 constituted the first major political earthquake, but the state responded with brutal repression in the massacre of 2 October. Agrarian and urban social movements that emerged in the 1970s constituted further pressure for the government to introduce limited political liberalization. Initially this took the form of opening electoral spaces to formerly forbidden political parties, left and right (Foweraker and Craig, 1990). The government's limitations in dealing with the ravages of the 1985 earthquake in Mexico City led to further demands from civil society for political opening. As a result, political participation has significantly increased in Mexico, but the central pieces of an authoritarian regime remain alive and well. This section provides an overview of the main features of Mexico's political system, all of which will have to experience a fundamental change if a significant transition to democracy is to emerge.

There have been several schools interpreting the Mexican political system, which has been variously characterized as a one-party "democracy," a perfect dictatorship, a benign dictatorship, and an authoritarian or a semiauthoritarian regime. The first classification came from optimistic political scientists or sociologists studying Mexico in the 1950s. After the 1960s, however, most observers came to agree that the Mexican regime was indeed authoritarian (Hellman, 1983; Levi and Szekely, 1987; Molinar Horcasitas, 1993). The concern in this section is not to address this general aspect of the Mexican system but its specificities. What makes the Mexican regime different from other authoritarian systems, and what has accounted for its durability and stability for the better part of over six decades?

Before the political reform of 1978, left-wing political parties were barred from legal participation in elections, although several political parties were formally part of the "opposition." These parties were the Partido Acción Nacional (PAN), the Partido Auténtico de la Revolución Mexicana (PARM), and the Partido Popular Socialista (PPS). Yet they actually functioned as virtual appendages of the ruling PRI. Even PAN, which has been clearly on the right of the PRI, often negotiated seats in Congress in exchange for accepting the loss of a gubernatorial post or several municipalities to the PRI.

In recent years, however, there has been an increasing militancy of the rank and file of PAN in defiance of its leadership's pragmatism. For instance, in 1994 the national leadership was quick to accept defeat in the municipal elections of Monterrey, the second industrial city, but the local Panistas took over city hall. After three weeks the government was forced to recount the votes, and it turned out that PAN had actually won. Its candidate was then allowed to take office. Given that PAN's economic platform is hardly distinguishable from the current PRI's neoliberalism, though, PAN has in effect been a cogovernment party since 1989.

The Partido de la Revolución Democrática (PRD) emerged out of the fusion of several leftist political parties and a splinter from the PRI that had formed a coalition to propose Cuahutemoc Cárdenas for president in 1988. Soon after these elections, the coalition became a formal political party and fielded the same presidential candidate in 1994. Considered a center-left party, the PRD includes former communists as well as Trotskyists and former PRI nationalists. This party was the most critical of the 1988 and 1994 presidential elections, arguing that there was massive electoral fraud. In the aftermath of the 1988 elections, its policy was to not negotiate with the government, and it kept this intransigent position throughout the Salinas administration (1988–1994), but recently the PRD has been more willing to negotiate with the state.

Given that political parties other than the PRI have not played a crucial role in the Mexican system, aside from legitimating the electoral process, one must look elsewhere for its distinctiveness. Six features of the Mexican political system distinguish it from totalitarian or other authoritarian systems. The first and most pervasive is the virtual fusion of the state and the ruling party, a linkage that resembles the case in the former Soviet Union except that in Mexico there have also existed opposition political parties. Such fusion makes it extremely difficult for any opposition political formation to have a significant chance of winning in the electoral game. If one adds to the picture the notoriously corrupt structures of the state, it becomes clear that the PRI has a large number of financial and political advantages over its competitors. Even symbolic elements, such as the fact that the PRI's emblem has the same colors as the national flag (green, white, and red), contribute to the image of the PRI and the state as a single entity. For example, the major social expenditures of the government are usually accompanied with colorful propaganda that evokes the PRI's emblem, just as it might evoke the national banner. Therefore, increased government social expenditures during electoral periods clearly favor the PRI's candidates.

The issue of PRI-state fusion has become so prominent in Mexican politics that Ernesto Zedillo promised to do away with it when he was the PRI's presidential candidate in 1994. Although there was some rhetoric to this effect in the first few weeks into his administration, which started 1 December 1994, by early 1995 it was clear that the PRI-state alliance was in business as usual.

Related to this linkage is statism, the second feature of Mexico's political system: The state plays a paramount role in the economy and society. "State institutions have generally had far more prestige, resources, and influence than private, independent, or non-profit organizations have had" (Camp, 1993:12). The most significant example of the state's power in Mexico is the fact that it was able to follow the ISI strategy and policies for decades and then to shift the course of economic development completely to EOI along neoliberal lines in less than a decade. Perhaps because the most prominent members of the political class have also become an important component of the economic ruling class, such an apparently contradictory outcome has materialized: that a strong state decides to introduce neoliberalism, which involves assigning to the private sector and the market, rather than to the state, a privileged role. A central attribute of Mexico's statism is that the PRI's major boss is the head of the state, the president.

"Presidentialism" is thus the third feature of Mexico's authoritarianism: The institution of the presidency in particular and of the executive branch in general far outweighs the legislative and judicial branches of government, a feature that makes them and any other autonomous authority ineffectual. Lorenzo Meyer (1993) has gone so far as to suggest that presidentialism is the greatest single obstacle to democratization in Mexico. This is so because the institution of the presidency is so powerful that it is beyond the law (Garrido, 1989). During the administration of Carlos Salinas de Gortari (1988–1994), for instance, many of his decisions were "not . . . legally implemented, whether they involved criminal matters, such as arresting a drug dealer, or were purely political, like his removals of state governors" (Camp, 1993:177).

Fourth, organized interest groups in society relate to the state through "corporatist structures." These provide for the mechanisms by which interest groups channel their demands and the state responds. However, as in all corporatist relations found in Latin America and elsewhere, the state always has the upper hand: It acknowledges or not, promotes or hinders, the formation of corporatist organizations. Thus, although corporatism does entail reciprocity and a certain capacity for subordinate groups to shape policy, it places social organizations in a dependent relationship with the state. As Camp put it, corporatism "facilitates the state's ability to manipulate various groups in the state's own interest" (1993:12). The result is that corporatist relations grant the state an enormous capacity for co-optation of autonomous or challenging groups. Jonathan Fox and Luis Hernández aptly phrased the dilemma for grassroots movements trying to change the political system while remaining autonomous in the following question: "What kinds of new styles and institutions make it possible to change the system even more than one is changed by it?" (Fox and Hernández, 1992:193).

Corporatism has been based on the mass organizations affiliated to the ruling PRI since the foundation of its ancestor, the Partido Nacional Revolucionario (PNR), in 1929. The three key organizations from the outset have been the CTM (Confederación de Trabajadores de México, or Confederation of Mexican Workers); the CNC (Confederación Nacional Campesina, or National

Peasant Confederation); and the CNOP (Confederación Nacional de Organizaciones Populares, or National Confederation of Popular Organizations), whose name was changed in 1993 to FNOC (Federación Nacional de Organizaciones y Ciudadanos, or National Federation of Organizations and Citizens). These three organizations have played a critical role of social control and have secured an electorate for the PRI. One widely criticized practice is that members of these organizations are collectively affiliated to the PRI and are expected to vote for it during elections. If they do not, they may confront severe penalties from the bosses of their organizations. Among the spoils that leaders of these organizations get for their loyalty to the PRI are government positions and seats in Congress representing the party. There are other organizations in the labor movement that belong to the PRI, even though not to the CTM, such as CROC (Revolutionary Confederation of Workers and Peasants) and CROM (Regional Confederation of Mexican Workers). Similarly, other peasant organizations loyal to the PRI include CAM (Mexican Agrarianist Council) and CCI (Independent Peasant Council).

Fifth, although authoritarian, the Mexican regime does allow greater access to decisionmaking processes than do totalitarian systems. Furthermore, decisionmakers change frequently, with the presidency limited to a six-year term. In the words of a reporter for the conservative British weekly *The Economist*, "Mexico is a benign dictatorship which is moderated, as in any system of benign absolutism, by the regular assassination of its dictator. The system has survived only because no individual is allowed to hold power for more than six years" (Grimond, 1993:22).

Finally, the sixth feature of the Mexican regime is that there is a self-selecting political and technocratic bureaucracy in the state's power structure. An enormous problem for democracy created by this self-designated group is that it lacks constituent responsibilities. Because of this, Mexican politicians "have generally been pragmatic, doing whatever is necessary to remain in office rather than pursuing a committed, ideological platform" (Camp, 1993:13). Among the factions within the PRI-state, the "dinosaurs" are the most resistant to political opening and modernization. Between dinosaurs and technocrats are the so-called políticos, or experienced career politicians who have held various offices by popular election or within the corporatist mass organizations. Technocrats are those politicians who move up the ladder merely through positions in government. Although Carlos Salinas was usually identified as a technocrat and initially viewed as a political modernizer, his administration clearly favored economic restructuring over democratic transition.

If anything, what the PRI-state technocrats have been trying to do since the first electoral reforms of 1978 is "modernize" the authoritarian political system to stay in control. Emerging forces in civil society, however, want to democratize the political system (Bartra, 1993). It is between these two pressures that current political developments are evolving in Mexico. Thus, the main question is whether the system will be reformed from above or transformed from below. Some political reforms have begun to take place merely under the impetus of economic reform. Yet the main implication of such reforms is to modernize authoritarianism rather than transform it.

For instance, the old corporatist structures of the CNC and the CTM have been among the most important casualties of economic restructuring in the past decade (Bartra, 1993; Méndez and Quiroz, 1992; Middlebrook, 1991). If it is true that these organizations continue to be crucial to the PRI and the state, they are a far cry from what they were in the 1940–1980 period (Teichman, Chapter 8, this volume). The role they used to play in social control and recruitment of voters for the PRI was broken down during the 1980s. This was demonstrated in the greatly contested (and severely tainted) presidential elections of 1988, when the PRI officially won with merely a plurality of the total votes cast, 48.7 percent (Cornelius and Craig, 1991:1), and then again in 1994 (Semo, Chapter 6, this volume).

The Salinas administration pursued aggressively a strategy of moving the terrain of politics from a form of corporatism based on mass social organizations, such as the CNC and the CTM, to a new form of political relationship based on PRONASOL (Programa Nacional de Solidaridad, or National Solidarity Program). PRONASOL has involved the creation of multiple organizations that make up a new electoral constituency for the PRI (Dresser, 1991; Cornelius et al., 1994).

PRONASOL was announced by Carlos Salinas de Gortari on 1 December 1988, the first day he assumed the presidency of Mexico. Along with a generally neoliberal economic program, PRONASOL was supposed to address the most severe problems of poverty in cities and the countryside with increased social spending approved and administered by the executive branch of government. Recent statistics show the gravity of the problem: There are 41.3 million Mexicans living in poverty, which represents about 50 percent of total population (81.2 million). Furthermore, 17.3 million of the total live in extreme poverty (Peón Escalante, 1992:14).

The key change instrumented through PRONASOL is that the relationship between the state and the corporatist organizations, which used to mediate the relationship of the state with the masses, is now being supplanted by direct links between the state and a large number of "solidarity committees" in civil society. The new approach bypasses the old corporatist structures and links the president directly with thousands of local-level organizations. In fact, PRONASOL has been credited with having organized or acknowledged a total of 150,000 solidarity committees by early 1994, all of which receive funds directly from the executive branch for rural or urban projects (such as production, road construction, education, running water, health, and electricity). The condition for people to get such funds is that they be organized and constitute a solidarity committee. This is why so many organizations have proliferated in the past few years. This neocorporatist structure has several implications for the state and electoral politics.

First, the state is able to control the financing of new or preexisting organized groups while securing their loyalty to the PRI-state:

> Solidarity's funds tend to be spent where the PRI feels most threatened electorally. For example, $135 M was spent [in 1992] in the state of Michoacán, where the PRD is strong. This amounts to 6% of Solidarity's estimated annual budget of 6.8 billion pesos ($2.2 billion). On the whole, spending tends to be concentrated in the countryside, where it is easier to garner political support in return for material benefits (and admittedly, because that is where most of the poor live) (Wood, 1993:12).

Second, since most PRONASOL financing is channeled through municipal presidencies, the old power structures are being marginalized from the new system, or at least they are left with diminished and more conditioned power. In Roger Bartra's view, PRONASOL buys political intermediaries that make up and organize the system's "popular base" (1993:114).

Thus, in organizing the new solidarity committees, the Salinas administration attained two goals: On the one hand, it competed with the traditional left-wing organizations for their social constituency; on the other, it evaded traditional corporatist structures while generating parallel structures, independent from traditional PRI organizations, such as CNC (Moguel, 1992a:44). In fact, Salinas tried to accomplish not only an economic restructuring of Mexico but also a political modernization that involved his own party (Harvey, 1993). Such "modernization of authoritarianism" (Cornelius et al., 1989a), however, might not necessarily signify a greater representation for subordinate groups and classes but merely a greater electoral efficiency for the PRI-state. This is an important difference between old corporatism and neocorporatism: Under the former, social constituencies were in a better position to press for their demands.

PRONASOL's electoral efficacy was demonstrated in the presidential and congressional elections of 21 August 1994, regarded by the international press as the cleanest in Mexican history. Although Alianza Cívica (made up of more than 400 nongovernmental organizations) discovered irregularities in the electoral process in as many as 78 percent of the balloting locations, it is unlikely that such irregularities would have altered fundamentally the global results. However, the margin of victory would not have been as comfortable as official results claim: PRI, over 48 percent of valid ballots cast; PAN, 27; PRD, 17 (with the rest divided among six other parties). Still, the candidate of the right-of-center PAN, Diego Fernández, declared that the triumph on 21 August was not the PRI's; it was a triumph of PRONASOL, PROCAMPO (a program of rural subsidies introduced just prior to the elections, in November 1993), and Televisa (the national, near-monopoly, progovernment private television network).

Indeed, PRONASOL's performance has led some observers, including a reporter for *The Economist*, to comment on the mismatch between political and economic reforms under the Salinas administration, in that it in fact strengthened presidentialism: "The result is to perpetuate the Mexican tradition of rule by a strong man. This is the reverse of modernization. The contrast with the reforms in the economic sphere are obvious and troubling, and sow the seeds for future conflict" (Wood, 1993:12). These words proved to be prophetic. Less than a year after they were published, the Indian-peasant rebellion in Chiapas broke out and as of late 1995 remained unresolved by the Mexican state (Harvey, Chapter 10, this volume; Otero et al., forthcoming 1996).

Furthermore, the 1994 electoral results continue to reflect the formidable problems for a democratic transition in Mexico, among them that (1) the state pours its enormous resources to the electoral advantage of the PRI; (2) the outgoing president, as chief of the PRI, handpicks his successor; and (3) the corporatist organizations of the PRI exert multiple pressures for their members to attend PRI rallies and ultimately to vote for its candidates. All of this has been documented profusely before and after the elections in the Mexican dailies of national circulation (e.g., *La Jornada, El Financiero, Reforma*) and in various political weeklies (e.g., *Proceso*). Thus, if we take to heart the suggestion of *The Economist* reporter, we would conclude that neoliberal economic reform must involve political "modernization," which he apparently equates with "democracy." The question is whether indeed neoliberalism must be accompanied by some form of political democracy.

Organization of This Book

As the title of this book implies, there are a number of alternative development paths that Mexico can take. The chapters that follow are devoted to an exploration of Mexico's economic and political restructuring in the midst of the country's economic integration into North America. Some of the most crucial social actors of the past several decades are studied in detail: peasants, workers, women, Indian peasants, the Catholic Church, the domestic private sector, transnational corporations, and the state itself. What roles have they played during the age of import-substitution industrialization? Who are the key social and political actors, both domestic and international, involved in promoting or resisting the new economic model? What is the role of the state? In what ways is the state itself being restructured to accommodate to the neoliberal reform? Is it possible to combine radical economic liberalization with political democratization? The goal of this book is not to formulate predictions of the future but to identify the key political and economic variables that are likely to shape possible future scenarios.

Given the preeminence of trade and NAFTA in the current context of the North American region, Chapter 2 by Gustavo del Castillo V. addresses the process by which NAFTA came to be proposed and passed in the three countries involved as part of the struggle for neoliberalism and enhancing the globalization of the economy. Del Castillo traces this process through the recent history of U.S.-Canadian and U.S.-Mexican relations and other multilateral agreements such as GATT. His chapter sets the international context for the rest of the book, which focuses on the national dynamics of Mexico and their linkages to global processes.

The next three chapters deal with critical sectors of the Mexican economy and its social agents, each of which has been deeply affected by neoliberalism. In Chapter 3, Marilyn Gates addresses economic restructuring in agriculture. This is not by chance, because agriculture is the least capitalistically developed sector of the Mexican economy. About half of total agricultural and forestry land surface is in the hands of *ejidatarios,* the beneficiaries of agrarian reform after the 1917 Constitution and one of the main results of the 1910–1920 revolution. Most producers in the *ejido,* or the so-called social sector of agriculture, produce at subsistence or infrasubsistence levels and are not able to sustain their families solely through agriculture (CEPAL, 1982). Therefore, the recent neoliberal reforms have hit hardest in this sector.

Gates discusses at length the issues relating to economic restructuring in agriculture prompted by the first debt crisis of the early 1980s. Given the symbolic as well as real importance of the peasantry to Mexican society, she proposes that the changes implemented by the Salinas administration will have far-reaching implications for Mexican agriculture. Rather than representing a "refunctionalization" of the peasantry into the agricultural sector, neoliberal policies are seen to be a logical extension of policies oriented toward global imperatives, despite their populist overtones.

As for the manufacturing sector, Enrique Dussel Peters offers in Chapter 4 an analysis of the structural transformation brought about by neoliberal reform. Although the main intent of the reform was to reorient industry toward exports, Dussel Peters documents how this process has actually resulted in an industry overly dependent on the intensive importation of parts and equipment. He first provides the macroeconomic context in which liberalization was undertaken and then examines which industries benefited and which were hurt by this process. He presents a detailed breakdown of industries, looking at their interconnections, their level of concentration, their trade balances, and the extent to which transnational corporations dominate in a given industry. For instance, the car industry has been hailed as a major new manufacturing exporter, but analysis of its relationship with the auto parts supplier industry shows that in terms of value the latter's imports have more than offset car exports. It is precisely this paradox of the extent to which the manufacturing sector has relied on imports that explains the increasing trade deficits that accrued to Mexico from 1990 to 1994 and led to the crisis of 1995. Dussel Peters argues that an adequate industrial policy could have avoided this pitfall but was conspicuously absent during the neoliberal reform.

Gary Gereffi directs his attention in Chapter 5 to a sector of the Mexican economy in which transnational corporations have also had an overwhelming presence: the maquiladora industry. By contrasting what he calls the "old" and the "new" maquiladoras, Gereffi highlights some of the key issues concerning the contribution of the maquiladora sector toward Mexico's development objectives. He builds several possible scenarios and argues that the feasibility for each to materialize depends largely on state policy and not only on corporate strategies. Furthermore, Gereffi argues that (1) the stereotype of the maquiladora plant as an unsophisticated, labor-intensive operation is no longer accurate; (2) Mexico's maquiladora program is different in many ways from the East Asian newly industrializing countries (NICs) to which it is often compared; and (3) NAFTA will have important implications for future developments of the maquiladora sector.

Whereas the chapters outlined thus far raise important questions as to the viability of the Mexican economy and the role of state policies, subsequent chapters concentrate on the political system. Ilán Semo begins in Chapter 6 by addressing the question of Mexico's democratic transition. Comparing Mexico's political process to its counterparts in East European and South American countries, Semo proposes that democratic transition processes may follow one of two alternative routes: a democracy of elites or a societal democracy. In the first one a concentrated state is constituted, with a marked separation between political society and civil society. In contrast, a diffuse state emerges in societal democracy, whose representational forms are based not only on universal voting by the citizenry but also on the representation of a multiplicity of particular social interests.

To the extent that general competitive elections are still not achieved in Mexico, Semo argues that this country finds itself in a pretransition phase, with a predominant trend toward the emergence of a democracy of elites. However, in the very process of transition, the democratization process could change its nature. Semo then explores the crisis of legitimacy of the PRI and the routes to change that have been put in place as well as their possible results.

Whereas peasants and workers have been mostly spectators and victims of the restructuring process, the leading organizations of the private sector have been at the forefront in shaping the new economic model of Mexico. Francisco Valdés Ugalde in Chapter 7 focuses on the role of the private sector in the transformation of the Mexican polity and ultimately the Mexican state. He explores the institutional preconditions and consequences of this transformation. Valdés Ugalde addresses the specific ways in which private interests can dominate and transform Mexican society, not only in the political sphere according to partisan interests but also in the areas of culture, ideology, public opinion, economics, and all of social life, as represented by the institutions of civil society. One question he raises is the extent to which the new Mexican state will be able to continue to maintain political stability while reconciling the contradictory tendencies of economic reform and social justice.

Another central aspect of Mexico's development model and political system has been the corporatist relationship between industrial workers and the state. In Chapter 8, Judith Teichman explores the transformations of the structures that have defined this relationship. She argues that Mexico's current economic restructuring program has been a crucial influence in accelerating the breakdown of Mexico's corporatist and clientelist political arrangements. Because these arrangements have ensured the dominance of the PRI since the formation of the PNR in 1929, the erosion of the corporatist state can be expected to produce a decline in support for the PRI or a gradual move toward some form of neocorporatism to replace the old system. This shift could lead to a situation of increased political instability if economic activity remains stagnant even under liberalization, which would raise the specter of repression and continued instability. It is more likely, however, that the gradual transformation of the state apparatus and a redefining of state-labor relations will take on some form of neocorporatism.

It is now well established that popular social movements have had a crucial role in the introduction of significant changes in the political system in Mexico (Cornelius and Craig, 1991; Foweraker and Craig, 1990) and elsewhere in Latin America (Eckstein, 1989; Escobar and Alvarez, 1992). One of the contradictions of social movements is that the leadership continues to be largely male, while the constituency is predominantly female. This is particularly true of urban social movements and increasingly so in rural-based movements. One reason women are so involved in social movements is that neoliberalism has had a tremendously negative effect on the possibilities for reproduction of household units, and women have been traditionally responsible for this in male-dominated societies.

Lynn Stephen in Chapter 9 explores the role of women's grassroots political activism in the 1990s by focusing on the cases of social movements in Mexico City and the state of Chiapas. She argues that women and children have felt the consequences of neoliberal reform in the harshest manner. With the dwindling of material resources and social services to maintain their families, women began to alter their consumption patterns and their strategies to engage in paid and unpaid work. In most cases the crisis was "privatized," which resulted in increased domestic workloads for women. This burden has been a triggering factor to increase the participation of women in social movements. Analysts of women's movements have established a dichotomy between feminist or strategically oriented movements that challenge women's gender oppression and feminine or practical movements that focus on subsistence issues along traditional gender roles, but Stephen argues that Mexican women are making this dichotomy irrelevant. They are bridging this division by demanding democratization of organizations and of the home, the right to basic survival and health, respect for women's physical integrity and control over their bodies and reproduction, and political representation. Therefore, women's presence in social movements has become a critical factor in cultural demands for increased democratization in all spheres of social life, including the formal political system.

While Stephen deals with both urban- and rural-based social movements, Neil Harvey in Chapter 10 addresses the social conditions that account for the emergence of an armed, rural-based uprising led by the EZLN in the southeastern state of Chiapas. This state began to experience the consequences of neoliberalism in the countryside early on. The Mexican government abandoned many of the protective policies it once had for the most disadvantaged groups in society. Coffee, for example, is one of the main crops in Chiapas, grown by both large and small producers. The most recent crisis began in 1989, after coffee prices collapsed in the world market and after the government had already dismantled IMECAFE, the state agency that used to regulate coffee prices and was in charge of commercialization (Downing, 1988). Even though Chiapas received the largest expenditures by PRONASOL of any state, that was not enough to contain the uprising by the EZLN. Major changes in agricultural policy have resulted from the passage of NAFTA in order to adjust agriculture to the internationalization of Mexico's economy. Harvey explores the extent to which these reforms accentuated existing inequalities in Chiapas, why the government was unable to defuse land conflicts through the policy of *concertación* (consensus building), and what the EZLN rebellion might imply for the future of campesino and indigenous movements in Mexico.

Despite the relative vigor of social movements in Mexico in the past two decades, they face a new and daunting problem: The nation-state is losing ground as the central terrain of political struggle. NAFTA and the process of continentalization of the economy involve many policy decisions that transcend the level of the nation-state. One response from social movements has been the attempt to build cross-border coalitions for action and solidarity.

Barry Carr in Chapter 11 thus addresses some key strands in labor internationalism in which North American and Mexican workers have been involved in this century. He notes that the vitality of these forms of internationalism depended on several factors. Ideology, however, was central: the various "isms" or grand narratives such as anarchism, Marxism, and communism. Anarchism ended with the Spanish Civil War; the latter two have been severely weakened by the collapse of the Cold War. Carr then identifies the new forms of transborder internationalisms that have emerged during the 1990s, partly in response to the challenges posed by free trade and NAFTA. By looking at specific examples of current transborder networking and future prospects, Carr also identifies the key factors that both promote and constrain international labor solidarity and cooperation.

In the concluding chapter I briefly recapitulate the issues discussed in this volume and propose research agendas for understanding and shaping Mexico's future. Changes are taking place so rapidly that multiple efforts are needed for our understanding to keep abreast of the reality facing Mexicans and therefore North Americans. Finally, several alternative future scenarios, based on the analyses of all the contributors to this book, are constructed. They include various combinations of economic and political variables. The viability of each scenario is discussed in terms of the principal global processes and national-level forces that combine in its configuration. It is hoped that identification here of the major parameters and social forces that will shape the future will contribute to enhancing the prospects of the more humane economic and political alternatives.

Notes

1. Citing Francisco Weffort, Seymour Martin Lipset argued that "although 'the political equality of citizens . . . is possible in societies marked by a high degree of [economic] inequality,' the contradiction between political and economic inequality 'opens the field for tensions, institutional distortions, instability, and recurrent violence . . . [and may prevent] the consolidation of democracy'" (1994:2, bracketed phrases added by Lipset).

2. The obstacles are large but not insurmountable: "The histories of social movements in each country are too different to have produced clear-cut trinational counterparts. Business and government elites, in contrast, have known each other well all along, so social organizations have had to begin to catch up quickly. With NAFTA, domestic politics became foreign policy and foreign policy became domestic politics" (Fox, 1992:4).

3. By two measures of inequality, the high and low income quintiles and the Gini coefficient, U.S. society has become sharply polarized in the past two decades, whereas inequality had narrowed from 1929 to 1969. "In 1992 the top 20% of American households received 11 times as much income as the bottom 20%, up from a multiple of 7.5 in 1969. The effect was to give the richest 20% of households a 45% share of the country's total net income in 1992, a post-war high, and the poorest 20% of households a mere 4% share. The Gini coefficient rose from 0.35 to 0.40 over the same period" (*The Economist*, 1994a:19). In the Gini coefficient, the more a country approaches 0.0, the greater its income distribution; the more it approaches 1.0, the greater its inequality. A further measure of polarization in the United States is that "the poorest 10% of American families suffered an 11% drop in real income between 1973 and 1992; the richest 10% enjoyed an 18% increase in real income" (*The Economist*, 1994a:20).

4. Among specific conditions of the rescue package are that the Mexican government is to limit credit expansion to 10 billion pesos for all of 1995; limit money growth to below the rate of inflation; maintain "substantially positive" interest rates; raise $12 billion to $14 billion through privatizations and concession operations over the next three years; increase transparency of the Central Bank with timely published statistics; and make some information available on the Internet (Carrington and Torres, 1995).

5. Ironically, the first cabinet position ever to be occupied by a member of an opposition party in modern Mexico is that of the head of the Attorney General's Office (Procuraduría General de la República, PGR). Antonio Lozano is a member of the right-of-center PAN, and he has been used to do Zedillo's unpleasant job of launching a war against the Chiapas Mayan people, for 20,000 Indians were displaced from their communities in their attempt to escape from the kind of human rights abuses they were subjected to in the initial phase of the uprising in 1994. In some communities identified as Zapatista, the army destroyed several houses and all kitchen and agricultural utensils, thus eliminating the material conditions for subsistence of the peasant households.

6. As *Business Week* reporters observed about the 1995 crisis, it "is apt to lead to major restructuring of the Mexican economy. Struggling small banks will be snapped by larger domestic or foreign institutions. Likewise, many of the big export-oriented manufacturers will wind up in a position to acquire smaller competitors. That risks strengthening the near-monopoly positions of some companies and skewing wealth distribution even further" (Smith et al., 1995:62).

Bibliography

Aglietta, Michel. 1979. *A Theory of Capitalist Regulation: The U.S. Experience*. London: New Left Books.

Barkin, David and Blanca Suárez. 1982. *El fin de la autosuficiencia alimentaria*. Mexico City: Nueva Imagen.

Bartra, Roger. 1993. *Oficio mexicano*. Mexico: Grijalbo.

Bradsher, Keith. 1995. "The World Shifted, But Not Mexico." *New York Times*. 2 January.

Camp, Roderic Ai. 1993. *Politics in Mexico*. New York and Oxford: Oxford University Press.

Canak, William, ed. 1989. *Lost Promises: Debt, Austerity, and Development in Latin America*. Boulder and London: Westview.

Carrillo, Teresa. 1992. "Building Transnational Networks Among Grassroots Organizations: Recent Experiences from Mexican Women's Movements." Paper presented at the XII Meetings of the Latin American Studies Association. Los Angeles, Calif., September.

Carrington, Tim, and Craig Torres. 1995. "U.S. Unveils Rescue for Mexico." *Wall Street Journal*. 22 February.

Castañeda, Jorge G. 1993. *La utopía desarmada: Intrigas, dilemas y promesa de la izquierda en América Latina*. Mexico: Joaquín Mortis.

CEPAL (Comisión Económica para América Latina, written by Alejandro Schejtman). 1982. *Economía campesina y agricultura empresarial: Tipología de productores en México*. Mexico: Siglo XXI Editores.

Cornelius, Wayne A., and Ann L. Craig. 1991. *The Mexican Political System in Transition*. La Jolla, Calif.: Center for U.S.-Mexican Studies, University of California, San Diego.

Cornelius, Wayne A., Ann L. Craig, and Jonathan Fox. 1994. *Transforming State-Society Relations in Mexico: The National Solidarity Strategy*. U.S.-Mexico Contemporary Perspectives Series, 6. San Diego: Center for U.S.-Mexican Studies, University of California, San Diego.

Cornelius, Wayne A., Judith Gentleman, and Peter H. Smith. 1989a. "Overview: The Dynamics of Political Change in Mexico." Pp. 1–54 in Cornelius et al., 1989b.

———. 1989b. *Mexico's Alternative Political Futures.* San Diego: Center for U.S.-Mexican Studies, University of California, San Diego.

de Janvry, Alain. 1987. "Latin American Agriculture from Import Substitution Industrialization to Debt Crisis." Pp. 197–229 in W. Ladd Hollist and F. LaMond Tullis, eds., *Pursuing Food Security: Strategies and Obstacles in Africa, Asia, Latin America, and the Middle East.* Boulder and London: Lynne Rienner Publishers.

de Janvry, Alain, Elisabeth Sadoulet, and Linda Wilcox Young. 1989. "Land and Labour in Latin American Agriculture from the 1950s to the 1980s." *Journal of Peasant Studies,* 16(3): 369–424.

de Palma, Anthony. 1995. "Burden of Proof on Mexico's President Tonight." *New York Times.* 2 January.

Downing, Theodore E. 1988. "A Macro-Organizational Analysis of the Mexican Coffee Industry, 1888–1977." Pp. 175–193 in Philip Quarles van Ufford, Dirk Kruijt, and Theodore Downing, eds., *The Hidden Crisis in Development: Development Bureaucracies.* Tokyo and Amsterdam: United Nations University and Free University Press.

Dresser, Denise. 1991. *Neopopulist Solutions to Neoliberal Problems: Mexico's National Solidarity Program.* Current Issue Brief No. 3 San Diego: Center for U.S.-Mexican Studies, University of California, San Diego.

Eckstein, Susan. 1989. *Power and Popular Protest: Latin American Social Movements.* Berkeley: University of California Press.

Economist, The. 1994a. "Inequality." 5 November, pp. 19–21.

———. 1994b. "The Two-Door Policy on Trade." 1 October, pp. 29–30.

———. 1995a. "The Egg on Zedillo's Face." 7 January, p. 31.

———. 1995b. "Putting Mexico Together Again." 4 February, pp. 65–67.

Edwards, Sebastián. 1991. "Structural Adjustment Reforms and the External Debt Crisis in Latin America." Pp. 129–168 in Patricio Meller, ed., *The Latin American Development Debate: Neostructuralism, Neomonetarism, and Adjustment Processes.* Boulder: Westview.

Escobar, Arturo, and Sonia E. Alvarez, eds. 1992. *The Making of Social Movements in Latin America: Identity, Strategy, and Democracy.* Boulder: Westview Press.

Evans, Peter. 1979. *Dependent Development: The Alliance of Multinational, State, and Local Capital in Brazil.* Princeton: Princeton University Press.

Foweraker, Joe, and Ann L. Craig, eds. 1990. *Popular Movements and Political Change in Mexico.* Boulder and London: Lynne Rienner Publishers.

Fox, Jonathan. 1992. "Agriculture and the Politics of the North American Trade Debate." *LASA Forum,* 23(1):3–9.

Fox, Jonathan, and Luis Hernández. 1992. "Mexico's Difficult Democracy: Grassroots Movements, NGOs, and Local Government." *Alternatives,* 17(2):165–208.

Friedland, William. 1984. "Commodity Systems Analysis: An Approach to the Sociology of Agriculture." Pp. 221–235 in Harry K. Schwarzweller, ed., *Research in Rural Sociology and Development.* Greenwich, Conn.: JAI Press.

Garrido, Luis Javier. 1989. "The Crisis of *Presidencialismo.*" Pp. 391–416 in Cornelius et al., 1989b.

Gates, Marilyn. 1993. *In Default: Peasants, the Debt Crisis, and the Agricultural Challenge in Mexico.* Boulder: Westview Press.

Gereffi, Gary. 1994. "Rethinking Development Theory: Insights from East Asia and Latin America." Pp. 26–56 in Kincaid and Portes, 1994.

Gereffi, Gary, and Miguel Korzeniewicz, eds. 1994. *Commodity Chains and Global Capitalism.* Westport, Conn., and London: Praeger.

Golden, Tim. 1995a. "Behind Mexico's Hard Line, a Political Shift." *New York Times.* 12 February.

———. 1995b. "A Mexican Zigzag." *New York Times.* 18 February.

Grimond, John. 1993. "Under Construction: A Survey of Latin America." *The Economist,* 13 November.

Harvey, Neil. 1993. "The Difficult Transition: Neoliberalism and Neocorporatism in Mexico." Pp. 4–26 in Neil Harvey, ed., *Mexico: Dilemmas of Transition.* London and New York: The Institute of Latin American Studies, University of London, and British Academic Press.

Hellman, Judith Adler. 1983. *Mexico in Crisis.* 2d ed. New York: Holmes and Meir.

Kenney, Martin, and Richard Florida. 1994. *Beyond Mass Production: The Japanese System and Its Transfer to the U.S.* New York and Oxford: Oxford University Press.

Kincaid, A. Douglas, and Alejandro Portes, eds. 1994. *Comparative National Development: Society and Economy in the New Global Order.* Chapel Hill: University of North Carolina Press.

Kochan, Thomas A., Harry C. Katz, and Robert B. McKersie. 1989. *The Transformation of American Industrial Relations.* New York: Basic Books.

Kuttner, Robert. 1991. *The End of Laissez-faire: National Purpose and the Global Economy After the Cold War.* New York: Alfred Knopf.

Levi, Daniel C., and Gabriel Szekely. 1987. *Mexico: Paradoxes of Stability and Change.* 2nd ed. Boulder: Westview Press.

Lipietz, Alain. 1992. *Towards a New Economic Order: Postfordism, Ecology, and Democracy.* New York: Oxford University Press.

Lipset, Seymour Martin. 1994. "The Social Requisites of Democracy Revisited." *American Sociological Review,* 59(1):1–22.

McMichael, Philip, and David Myhre. 1990. "Global Regulation Versus the Nation-State: Agro-Food Systems and the New Politics of Capital." *Radical Review of Political Economy,* 22(1): 59–77.

Meller, Patricio. 1991. "IMF and World Bank Roles in the Latin American Foreign Debt Problem." Pp. 169–206 in Patricio Meller, ed., *The Latin American Development Debate: Neostructuralism, Neomonetarism, and Adjustment Processes.* Boulder: Westview.

Méndez, Luis, and José Othón Quiroz. 1992. "Respuesta obrera y acuerdos concertados." *El Cotidiano* (Mexico City), 8(49): 94–105.

Meyer, Lorenzo. 1993. "El presidencialismo: Del populismo al neoliberalismo." *Revista Mexicana de Sociología,* 55(2): 57–83.

Middlebrook, Kevin J., ed. 1991. *Unions, Workers, and the State in Mexico,* U.S.-Mexico Contemporary Perspectives Series, 2. San Diego: Center for U.S.-Mexican Studies, University of California, San Diego.

Moguel, Julio. 1992a. "Cinco críticas solidarias a un programa de gobierno." *El Cotidiano* (Mexico City), 8(49): 41–49.

———. 1992b. "Caminos del movimiento urbano popular en los ochenta." *El Cotidiano* (Mexico City), 8(50): 221–226.

Molinar Horcasitas, Juan. 1993. "Escuelas de interpretación del sistema político mexicano." *Revista Mexicana de Sociología*, 55(2): 3–56.

Otero, Gerardo, Steffanie Scott, and Christopher Balletto. Forthcoming 1996. "Neoliberalism and New Technologies in Mexico's Agriculture: Social Polarization, Environmental Damage, and the Chiapas Rebellion." In James Davis, Thomas Hirschl, and Michael Stack, eds., *The Cutting Edge: Readings in High Technology, Social Class, and Revolution.* London: Verso.

Peón Escalante, Fernando. 1992. "Solidaridad en el marco de la política social." *El Cotidiano* (Mexico City), 8(49):14–19.

Petras, James, and Howard Brill. 1986. "The International Monetary Fund, Austerity, and the State in Latin America." Pp. 21–46 in James Petras, ed., *Latin America: Bankers, Generals, and the Struggle for Social Justice.* Rowman and Littlefield Publishers.

Sanderson, Steven E.. 1986. *The Transformation of Mexican Agriculture: International Structure and the Politics of Rural Change.* Princeton: Princeton University Press.

Sanger, David E. 1995. "Peso Rescue Sets New Limits on Mexico." *New York Times.* 22 February.

Shaiken, Harly. 1990. *Mexico in the Global Economy: High Technology and Work Organization in Export Industries.* San Diego: Center for U.S.-Mexican Studies, University of California, San Diego.

Smith, Geri, Elisabeth Malkin, Dean Foust, and Stanley Reed. 1995. "Is It Tough Love—or a Savage Crackdown?" *Business Week,* 15 May, pp. 62–63.

Thorup, Cathryn. 1991. "The Politics of Free Trade and the Dynamics of Cross-Boarder Coalitions in the U.S.-Mexican Relations." *Columbia Journal of World Business,* 26(2): 12–26.

Urías Brambila, Homero. 1993. "La ofensiva comercial de la diplomacia mexicana." *Comercio Exterior* (Mexico City), 43(12):1099–1106.

Van Young, Eric, ed. 1992. *Mexico's Regions: Comparative History and Development.* La Jolla, Calif.: Center for U.S.-Mexican Studies, University of California, San Diego.

Wall Street Journal. 1995. "Mexico's GDP Grows 3.1%." 2 February.

Whiteford, Scott, and Anne E. Ferguson, eds. 1991. *Harvest of Want: Hunger and Food Security in Central America and Mexico.* Boulder, San Francisco, and Oxford: Westview.

Wood, Christopher. 1993. "Mexico Survey." *The Economist,* 13 February, pp. 1–22.

2

NAFTA and the Struggle for Neoliberalism: Mexico's Elusive Quest for First World Status

Gustavo del Castillo V.

The image of a modern, restructured Mexico—a Mexico built on a new economic doctrine far different from the path it has followed since the revolution of 1910—is as deceptive as it is unrealistic. Unrealistic applies because few policymakers have taken the time to understand the rhythms of change and the modifications needed to turn dreams into reality; deceptive because the transformations necessary must go beyond those found in the formal neoliberal economic model that thrusts market mechanisms to the center of the laissez-faire temple. Few in the public sector have found ways to explain to private-sector entrepreneurs the needed changes. Often what has passed for rationality, such as the privatization of state-owned firms, is little more than a justification for the further enhancement of a few plutocrats in Mexico.

The North American Free Trade Agreement (NAFTA) was but a cornerstone of these new quicksand foundations. The quicksand arose because economic rationality could not be achieved from one day to the next while placing new demands on productive sectors and national entrepreneurs by integrating the Mexican economy into globalism. The selling of NAFTA, along with its compelling vision of the future, was carried out in Mexico as if this agreement were an end in itself and not an instrument (a set of rules) to help achieve economic progress. But just as NAFTA could not be an end in itself, neither was it the beginning of policy changes leading to the new economic model for Mexico. Profound changes had indeed occurred in Mexico's trade relations (especially with the United States) during the 1980s. In this chapter I analyze some of the policies leading up to NAFTA, what this agreement has meant for the peoples of North America, and its midterm prospects within the North American community.

The Road to NAFTA

The road leading to NAFTA was neither straight nor smooth. From a Mexican perspective, it was pocked with potholes, and many a worker, peasant, and hardworking businessperson was left on its wayside. It is my belief that Mexico took this path in a great leap of faith, mistaking NAFTA for that elusive "easy road" to economic growth and development.

Observers generally agree that up to 1976 Mexico had achieved success in two major areas challenging any developing country: It had sustained high rates of economic growth (surpassing the rate of population growth by 100 percent), and it had achieved this growth while holding down inflation rates. This had been accomplished through a strict regime of import substitution, principally of intermediate goods intended for industrial production as well as final consumer products (Solís, 1981). Between the end of World War II and 1975, the Mexican economy had undergone a substantial transformation, relying less on agricultural production and more on manufacturing (see Table 2.1).

The pattern shifted once again following the 1976 peso devaluation and the discovery of new petroleum reserves in Mexico. The results were the "petrolization" of the Mexican economy and its dependency on increasing oil exports (and on international demand factors) as well as domestic and international debt levels far in excess of individual GNP contributions (Bendesky and Godínez, 1989). These disproportionate levels of external and internal borrowing put heavy downward pressure on the value of the peso, forcing devaluations beginning in 1982 (in what Carlos Tello, then minister of finance, characterized as "a liquidity crisis") and continuing throughout the decade. The falling value of the peso created a hyperinflationary situation that did not come under firm control until the end of the Salinas administration in 1994.

One predominant factor characterized the decade: increasing reliance on the external sector to provide the necessary capital for investment in Mexico and to serve as a source of hard currency through Mexican exports. These two needs

TABLE 2.1
Sectoral Contributions to GNP at 1960 Prices (percent)

Sectors	1936	1956	1970	1975
Agriculture	20.8	17.1	11.6	9.6
Mining	4.1	1.1	1.0	0.9
Petroleum	2.8	3.0	4.3	4.7
Manufacturing	14.0	18.3	22.8	23.1
Construction	3.2	4.0	4.6	5.2
Electricity	0.9	0.9	1.8	2.1
Services	54.2	55.0	55.1	55.7

Source: Data from Leopoldo Solís, *La realidad económica mexicana: Retrovisión y perspectivas* (Mexico, D.F.: Siglo XXI, 1981), p. 171.

were addressed through bilateral agreements with the United States and through gradual reforms to Mexican laws that were perceived as barriers to foreign direct investment.[1]

Mexico's initial refusal to enter into the General Agreement on Tariffs and Trade (GATT) in 1979 stemmed from the belief that the country's petroleum reserves could generate enough wealth to obviate the need to change the Mexican economy in any fundamental way (Aguilar Camín, 1982). In other words, the policies of import substitution were to continue—even if the costs to the economy were high. Worse, policymakers saw no need to restructure Mexico's productive plant, on the assumption that economic inefficiency could be absorbed through the nation's oil wealth (Serrato, 1983). Yet most of the basic economic premises of the 1970s were wrong (especially the judgment that world oil prices would rise 7 percent annually until the year 2000), and it took Mexico the better part of thirteen years to "recover" from the crisis that began in 1982 (Secretaría de Patrimonio y Fomento Industrial, 1982). Jaime Corredor, one of the architects of Mexico's petroleum policy, concluded wrongly: "Under present world conditions of scarcity and increasing costs of conventional forms of energy, oil also signifies for Mexico the possibility of generating large financial surpluses that it can use to expand its efforts at social and economic development" (Corredor, 1983:155).

The Great Leap Forward:
The Elusive Quest for First World Status

Mexico's second great transformation, after its evolution from an agrarian to an industrial society, was the radical process that hurled the country into the global economy and particularly into a liberalized trade regime in North America. If the first great transformation was the result of endogenous actions, the second transformation—Mexico's great leap forward—was the result both of domestic decisionmaking and of trends and events in the world economy. Of particular interest here is the evolving economic role of the United States in the globalized economy and that country's search for a new regional or hemispheric hegemony.

Canada's response to U.S. and global economic challenges was as dramatic as that of Mexico. Canada opted for a free trade regime with the United States (almost a decade before Mexico chose this same path) in reaction to some of the same forces that induced Mexico to liberalize its economy during the 1980s (Lande and Grasstek, 1986). As Canada explored other, more limited options of economic integration with the United States, such as sectoral agreements (it already had the successful experience of the 1965 Auto Pact), the Canadians' restrained approach got little support in the United States, which preferred a wide-ranging free trade agreement like that finally negotiated in 1987. The

U.S.-Canada Free Trade Agreement (the FTA) served (for a variety of reasons) as the model for the North American Free Trade Agreement negotiated among Mexico, the United States, and Canada.[2] We should note that the negotiating agendas for both the FTA and NAFTA reflected concerns of critical importance to the United States, expressed bilaterally through the Understanding on Subsidies and Countervailing Duties and the Framework Agreement signed with Mexico and multilaterally in the negotiations of the Uruguay Round of the GATT.

Toward the end of the 1970s, a number of U.S. public figures—ranging from Senator Ted Kennedy to Ronald Reagan, then governor of California—proposed a free trading system in North America. Indeed, Mexico's extensive petroleum deposits had led governments of its neighboring countries (beginning with the Carter administration) to start considering it as a "middle-level" power. A wide-ranging debate ensued in Washington over how to relate to Mexico under these seemingly new conditions. The outcome was Presidential Review Memorandum 51, which outlined U.S. options and concluded by arguing that the "special and long-standing relationship" with Mexico should be continued. This discussion was largely abandoned with the onset of the 1982 economic crisis, when Mexico lost its status as a "middle power" and reverted to being perceived once again as an underdeveloped country with an underdeveloped economy. Trade and commercial negotiations would have to wait until Mexico's economy regained some semblance of stability. This recovery began to occur in 1985.

During this same period, beginning with the Tokyo Round, the U.S. trade agenda in multilateral negotiations had begun to emphasize those areas in which the United States felt it had a comparative advantage. In a world of changing trade patterns, fields characterized by high inputs of knowledge and communications demanded multilateral solutions—not measures such as tariff reductions that had been adequate to resolve the simpler trade problems of the past. These areas encompassed intellectual property, patent rights, banking and financial services, agriculture, and the treatment of foreign direct investment, among others (Grey, 1990; Riddle, 1986). This agenda was carried over from the multilateral arena of GATT to bilateral interactions with countries like Canada—where these concerns were addressed in the FTA—and Mexico—with which the United States signed the Agreement on Subsidies and Countervailing Duties in 1985 and a Framework Agreement in 1987. Obviously the negotiation of a free trade regime between Mexico and the United States would have not only to address major tariff reductions but also to incorporate the most salient issues of this multilateral agenda.

Because Mexico was not the first country to sign a free trade agreement with the United States, the negotiations would now also have to include the issues covered by the U.S.-Canada Free Trade Agreement. In other words, the "Canadian presence" would set a series of parameters for any bilateral U.S.-Mexican

FTA and would exert even more influence if the negotiations became tripartite in nature, involving the whole of North America. These new issues involved such areas as the exploitation of energy resources, labor exchanges (even if only on a very limited scale), auto production, and the old standby, agricultural subsidies. Other issues—environmental protection and labor rights—were not touched on in the bilateral FTA, but they were introduced into the NAFTA negotiations. The manner of their incorporation into NAFTA reflects the participation of new actors in the trade debate in Washington in association with traditional opponents of free trade (such as the AFL-CIO). The alliance between environmentalists and labor proved so successful that these actors were able to introduce their issues into the NAFTA agenda as the Bush administration was seeking fast-track negotiating authority in 1991. In order to secure this authority, the Bush administration had to satisfy environmental groups' demands that free trade with Mexico be accompanied by environmental protections (especially in the U.S.-Mexican border region) and that labor rights be protected in Mexico. According to critics of the developing free trade agreement, negotiations along these two dimensions would "level the trading field" and keep Mexico from gaining unfair trading advantages.

These provisions were outlined in a White House memorandum to the leaders of the U.S. Congress (Senator Bentsen, chairman of the Finance Committee, and Representative Gephardt, majority whip in the House of Representatives) in an attempt to gain their support for the fast track in summer 1991. This agenda percolated through the negotiating process until the Clinton administration promised to negotiate environmental and labor-rights "side agreements," complementary to the main trade agreement, in order to broaden the base of support for NAFTA. With these side agreements, the NAFTA proposal began to incorporate some elements of the agenda that had evolved in the European Community, but there has been as yet little thought in North America of institution building on a European scale.

Canadian participation in the NAFTA negotiations introduced new possibilities along two fronts. First, the fact that the U.S.-Canada Free Trade Agreement was already in place facilitated progress with the NAFTA negotiating agenda because many key issues had already been resolved on a bilateral basis, and this resolution could be carried over into the trilateral agreement (Hart, 1991). Second, the Canadian presence in NAFTA would give Mexico a model and a partner with ample experience in multilateral dealings and in negotiating with the United States on a bilateral basis—and not just on trade issues. Under the right conditions, this experience could be invaluable to Mexico; the combined experience of Mexico and Canada could serve as a counterweight to the United States in the context of the developing tripartite relationship.

If for analytical purposes we momentarily separate the NAFTA negotiating agenda from the economic structural conditions of the three partners in North America, we find some notable and distinctive economic differences as well as some surprising similarities. In analyzing these similarities and differences, we must ask whether the economic conditions driving these three countries into each other's arms are the result of passion or pragmatism. How can such diverse economies end up with foreign trade policies so similar? How can Canada and Mexico, both distrustful of the United States because of past humiliations and punitive trade actions levied against them, want to join in an agreement that frees all trade among them? Could it be that a continentwide free trade agreement offers a basis for dispelling distrust and encouraging a more equitable trading environment? Given that the United States is the largest and most important trade partner of both Mexico and Canada, is it better to deal with that country in a bilateral fashion rather than through the GATT system?

Both Mexico and Canada had suffered from severe trade-restricting actions levied by the United States since the early 1980s. During this time, most U.S. countervailing and antidumping orders targeted Canada, Mexico, and Japan— the largest trade partners of the United States (Trebilcock and York, 1990). At this same time, the United States began stricter enforcement of section 301 of its trade law dealing with unfair trade practices on the part of other countries, a move that further threatened exports from countries like Mexico (which, though not on the 301 hit list, was affected peripherally). In other words, Mexico and Canada had no guaranteed access to the U.S. market, and further, they had no assurance that they would receive an administratively fair and nonpolitical hearing in the United States if trade actions were brought against them.

It is within this context that we must view some of the recent trade-liberalizing actions taken by Canada and Mexico in their pursuit of a more stable trade regime in North America. This common approach does not mean that Canada and Mexico have identical economic interests vis-à-vis the United States, nor does it explain U.S. acquiescence in the quest for continentwide free trade. This leads one to wonder what force is driving the United States toward a series of bilateral or trilateral free trade agreements. Is it a new Good Neighbor policy? If so, what is the carrot, what is the stick?

There is little doubt that the U.S. loss of hegemony (loosely defined) is one driving factor (Bergsten, 1988). Probably the most important way in which this factor has influenced U.S. foreign economic policy is that the country's fear of being overtaken by the more productive economies of Japan and the European Community led the United States to seek new spheres of influence and new mechanisms for expressing its power within these spheres. A second important factor shaping U.S. foreign economic policy was past inability of the United States to "push" its agenda and get a quick, favorable outcome in the Uruguay Round. The difficulties encountered in the GATT negotiations, the multiple delays, and the apparent unwillingness of old partners to see things from the U.S. perspective combined to convince the United States of the need to seek new bilateral mechanisms (which are not necessarily incompatible with GATT) in order to further certain policy aims. Finally, there is a perception (rarely espoused publicly by U.S. policymakers) that trade blocs such as the European Community, and perhaps others guided by Japan in the Far East, would be exclusionary in nature, threatening an already weakened U.S. balance-of-payments situation and, more important, endangering the old world order established at Bretton Woods, where the United States dictated, in a spirit of cooperation, the rules of postwar life. Under a system of economic blocs, the old cooperation could give way to conflict, and the United States would no longer be able to dictate solutions as it had done for the past forty years.

It has been suggested elsewhere that the North American Free Trade Agreement and the Enterprise of the Americas Initiative represent a strategic response on the part of the United States as the challenges posed by Japan and the European Community (EC) threaten to diminish the economic hegemony that the United States gained following World War II (del Castillo V., 1995a; Milner, 1993). This might sound like a simple proposition (or an extension of dependency theory), but in fact it involves new approaches to the management of advanced capitalist production, now generalized throughout the world after the collapse of the state-socialist alternative (Thurow, 1992).

The conflict over new approaches to capitalist evolution arises because of the gradual but determined forging of a new ideology in the United States by the Republican Party, beginning with the election of Richard Nixon to the presidency in 1968 and continuing through the end of the Bush administration in 1992. These years of Republican control of the White House resulted in the discrediting of the state as a relevant social actor and involved the rediscovery of Adam Smith's faith in market forces as the determinant factor in economic exchange and in the allocation and distribution of wealth in society.

In contrast, the process of European integration depended on the active intervention of the state of each EC country in defining social and economic welfare, both nationally and on a transnational and community basis. Clearly, in the European tradition the state continues to be an important social actor (Fitzgerald, 1980). The same is true of Japan. Japan's experience in developing an industrial policy after World War II emphasized the critical role of the state, and this same activist tradition emerges in the push toward economic development in new regional economic actors such as Korea, Taiwan, and China. These experiences have all involved active state participation in managing and defining capitalist practices and strategic economic goals.

This tradition of state intervention is relevant to the processes of economic integration in North America because at stake from the U.S. perspective is whether Canada and Mexico will play by U.S. rules after receiving preferential trading status. In other words, the success of the FTA or NAFTA depends on the extent to which the countries involved adhere to the ideology in which different levels of state actors attempt to foster economic activity while attempting to minimize government regulatory activity as recently demonstrated by the Republicans' "Contract with America." Canada's and Mexico's adoption of this neoliberal ideology benefits the United States in a number of ways.

First, it furthers the ideology of nonintervention by the state while giving free rein to so-called market forces as the final arbiters between economic actors in the society, in contrast to the position adopted in both the European Community and Japan. Second, it consolidates North America and the rest of Latin America in the U.S. camp. And third, having succeeded in this endeavor, it prompts the nations of Latin America to put pressure on the multilateral system (GATT) to adopt, or bring international trading rules in close alignment with, the developing hemispheric belief in economic nonintervention.

In this context, the FTA and NAFTA take on strategic significance for the United States. If the U.S. position on the diminished role of the state is reinforced, the nations receiving preferential trade treatment will have to operate within strict parameters. This is the case, for instance, when drawing up development plans or industrial policies in order to avoid noncompliance with negotiated formulas, since failure to observe the terms of a trade agreement could carry costly consequences in terms of these countries' relations with the United States.

Thus, the maintenance of this system of beliefs, operationalized through a formal trade agreement in the Americas, constitutes a trade system in competition with the advanced EC system and the developing Pacific Basin system. Because system maintenance is of strategic importance, countries that involve the state to any significant degree—through the application of subsidies or a lukewarm enforcement of sanctions against intellectual property violators, for example—will now not only violate U.S. trade law but will also threaten the entire trade system being developed under U.S. auspices.

In today's globalizing economy, countries and regions are being forced to find new ways to produce goods, to organize the workforce, and to market traditional and new products (including information) in ways in which the nation-state may not be the most relevant unit of analysis. Nevertheless, many of the decisions that direct this globalization process are affected by the nation-state, an intellectual creation of the eighteenth and nineteenth centuries. These decisions range from policies that lead to international trade agreements to restrictions on foreign investment on domestic soil. In this respect, the process of private production (loosely defined) and decisionmaking in the public sector are out of phase, with mismatching units trying to interface.

Global production now is thus characterized by the speed with which a product can be modified or new products can be introduced into the market, whereas nation-states are characterized by institutional arrangements entailing slow response times that result from the participation of multiple actors, such as parliaments and their committees, public hearings, rounds of discussions, and so on (del Castillo V., 1995b). Faced with this paradox, the nations of

North America have opted for economic integration as a way to meet the challenge inherent in these new ways of organizing capitalist production. When Marx observed the relationship between the developing characteristics of industrial capitalism and the nation-state in the nineteenth century, he saw few contradictions as far as governmental structures being developed and the class interests they represented; in other words, structures and process were closely linked. This linkage was so strongly established that Marx described the state as an agent of the capitalist class. In today's North America this linkage is not so clear. In fact, many analysts concede that economic integration, especially in certain sectors, is proceeding independently of government actions. Many critics of the process of North American integration have argued that this global capitalist class is outside of governmental control, and they criticize the trade agreements signed by governments as secondhand actions that tend to follow from private-sector decisions. In this context, NAFTA must be conceptualized as an attempt by the three governments of the region to gain some control over the process of economic integration through a transnational approach.

Although debates and accords focus on matters of trade and investment in North America, we must remember that socioeconomic factors are not independent one from another; in this respect, the role and operation of the contemporary state are still of primary importance. A related consideration comes into play, especially when dealing with trade issues: the role of economic doctrine in forging public policies and setting the parameters for relations between the state and the private sector. This factor, always present, becomes particularly relevant with the end of the ideological conflicts of the Cold War and the emergence of new questions about how modern neocapitalist economies function in a world of globalized production under different ideological regimes and different areas of influence, as was briefly discussed in earlier pages.

Some of these considerations are of special significance in North America given that the region comprises three nations with different historical traditions. Moreover, Canada and Mexico have had to coexist with the richest capitalist country, a world hegemon, as their neighbor, and thus many aspects of their economic integration must be related to questions about the relationship among asymmetrical partners. Canadian scholars have addressed this issue of asymmetry in the "hub and spoke" model of trade relations (Lipsey, 1990). This model suggests that there are grounds for concern among trade partners of the United States. According to this model, the most important trade partner will concentrate trade benefits with a number of peripheral nations, which will then be isolated one from another and derive little benefit from liberalized trade (Servín, 1992). Less developed nations entering into such an arrangement will continue in their regional isolation, unable fully to rationalize economic production and specialization because the established trade patterns emphasize whatever elements of production are most beneficial to the hub country. Under this type of arrangement, free trade does not operate as an adjustment mechanism, as an economic rationalizer with which to confront the forces of globalization and neocapitalist production.

We must recognize that NAFTA is more than a trade arrangement that has gone beyond the U.S.-Canada FTA and GATT in restructuring trading arrangements among countries. More than anything, it represents the search for a regional response to the evolving neocapitalist system wherein North America as a region must compete with the European Community and the countries of the Pacific Basin under rapidly changing conditions and in which both the trade rules and actual systemic production are as yet undefined.

In this respect, NAFTA represents an attempt to respond to high *degrees of uncertainty, not only in global* terms (that is, regarding the relations of each of the participant countries with the rest of the world) but also among the member countries of North America. The agreement should be seen, therefore, as an institutional response to an uncertain and changing world economic order. NAFTA must be evaluated in relation to the economic issues it was meant to address—the flexibility of production and increasing competition from less developed regions of the world and from established centers of industrial and technological innovation in the European Community and East Asia. The questions to be asked, then, are these: How can NAFTA become an instrument that helps each country of the region adjust to global competition and rationalize production among the three nations? Can NAFTA as an institution address changing conditions between the region it represents and other productive regions of the world? And can it address changing conditions within the North American region itself?

NAFTA and the Uruguay Round of GATT

Existing conditions foretell the need for a highly flexible instrument with which to resolve future trade conflicts. For now, NAFTA has adopted the problem-solving chapters written into its predecessor, the U.S.-Canada FTA; it remains to be seen whether this instrumentation can adequately address the legitimate interests of all NAFTA partners. The experience with conflict resolution under the FTA seems to be highly positive and much more efficient than the GATT conflict resolution structure (Winham, 1993). This is especially significant in light of the marked asymmetry that characterizes the North American trade partners.

In terms of needed flexibility, one of the characteristics of NAFTA is that it is not a closed document but instead is composed of multiple working groups in charge of refining the original document; in other words, like the GATT structure, it is a constant negotiating and consultations forum (Chapter 20, Article 2006) intended to address those dimensions appearing in the original document. These are the obvious areas of tariff reduction but also encompass difficult dimensions that had been under negotiation in the Uruguay Round, such as financial services, the treatment of foreign investment, agriculture, government procurement, and protection for intellectual property and patent rights. NAFTA provides for the existence of permanent working groups for all of these areas and ought to be able to deal with potential problems arising from these issues as the process of economic integration goes forward. The eight committees and six working groups specified in Annex 2001.2 are responsible for issues ranging from rules of origin to the temporary entry of professional workers.

Yet the economic crisis in Mexico that began in December 1994, just after NAFTA had been in operation for twelve months, indicates that further instruments have to be in place to address the issues of economic asymmetry among the North American partners and the different effects economic liberalization has on them. In this context, it may be possible to argue that before NAFTA can be widened further, issues of fundamental importance must be resolved and specific instruments put in place to deal with the nature of economic asymmetry, since these issues are also very much in the forefront of economic discussions in Latin American countries wishing to become members of NAFTA under Chapter XXII, Article 2204. In other words, before further widening can take place, deepening ought to occur to address the problems previously mentioned.

One obvious characteristic of NAFTA is that it abolishes the "special and differential treatment" under which many developing nations had been incorporated into GATT. Under NAFTA, Mexico was to enter into a free trade agreement with Canada and the United States under conditions of equality without any special treatment and with the only *protection* granted to be the different phase-in periods of NAFTA, which defers incorporation of certain weak Mexican sectors to the end of the fifteen-year final phase-in period, such as Mexico's agricultural sector.[3]

Yet the most recent Mexican economic crisis manifests the problems that can arise from trade agreements that are not flexible enough to deal with fast-changing economic situations (import and monetary policy) causing enormous trade deficits, current account imbalances, and immediate pressures on weak currencies. Both NAFTA and GATT allow some measure of protection from imports under *emergency action* procedures (Chapter 8 of NAFTA and Article XIX of GATT), *safeguard measures* (for instance, under the General Agreement on Trade in Services, GATS, of the Uruguay Round), and as a result of *balance-of-payments* problems (NAFTA Article 2104). Most of these protective measures by an injured party are temporary and require some form of restitution to the country being closed off by protection.

These protective measures are, in a sense, traditional in nature, oriented toward restricting the flow of goods or services (GATS). Unfortunately, these instruments offer little protection against speculative activities that are global in nature but that—for a number of reasons—affect some countries much more deeply than others.[4] These activities involve actions against currency stability and therefore affect not only a currency's value but also the nature of free trade itself by endangering the base of trade, which is the stability of the currencies involved that facilitate commercial and service transactions. The end result of these activities is that they lead to what has occurred in Mexico since December 1994: currency devaluations, inflationary spirals, and tight fiscal and monetary policies—all of which also endanger the possibilities for free trade.

Conclusion

In view of this analysis, NAFTA and the recently concluded Uruguay Round are inadequate instruments to deal with economic near-calamities of the type that face Mexico. These are the direct result of the nature of capital in general, always in search of the highest rates of returns in secure environments. In particular, the problems arise from a number of factors, including the specific composition of investment capital and the mobility of capital. With regard to the composition, one would have to differentiate between short-term speculative capital, which was predominant in the new capital flows to Mexico between 1990 and 1994, and long-term foreign direct investment in productive assets. Capital mobility, on the other hand, has been greatly accelerated by modern computational technologies. Therefore, when there is a high risk—real or imagined—speculative capital can flow out of a country just as soon as it flowed in and deeply aggravate the initial conditions of risk.

The effects that investment measures have on trade matters is not an unknown subject to past trade negotiations (Curtis and Vastine, 1971; Winham, 1986). More recently the particular focus on investment measures has been related to the question of what role foreign investment plays in the economic restructuring of less developed nations. It was in this context that the Uruguay Round negotiating group on trade related investment measures (TRIMs) began discussions in 1987 on the following mandate: "Following an examination of the operation of GATT Articles related to the trade restrictive and distorting effects of investment measures, negotiations should elaborate, as appropriate, further provisions that may be necessary to avoid such adverse effects on trade" (cited in Stewart, 1993:103).

For developing countries, the issue of whether a government could use investment measures to direct or restrict investments was interpreted as being outside the purview of GATT, and they opposed negotiations on TRIMs. Others argued that further GATT discipline on TRIMs was unnecessary because rules already existed under Articles III and XI. Many of these countries argued against the concept of *prohibition* (denying policymakers the authority to set investment policy) on the grounds that investment measures ought to be evaluated by their effects (similar to the concept of *injury*) and be dealt with under those terms. Under the Dunkel draft of December 1991, there were three different phase-in periods depending on the status of a country; the categories were developed, developing, and least developed nations. The Uruguay Round Final Act leaves participation on the TRIMs accord up to the individual participant countries. This brief discussion outlines the context of the Uruguay Round discussions on acceptable disciplines to be brought to bear in case a government utilizes investment measures so as to impact on third-party investments. As can be seen, the TRIMs agreement does not address the issue of possible regulatory instruments a country may employ in order to obtain an orderly inflow or outflow of investment.

NAFTA also concerns itself with trade in *financial services* under Chapter 14. There are four principal areas of concern under Chapter 14 as it treats the operations of the financial sector: (1) Article 1403 protects a participant country's right of regulation; (2) Article 1404 establishes the conditions under which the financial institutions of NAFTA members may operate in each other's territory (Article 1407 deals with the issue of national treatment for these services); (3) Article 1405 addresses the issue of supply of financial services; (4) finally, Articles 1413–1416 deal with consultations and conflict resolution of financial services disputes. But, as may be appreciated, none of these matters touches on the question of how regulated financial institutions may themselves or through government action control the flow of capital on a transborder basis. Yet Articles 1410:1(c) and 1410:2 do hint at the possible problems associated with market-driven flows of cross-border capital because they state a party's right to ensure the integrity and stability of a country's financial system (as long as the measures are not discriminatory). Article 1410:2 states that "Nothing in this Part applies to non-discriminatory measures of general application by any public entity in pursuit of monetary and related credit policies or exchange rate policies." In other words, if national stabilization policies are allowed under NAFTA, the development of disciplines on a continental or multilateral basis (under the new World Trade Organization, WTO) focusing on the issues of capital mobility and the destabilization effects these have on all nations, particularly developing countries such as Mexico, would go a long way toward providing economic stability.

At a minimum, these disciplines might focus on the composition of investments in a country's national accounts—that is, desirable ratios of short or hot investments vis-à-vis direct productive investment—as a means of ensuring macroeconomic stability. Related to this and in line with the Dunkel draft of 1991, countries in different stages of development would be subject to different investment ratios. Just as most economic integration efforts permit the fluctuation of a country's exchange rates within certain band limits, the same principle ought to apply within the stock markets of developing nations in order to control widely swinging negative trends. For instance, automatic "slow-down" procedures on paper transactions could be activated if the aggregate stock begins to deteriorate, as happened during Black Monday in the United States on 19 October 1987. Finally, the public sector's emission of bonds also has to be analyzed carefully and regulated to fall within certain ratios (pegged to individual GNP growth or productivity gains or as a ratio of the budget deficit). This would ensure that the public-sector debt would not add to the natural pressures on a country's currency and would forestall the need for emergency actions.

These measures are evident and necessary as countries throughout the world decide to liberalize their economies and let them be regimented by market forces. They would appear to be essential under integration schemes such as NAFTA that link countries with very different levels of development and in which economic asymmetries put enormous pressures on the least developed partner. Without such measures, NAFTA is an incomplete and deformed instrument that needs to be deepened to account for these dimensions. Otherwise the economic and political pressures to scrap it will increase as further distortions manifest themselves (such as the Clinton emergency rescue package for Mexico), which will only increase the costs the retiring partner will have to pay in a now hostile North America.

Notes

1. The first agreement, entitled "U.S.-Mexico Understanding on Subsidies and Countervailing Duties," was signed in 1985. A second generalized agreement, a Framework Agreement, was signed in 1987. Both of these bilateral agreements "liberalized" bilateral trade and set a framework for continued trade negotiations. During this same period Mexico and the United States had undergone further bilateral negotiations as a requisite for Mexico's entry into GATT in 1986 (del Castillo V., 1985, 1986, 1989).

2. Personal interview, G. del Castillo V. with M.B., External Affairs, Ottawa, Canada, 1 October 1991.

3. Certain Mexican economic activities are completely excluded from NAFTA, such as Mexico's energy sector. It would be difficult to classify these exclusions as *protection* in the way it usually is treated in the trade literature. Yet the energy sector is composed of multiple economic activities, and NAFTA opened many of these activities to foreign actors, such as investment and operation in the secondary petrochemical industry. Legislation passed in early 1995 modified the regulatory law associated with Article 27 of the Mexican Constitution to permit the storage, transport, and distribution of natural gas but not crude petroleum.

4. Much of the Mexican December peso crisis was attributed by Mexican policymakers to the uncertainty created around the supposed political instability in Chiapas and the murder of the PRI's presidential candidate, Luis Donaldo Colosio, early in 1994 and the later assassination of the PRI's executive secretary, José Francisco Ruiz Massieu.

Besides these official pronouncements, one cannot discount a monetary policy that increased money supply by 20 percent during 1994, clearly for electoral reasons, and the emission of dollar-denominated treasury bonds, many of them with short-term maturity dates. The dumping of pesos by these bondholders has also accelerated the inflation rate in the country, estimated at over 50 percent for 1995.

Bibliography

Aguilar Camín, Héctor, ed. 1982. *El desafío mexicano*. Mexico City: Ediciones Océano.

Bendesky, León, and Víctor M. Godínez. 1989. "La deuda externa de México: Un caso de cooperación conflictiva." In Riordan Roett, ed., *México y Estados Unidos: El manejo de la relación*. Mexico, D.F.: Siglo XXI, 1989.

Bergsten, C. Fred. 1988. *America in the World Economy: A Strategy for the 1990s*. Washington, D.C.: Institute for International Economics.

Corredor, Jaime. 1983. "The Economic Significance of Mexican Petroleum from the Perspective of Mexico–United States Relations." Pp. 137–165 in Clark W. Reynolds and Carlos Tello, eds., *U.S.-Mexico Relations: Economic and Social Aspects*. Stanford, Calif.: Stanford University Press.

Curtis, Thomas B., and John Robert Vastine Jr. 1971. *The Kennedy Round and the Future of American Trade*. New York: Praeger Publishers.

del Castillo V., Gustavo. 1985. "U.S.-Mexican Trade Relations: From the Generalized System of Preferences to a Formal Bilateral Trade Agreement." La Jolla, Calif.: Center for U.S.-Mexican Studies, University of California, San Diego, 1985.

———. 1986. *México en el GATT: Ventajas y desventajas*. Tijuana: El Colegio de la Frontera Norte.

———. 1989. "Política de comercio exterior y seguridad nacional en México: Hacia la definición de metas para fines de siglo." *Frontera Norte*, 1 (January-June), pp. 25–48.

———. 1995a. "Private-Sector Trade Advisory Groups in North America: A Comparative Perspective." In Gustavo del Castillo and Gustavo Vega, *The Politics of Free Trade in North America*. Ottawa: Centre for Trade Policy and Law, Carleton University, forthcoming.

———. 1995b. "Convergent Paths Toward Integration: The Unequal Experiences of Canada and Mexico." Pp. 91–106 in Donald Barry, ed. *Toward a North American Community? Canada, the United States, and Mexico*. Boulder: Westview Press.

Fitzgerald, E.V.K. 1980. "The Restructuring of the Mexican and U.S. Economies: A European View." The Hague: Institute of Social Studies. Prepared for the meeting of the "Chapultepec Group," Stanford University, November.

Grey, Roy de C. 1990. *The Services Agenda*. Halifax, Nova Scotia: The Institute for Research on Public Policy.

Hart, Michael. 1991. "Elementos de un acuerdo de libre comercio en América del Norte." Pp. 319–352 in Gustavo Vega C., ed., *México ante el libre comercio con América del Norte*. Mexico, D.F.: El Colegio de México/Universidad Tecnológica de México.

Lande, Stephen L., and Craig Van Grasstek. 1986. *The Trade and Tariff Act of 1984: Trade Policy in the Reagan Administration*. Lexington, Mass.: Lexington Books, D.C. Heath.

Lipsey, Richard G. 1990. "Canada at the U.S.-Mexico Free Trade Dance: Wallflower or Partner?" *Commentary*, no. 20. Toronto: C.D. Howe Institute.

Milner, Helen. 1993. "Trading Places: Industries for Free Trade." Pp. 141–172 in John S. Odell and Thomas D. Willett, eds., *International Trade Policies: Gains from Exchange Between Economics and Political Science*. Ann Arbor: University of Michigan Press.

Riddle, Dorothy I. 1986. *Service-Led Growth: The Role of the Service Sector in World Development*. New York: Praeger.

Secretaría de Patrimonio y Fomento Industrial (SPFI). 1982. *Programa de Energía: Metas a 1990 y proyecciones al año 2000*. México: SPFI.

Serrato, Marcela. 1983. "Las dificultades financieras de México y la política petrolera hacia el exterior." Pp. 287–303 in Olga Pellicer, ed., *La política exterior de México: Desafíos en los ochenta*. Mexico: Centro de Investigación y Docencia Económicas.

Servín, Andrés, ed. 1992. *El grupo de los tres*. Bogota: Fundación Friederich Ebert de Colombia (FESCOL).

Sheahan, John. 1991. *Conflict and Change in Mexican Economic Strategy: Implications for Mexico and for Latin America*. La Jolla, Calif.: Center for U.S.-Mexican Studies, University of California, San Diego.

Solís, Leopoldo. 1981. *La realidad económica mexicana: Retrovisión y perspectivas*. Mexico, D.F.: Siglo XXI.

Stewart, Terence P., ed. 1993. *The GATT Uruguay Round. A Negotiating History (1986–1992)*. Deventer, The Netherlands: Kluwer Law and Taxation Publishers.

Thurow, Lester. 1992. *Head to Head: The Coming Economic Battle Among Japan, Europe, and America*. New York: Morrow.

Trebilcock, Michael J., and Robert C. York, eds. 1990. *Fair Exchange: Reforming Trade Remedy Laws*. Toronto: C.D. Howe Institute.

Winham, Gilbert R. 1986. *International Trade and the Tokyo Round Negotiation*. Princeton: Princeton University Press.

———. 1993. "Dispute Settlement in NAFTA and the FTA." In Pp. 251–270 in Michael Walker and Steven Globerman, eds., *Assessing NAFTA: A Trinational Analysis*. Vancouver, B.C.: The Fraser Institute.

3

The Debt Crisis and Economic Restructuring: Prospects for Mexican Agriculture

Marilyn Gates

Outlined in this chapter are the main directions of the Salinas administration's agricultural modernization strategy within the context of the progression of Mexican agrarian policy since the onset of the debt crisis in 1982.[1] Also assessed is the potential of these initiatives for reversing the national agricultural crisis and improving the peasant condition. One question is whether the Mexican state, which to a large extent created the agricultural crisis through its interventionist policies, will now be able to plan its way out of it. More specifically, because the legacy of state intervention in peasant agriculture has been the creation of a bankrupt, modernized subsistence sector, adapted to an ethos of institutionalized failure, will organizational reforms and economic liberalization be sufficient to redress the social as well as the economic balance? A corollary to both of these questions is the issue of whether the Salinas reforms constitute a fundamentally new direction for Mexican agrarian policy or whether they are part of an ongoing process of refunctionalization of the peasantry, in keeping with the evolving needs of national and international capital.

Mexican agriculture has been the sector hit hardest by debt-crisis austerity and economic restructuring largely because it was already enmeshed in a long-standing crisis of its own, which had surfaced in visible form in the late 1960s. At that time, the growing need to import basic foods, an inevitable concomitant of the post-1940 import-substitution model wherein agriculture subsidized industrial expansion, together with increasing symptoms of rural unrest, made it imperative for the government to attempt to modernize the stagnant production of peasants on ejidos, the unique corporate land tenure category generated by the 1910–1917 revolution.[2] From 1970 until the onset of the debt crisis in 1982, Mexican public-sector expenditure on ejidal agricultural development

43

programs was massive, both in absolute terms and as a percentage of national budget. Rather than fostering an efficient, expanded productive base, however, the net result of this big-spending statist approach to promoting wide-ranging rural development was the institutionalization of "la industria de siniestros" (the industry of disasters), in which crop failure, corruption, and chronic indebtedness became the norm.

These contradictions have been exacerbated under the debt crisis and economic restructuring, as ongoing problems such as overcentralized state planning, bureaucratic corruption, the stranglehold of intermediaries, climatic vicissitudes, inadequate credit, infrastructural bottlenecks, and the displacement of subsistence crops by export production and cattle have become particularly acute now that they are not being offset by massive public-sector capital influx. Meanwhile, the peasants have born the brunt of the government's austerity measures under a continuing strategy of subordinating the interests of the countryside to those of the city, agriculture to industry, and the peasants to the growing urban masses, despite the persistence of agrarian populist rhetoric.

The dsicussion in this chapter is organized in three parts. First is a review of the accelerating deterioration of Mexican agriculture under the de la Madrid administration (1982–1988), which was preoccupied with debt-crisis management and initial steps toward economic diversification and trade liberalization consistent with the International Monetary Fund's (IMF) structural adjustment conditions. Next is an examination of the package of reforms introduced by President Carlos Salinas (1988–1994), which were intended to restructure and recapitalize the stagnant agricultural sector in keeping with the dramatic opening of the economy overall. In general, these reforms are marked by a selective retreat from direct state intervention in the peasant sector, a substantial reduction in supports and subsidies, the encouragement of increased direct producer participation, and the promotion of collaborative ventures between agribusiness and peasants in an attempt to bring market forces back into agriculture. The conclusion presented in the final section is that despite a recent resurgence of government agricultural programs with populist overtones, the general trend in new policy is proproduction rather than propeasant in response to a complex of domestic and international forces that appears to be altering Mexico's agrarian structure radically, at least on the surface. Thus, although the pace of change in the Mexican countryside has quickened dramatically, overall the Salinas reforms constitute a logical extension of previous policies rather than a fundamentally new orientation. Nevertheless, the very rapidity of transition toward a free market economy, the implementation of the North American Free Trade Agreement (NAFTA) with the United States and Canada, and the prospects of Pan-American free trade will have significant repercussions for agricultural producers. For the peasant sector, in particular, the Salinas reforms add up to a substantial alteration in agrarian form if not in function, as the ejido and state-peasant relations are being reshaped to conform to global economic imperatives. These trends seem likely to continue under the Zedillo administration.

The de la Madrid Administration: Dealing with the Debt Crisis

Under the de la Madrid administration (1982–1988), Mexico made considerable progress in recovery from the immediate strictures of the debt crisis, as a result of drastic cuts in public expenditure and the government's willingness to comply with international pressures for trade liberalization and to initiate innovative debt-restructuring strategies. However, this external pragmatism was not translated into effective tactics for reducing the massive internal debt and spurring growth in stagnant domestic production. The Mexican people continued to pay a heavy price for their government's relative success in renegotiating the foreign debt and containing inflation throughout the presidency of Carlos Salinas de Gortari.

The impact of inflation, public-sector cutbacks, reduction of subsidies, and government austerity measures like wage and price controls has been particularly severe for those on the margins of the cash economy, such as the majority of Mexican peasants. However, in agriculture these effects were somewhat muted during the early years of the crisis, as the sector performed somewhat better than the shrinking economy at large from 1982 through 1986. This was the result in part of improved exchange rates for agricultural exports, favorable weather, and a small increase in government-guaranteed prices for staples, which reduced the long-standing disparity relative to nonagricultural prices.[3] An additional factor in this temporary upswing was the impact of increased direct government intervention in staple cultivation on the production units enabled by the 1980 agrarian reform legislation, the Ley de Fomento Agropecuario (LFA, Agricultural and Livestock Promotion Law).

A major thrust of the LFA was to stimulate the establishment of joint ventures between the private sector and ejidatarios, a highly controversial measure that appeared to threaten the cherished inviolability of the ejido as the most enduring revolutionary symbol of social justice for Mexico's peasants. The onset of the debt crisis, however, eliminated any possibility of enticing significant spontaneous reinvestment of private moneys in agriculture, as the few entrepreneurs who had risked investments involving the ejido were quickly driven out of business by the devalued peso, particularly if they owed money in dollars. Instead, the production units became essentially state-managed farms on ejidos or on the lands of small property owners associated for credit purposes, both of which received the lion's share of the now limited public resources available at the expense of subsistence-level peasants and independent private property owners.

By the mid-1980s, the relatively strong performance of the agricultural sector under the debt crisis proved to be illusory as attempts to raise production floundered in a sea of debt. This was the result of a combination of drastic increases in production costs, soaring interest rates, continued low official purchase prices for staples, and the long-term downward trend in world market prices for many agricultural products. De facto deficit production had become the norm in many state-directed ejidal agricultural projects over a decade earlier, as massive government investments involving heavy subsidies often turned out to be expensive mistakes at both the planning and implementation levels. Under the debt crisis, many ejidatarios in these inefficient projects fell into default, unable to repay their high-cost loans at the marginal level of operations standard in the modernized peasant sector.

In this climate, corruption flourished under what has become widely known as la industria de siniestros, primarily involving credit and crop insurance fraud. Unscrupulous members of the agrarian bureaucracy, in particular from the Banco Nacional de Crédito Rural (BANRURAL, the National Rural Credit Bank) and the Aseguradora Nacional Agrícola y Ganadera (ANAGSA, the National Agency for Agricultural and Livestock Insurance), acting alone or in collusion with ejidal authorities, initiated elaborate schemes to defraud government agencies. Frequently, these swindles involve arranging credit and insurance for fictitious operations or obtaining compensation for actual crops declared a siniestro total (total disaster) when, in fact, the majority is harvestable. For many ejidatarios at marginal levels of production, the latter deception has become the only way to avoid repeated loan default and subsequent ineligibility for future credit. Furthermore, many peasants feel entitled to credit and other subsidies, irrespective of the harvest outcome, as part of their rightful due as ejidatarios, promised social justice under the 1917 Constitution and still awaiting payment in full. As a consequence, an ethos of institutionalized failure has been inculcated in the modernized peasant sector, wherein deficit and debt have become the norm and deceit is the only reliable economic strategy given the inefficiencies of production. Such a mentality, once established, is hard to alter and obviously militates against the success of future developments.

These problems have been compounded by extensive cutbacks in the agrarian bureaucracy after years of unchecked state growth. One example is the Secretaría de Agricultura y Recursos Hidráulicos (SARH, the Ministry of Agriculture and Water Resources, which in January 1995 was renamed Secretaría de Agricultura, Ganadería, y Desarrollo Rural [SAGDR, Ministry of Agriculture, Livestock, and Rural Development]), which is the lead agency in the modernized ejidal sector. The majority of the jobs in that agency affected by cutbacks involved middle- and lower-level administrative, secretarial, technical, and support staff. In addition to generalized restraint, austerity budgets resulted in the elimination of major SARH projects and programs, including the closure of key research institutes. For many ejidatarios who had become accustomed to the constant influx of new government funds to compensate for the failure of past development strategies, the abrupt withdrawal of official supports acted as a major disincentive to production in an already highly unprofitable and inefficient system.

The pace of economic liberalization via deregulation, tax reform, and privatization, gradual at first, accelerated after 1986 when Mexico entered the General Agreement on Tariffs and Trades (GATT). However, these major restructuring initiatives had little immediate effect in terms of the promotion of economic recovery. Inflation rose to 160 percent by the end of 1987, the economy overall continued to stagnate despite diversification efforts, and the internal debt burgeoned to 15 percent of gross domestic product (GDP) (*IMF Survey,* 10 July 1989) even though extensive efforts were made to cut government costs, for example through the sale of inefficient state enterprises.

In response to these worsening conditions, the de la Madrid administration introduced a comprehensive antiinflationary program in December 1987 based on a pact among the government, organized labor, the formal peasant organizations, and private business sectors, the Pacto de Solidaridad Económica (PSE, the Pact for Economic Solidarity). This program of wage and price controls succeeded in reducing inflation to 52 percent by the end of 1988. Nevertheless, economic activity remained weak, as real GDP grew by only 1.1 percent in 1988 despite increased private-sector investment activity, and consumption rose by less than 1 percent in real terms (*IMF Survey,* 10 July 1989).

The escalation of the agricultural crisis between 1986 and 1988 reflected the low priority given to the sector by the de la Madrid administration, which was preoccupied initially with renegotiation of Mexico's vast external debt and implementation of domestic austerity measures. However, in midterm, President de la Madrid's reform horizons broadened beyond the immediate crisis management level, as it became clear that the logic of internationally impelled restructuring required a major reorientation of the Mexican economy in order to diversify production away from petroleum dependence and open up the country to foreign trade.

By 1988, Mexican agriculture was widely acknowledged to be in chaos, in sharp contrast to the impressive recovery of the national economy overall, as the gross value of production fell by 3.2 percent to the lowest level in a decade (*El Financiero,* 4 April 1989). The crisis was particularly severe in the staple food crop sector as a result of a prolonged drought throughout much of the country. The dream of restoring self-sufficiency became increasingly remote with each disastrous crop cycle, as imports of basic foods rose from 8.5 million tons in 1981 to 10 million tons in 1988 (*Excelsior,* 11 April 1989)[4] and the population grew by some 7 million.[5] Meanwhile, international market prices of key agricultural imports such as maize spiraled also, tying up public-sector funds that otherwise could have been employed in sorely needed social programs or invested in economic infrastructure and other sectors neglected since the onset of the crisis.

The Salinas Administration:
Modernization, Restructuring, and "Solidarity"

In the midst of this struggle to attain a balance between short-term measures to contain inflation and initiatives to stimulate economic growth, which tend to act at cross-purposes, Carlos Salinas de Gortari, de la Madrid's budget minister, took over the presidency. In Mexico, such political transitions tend to be characterized by abrupt discontinuities in policies and programs, although the successor has been handpicked by his predecessor. This is largely because of the enormous personal authority vested in the chief executive office and the desire of each incoming president to place an individual stamp on the sexenio (six-year term). No such hiatus took place in the de la Madrid–Salinas transition as a result of the crisis exigency and because both individuals belonged to the new breed of técnicos (technocrats), foreign-educated professionals adept at economic management, rather than being old-style politicians preoccupied with orchestrating the traditional worker and peasant alliances with the state. Consequently, continuity and intensification of previous strategies were the hallmark of the Salinas regime, particularly with respect to austerity management and attempts to stimulate economic dynamism by reducing federal government interventionism and reversing protectionist policies.

Differences in presidential style did, however, become apparent. Whereas the trademark of the de la Madrid administration was caution, bold and rapid reform became the dominant motif under Salinas. De la Madrid talked extensively about moral renovation, but Salinas engaged in a tough and comprehensive anticorruption campaign that resulted in the apprehension of the notorious leaders of two of Mexico's strongest unions, a drug czar, a top financier, and other significant public figures, often political allies. De la Madrid held state agencies to austerity budgets; Salinas trimmed the government fat to the bone in many sectors, introduced significant government decentralization, streamlined economic procedures via extensive deregulation and tax reform, and initiated a widespread privatization drive resulting in the sale or closure of over 800 public enterprises, even finding buyers for some of the most inefficient ones such as Aeroméxico and Teléfonos de México (Teichman, Chapter 8, this volume).[6]

The most dramatic changes under President Salinas were in the economic sphere, particularly with respect to rapid and comprehensive measures to continue the economic opening via relaxation in the foreign investment law and tariff reduction. These reforms were integrated within an overall program of national economic and political modernization explicitly designed to "strengthen

[Mexico] in the global context and improve coexistence among Mexicans . . . to create a viable economy in a strongly competitive international environment and thus to generate employment and opportunities for all . . . to forge a more just, more generous, more valuable society for each one of us, more respected in the world" (Salinas de Gortari, 1990:1, my translation). In the political domain, Salinas envisioned "democracy consubstantial with the economic modernization of our country . . . a public service that serves rather than being served by power . . . a new political culture" (Salinas de Gortari, 1990:1, my translation).

Another high-profile area during the early part of the Salinas administration was the further renegotiation of the foreign debt under the widely publicized Brady Plan. This agreement, reached in March 1990, cut Mexico's debt service payments by $4 billion a year. Although less than was anticipated originally, it was sufficient to boost private-sector and foreign investor confidence in the economy and bring interest rates down to their lowest level since 1981. Most important, the savings appeared to give Salinas the impetus to devote attention to Mexico's chronic social problems and to devise specific initiatives to promote the recapitalization of agriculture, the Achilles heel of the Mexican economy.

The efforts of President Salinas to promote economic dynamism in agriculture were directed initially to attempt to eradicate the corruption fostered by the "industry of disasters" and improve the efficiency of the agricultural development agencies. Late in 1989, it was announced that BANRURAL, the rural credit bank for ejidos, would cease to employ field inspectors who had been in a prime position to initiate insurance and other frauds. At the same time, the agricultural insurance agency ANAGSA was abolished, having become notorious for corrupt practices as blatant as collecting indemnification for phantom crops. This agency was replaced in June 1990 by a new insurance company, AGROASEMEX, a parastatal affiliate of the Aseguradora Mexicana, which was to operate with only one-third the personnel employed by ANAGSA and without field inspectors. So far, this cleanup campaign has uncovered hundreds of major frauds at all levels, including among ejidal officers. However, petty swindles appear to have increased in the latest phase of the debt crisis, largely in response to massive decline in real wages to less than half of 1982 levels. With average salaries of less than $300 a month, agrarian bureaucrats often feel compelled, at the very least, to cheat on their gasoline allowances, to extort boxes of produce from the ejidatarios, and to rob their employers of time by padding their work sheets.

These new anticorruption measures were paralleled by a major restructuring of BANRURAL as a normal banking institution after two decades of paternalistically supervising deficit production. It now allocates credit only to those crops, regions, and producers where an adequate return on investment is virtually guaranteed. Thus, the majority of Mexican peasants have been excluded from bank credit programs since the 1989 summer agricultural cycle, when 1

million of the nation's almost 3 million ejidatarios fell into default, with over
1 billion pesos still remaining unpaid by the end of the year (*El Economista*, 1
February 1990).[7] In order to further reduce this delinquency level and provide
increased production incentives, BANRURAL interest rates were slashed 15.75
percentage points to 28 percent in 1990. Nevertheless, overdue loans as a percentage of total agricultural loans increased in 1993 from 11 percent to almost
15 percent, prompting the government to establish a special program to restructure delinquent accounts (U.S. Embassy, 1994). Interest rates soared to
over 70 percent after the December 1994 currency devaluation and the ensuing
crisis.

The formal agricultural strategy of the Salinas administration was articulated on a piecemeal basis over the term of office, but the emphasis was clearly
on the recapitalization of agriculture via a more flexible, balanced, and heterogeneous development model attuned to the different needs of various types of
producers, crops, and regions. This approach involved deregulation and disag-
gregation of the preexisting policies toward pricing incentives, subsidies, credit,
insurance, investment, technical assistance, organization, and training. Important elements in this strategy included institutional and legislative reform;
intensification of production through high technology; promotion of agribusiness in regional development corridors; restructuring, trimming, and decentralization of government development institutions; the liberation of most
crops except staples from official price controls; and the creation of an agricultural commodities exchange (SARH, 1990).

Overall, the intent was to open agriculture to the external market gradually
and selectively, to extend the linkages between the peasant and commercial sectors, and to provide support programs for marginal producers with "productive content that will give them economic viability in the medium term,
moving away from the administration of poverty in any shape or form"
(SARH, 1990:1, my translation). Thus, in tandem with the productivity thrust,
producer initiative and participation in policy generation were to be encouraged through dialogue, as the state engaged in a selective withdrawal from direct intervention in peasant agriculture. These goals were to be pursued by the
various agrarian agencies, collaborating in committees composed of representatives from all the institutions and interest groups involved, including formal
peasant organizations and ejidal delegates, and operating at national, regional,
and local levels.

While the watchword "concertación" (consensus building or concertation
[Collier, 1995]) sums up President Salinas's style of agrarian policy implementation, the content was dominated by the productivity imperative. This pre-
occupation with the restructuring of agriculture first and foremost as a
business enterprise rather than a social category was reflected in the unexpected appointment of Carlos Hank González as minister of agriculture in December 1989. Hank had an exceptional track record as a tough and efficient

public-sector manager and, in the past, had made no secret of his conviction that the ejido was an anachronism that Mexico could no longer afford.

A core component of the recapitalization strategy was contained in the 1990–1994 Plan Nacional de Modernización del Campo (National Plan of Rural Modernization), which gave additional impetus to associations between ejidatarios and the private sector. Such production units had been legalized in 1980, but few were created because of the financial exigencies of the debt crisis and a continuing lack of clarity with respect to constraints imposed by the corporate ejidal system, wherein usufruct tenure officially prohibited alienation of land before the new Agrarian Law of 1992.

Under the new "alliances for production," contracts between ejidos and private investors can be very flexible, permitting ejidatarios to receive income from the outright rental of lands, from wage labor on the agribusiness enterprise, and from profit dividends. These kinds of arrangements are not new; indeed, they have been the norm, though technically illegal, for U.S. agribusinesses operating on ejidal lands in the north since 1950 as well as in the large-scale agricultural projects initiated by the Mexican government in the 1960s and 1970s, such as Tabasco's Plan Chontalpa and Campeche's Edzná Project. However, such contracts can now be engaged in by any portion of the ejidal sector that can attract private capital and are not restricted to favored enclaves or state developments. The new system also demands a greater degree of production responsibility from ejidatarios, with the aim of fostering a business ethos in that sector as well as encouraging domestic in addition to international investment. Within a few months of announcement of the initiative, several major Mexican agribusinesses signed contracts with ejidos, including Maseca, El Trasgo, and Gamesa. The latter, a corporation concerned mainly with food processing, in June 1990 formed the first such society, the Vaquerías Project in the state of Nuevo León, to produce beans collectively on 2,500 hectares of irrigated ejidal land, funded equally by the enterprise and the government (Santos de Hoyos, 1990). In 1992 Gamesa was acquired by Pepsico, and in 1994 the Vaquerías Project was dissolved after disputes over profit shares.

Although the agricultural policy of the Salinas administration was oriented toward promoting productivity, profitability, and recapitalization, increased producer participation and responsibility were a recurrent theme underlying most of the reforms. This motif came to the fore in a dramatic program, the Programa Nacional de Solidaridad (PRONASOL, National Solidarity Program), announced in December 1988 during Salinas's inauguration. Four general principles guided the actions of PRONASOL: community initiative, popular participation and organization, coresponsibility, and "transparency, honesty, and efficiency in the management of the resources" (Salinas de Gortari, 1990:6, my translation). The intention was to stimulate self-sustaining economic and social dynamism by visibly demonstrating the solidarity of the state with popular necessities in a concerted thrust to overcome poverty through funding for specific productive and welfare initiatives.

In agriculture, under the new slogans of "confianza y esfuerzo propio" (confidence and one's own effort) and "pagar es corresponder" (to pay is to reciprocate) (Gobierno del Estado de Campeche, 1990), the Fondo de Solidaridad para la Producción (Solidarity Fund for Production) supported more than 400,000 peasants in 1,350 municipalities over the first year of operation. The program is a rural branch of PRONASOL and was intended to benefit peasants who cultivate lands of low productivity in high-risk zones, who are no longer eligible for BANRURAL credit under the restructured system, and who are not in default to the bank through personal delinquency at the time of application. Under PRONASOL, individual peasants could receive interest-free credit for up to four hectares of crops at $300,000 a hectare (a total of US$450), and no guarantee was required other than the promise of the producer: "palabra ofrecida, palabra cumplida" (word offered, word kept) (Salinas de Gortari 1990:7). The program was managed autonomously by local-level committees, and campesinos (peasants) received credit directly from the municipal government without the intervention of intermediaries. Additional incentives for loan repayment were that the funds collected would be allocated to "works of social benefit" at the discretion of each municipality and that lists of defaulters were published locally at the end of the agricultural cycle (Gobierno del Estado de Campeche, 1990).

PRONASOL marked a radical departure in Mexican agricultural development strategies in terms of the extreme level of decentralization involved, the high degree of interdevelopment agency consultation required, the emphasis on agent-producer collaboration rather than old-style paternalism, and the focus on the individual responsibility of the campesino rather than collective liability for debt, which had been the foundation of the official bank credit system and the cause of much default. Furthermore, campesinos who received PRONASOL funds were not compelled to grow a particular crop or employ a stipulated technical packet of agricultural inputs. Rather, the program aimed "to stimulate the incursion into new activities that recognize the experience of the campesinos" (Salinas de Gortari, 1990:7, my translation). In this way, President Salinas hoped that PRONASOL would "permit us to break the vicious circle that has linked agricultural credit to disaster and default while promoting corruption, deception, and paternalism" (Salinas de Gortari, 1990:7, my translation).

The implications of this bold move were clear in terms of underscoring the government's commitment both to increasing productivity without the chronic waste and diversion of funds endemic to such attempts in the past and to promoting individual responsibility and an ethos of success within the constraints of the ejidal system. However, whether PRONASOL has succeeded on either count is doubtful. This is particularly the case in view of the additional agricultural stresses occasioned by the move away from import substitution and self-sufficiency to a market-driven competitive structure, reflected in the sector's decline in GDP share from 8.5 percent in 1987 to 7.4 percent in 1993 (U.S. Embassy, 1994).

Critics of PRONASOL, including many peasants, saw the program as little more than a less than subtle attempt to boost flagging support for the Partido Revolucionario Institucional (PRI, Revolutionary Institutional Party) in the face of widespread discontent with years of austerity and little tangible evidence of economic recovery despite the rhetoric of dramatic reform. In particular, complaints about the prolongation of wage and price control pacts became vociferous even among ejidatarios, until recently among the most stalwart (if the most coerced) party faithful, at least at voting time. Thus, PRONASOL, often referred to as PRINASOL, was perceived as a typical populist strategy to buy votes before the crucial 1991 gubernatorial, senate, and congressional elections and was employed blatantly as a campaign tool prior to the August 1994 presidential elections (*Wall Street Journal,* 26 August 1994, 18 November 1994; Cornelius et al., 1994).

In a structural sense, the terms of reference of PRONASOL's agricultural activities seem likely to harden the boundary between peasants with possibilities for commercial agriculture and those relegated to subsistence production on a permanent basis. Officially, PRONASOL loans are not tied to basic crops. However, in view of the continuing government emphasis on promoting staple production, the lack of real alternatives in most regions, the high cost of fertilizer and other agricultural inputs, and the greatly reduced allocation of funds per hectare compared with official bank credit, most ejidatarios have no alternative but to continue to grow basic crops, such as maize and beans. Consequently, even with interest-free loans and slight increases in guaranteed rates, profits on the maximum four hectares funded tend to be minimal, at best, as a function of the low value of staples and the small surplus after household subsistence needs are satisfied.

These tendencies are supposed to be offset by the Programa de Apoyos Directos al Campo (PROCAMPO, the Program for Direct Supports to the Countryside) introduced in October 1993 to support farm income while encouraging farmers to select planting strategies on the basis of market forces. The intent is to rationalize crop production by abolishing guaranteed prices in favor of government payments on a per-hectare basis to all qualifying farmers, thus increasing access to subsidies for smaller producers. For example, in the past, only some 30 percent of corn producers (those with sufficient surplus to sell) benefited from the price support system (U.S. Embassy, 1994). Initially, the program covers basic crops including corn, beans, wheat, rice, sorghum, soya, barley, safflower, and cotton. For the 1993–1994 fall-winter crop cycle, each producer received 300 new pesos (approximately US$100 per hectare); this rose to 350 pesos per hectare for the 1994 spring-summer cycle, with full implementation in fall 1994 (SARH, 1993). Payments will continue over fifteen years (decreasing after the tenth year) in order to ease adjustment problems caused by the phasing out of all agricultural tariff and nontariff barriers under NAFTA by the end of this period.

Critics maintain that the bulk of PROCAMPO resources ended up in the hands of the larger producers and that payments to small farmers amounted to only 1.70 pesos a day, barely enough to buy a taco (*El Financiero,* 13 October 1993, 18 October 1993). Furthermore, it will take much more than an interim support program to make Mexican agricultural products competitive internationally, with the exception of selected fruits and vegetables (in particular, winter season, tropical, and other specialty items).[8] In any event, it seems that many peasants either did not apply for PROCAMPO payments or used them for basic household needs rather than for investment in equipment or improved agricultural practices that might boost competitiveness.

Thus, the overall implication of PRONASOL and PROCAMPO, together with the restructuring of BANRURAL operations and the renewed Alianza para el Bienestar (Alliance for Well-being) under Ernesto Zedillo's Administration (1994–2000), appears to be the repeasantization of those who have failed to perform under previous misguided government strategies for modernizing ejidal agriculture. In other words, the majority of peasants will be eligible, at best, for incentive programs likely to re-create household subsistence units with little or no economic surplus, through a return to reliance largely on low-value staples cultivated via traditional practices. At the same time, the few ejidatarios possessing good production records with priority crops in high-yield regions are to become full-fledged, high-technology farmers for whom agriculture will be a business rather than a marginal way of life, in collaboration with the state via the bank credit mechanism or the private sector by means of contracts (Singelmann and Otero, 1995). The government maintains that this opening up of the ejido constitutes neither a license for private enterprise to despoil the social sector nor a step toward the imminent dissolution of this previously sacrosanct land tenure institution. Whether these favored ejidatarios will become truly independent competitive farmers or de facto rural proletarians— wage laborers on their own land and lacking any real production autonomy— remains to be seen.

As far as PRONASOL is concerned, the lamentable fact is that some such program is desperately needed in order to bring a degree of immediate relief to those millions of rural Mexicans who are sinking daily into deeper poverty. The swing back to the PRI in the August 1991 midterm elections and the August 1994 presidential elections is indicative of PRONASOL's success in extensive spending on highly visible social programs, even if many peasants remain skeptical about the long-term implications of its agricultural component.

Peasant misgivings escalated in the wake of the radical changes to the land tenure system that were introduced to Article 27 of the Mexican Constitution

and passed in February 1992. This reform legitimates the various leasing, rent-
ing, and collaborative ventures encouraged by the Salinas administration and
marks an end to land redistribution to peasants. President Salinas insisted that
this reform would mean the transformation rather than the end of the ejido
and that change would be gradual and a matter of choice. An ejido would be
able to grant title only if a 66 percent majority of its members agreed, and the
new owners would be free to do as they pleased with their parcels (DeWalt et
al., 1994). Critics denounced the reform as counterrevolutionary and likely to
further concentrate land in the hands of the caciques (rural bosses) and multinationals as uncompetitive ejidatarios would be dispossessed for a pittance.

This significant step toward the abolition of the social property established
by the revolution underscores the government's determination to remove a primary obstacle to increased domestic and foreign investment in Mexican agriculture. Progress has been slow, however, in providing title to landholders, and
investment also continues to be sluggish because of this title problem, inadequate financial resources for rural development, the lack of a rural real estate
market, and fragmented land holdings (U.S. Embassy, 1994).[9] Furthermore, it
seems doubtful that any major investor, foreign or domestic, will be interested
in alliances for production on the marginal lands of the majority of ejidos in
southern Mexico, where such traditional predators on the peasantry as rural
bosses, cattle ranchers, and merchant middlemen are likely to make a killing
from appropriation or sales of newly privatized parcels. Thus it appears that
the quasi-privatization of the ejido will inevitably accelerate socioeconomic
differentiation and proletarianization. For the heirs of Emiliano Zapata's battle
for "land and liberty," the fruits of the revolution have been continuing subordination in a progression from the old hacendados (landlords) to the PRI
caciques and, more recently, the agricultural development bureaucracy. The future now seems to hold the "choice" of either accepting yet another set of masters (the chief executive officers of agribusiness), continuing the subsistence
struggle on the most impoverished land without the benefits and costs of state
paternalism, or taking the "liberty" of abandoning farming altogether.

Restructuring or Refunctionalization?
Prospects for Mexican Agriculture

In his evaluation of Mexican agricultural policy since the revolution, Arturo
Warman distinguished between "política agrícola" and "política agraria": The
former implies a technocratic production orientation emphasizing mechaniza-
tion and state-controlled modernization; the latter stresses the social function
of land and redistribution to the landless (Warman, 1978). These two facets
have interplayed in different ways at different times, each constraining the
other. The outcome has been the evolution of a highly distinctive relationship

between the Mexican state and the countryside over the course of the twentieth century, particularly as expressed in policies affecting the ejido. Política
agrícola and política agraria have been regarded as flip sides of the same coin,
but in recent years the productivity orientation has become paramount. Until
the consolidation of the debt crisis, this was marked by ever-increasing state intervention in the ejidal sector.

The ejido has evolved from initial revolutionary reform, which effectively
tied peasant labor to land, through five decades of infrastructural neglect by
the government, during which it served as a tranquilizing device and holding
tank providing cheap labor for commercial agriculture and subsidized food to
urban consumers, to the recent period of concerted state modernization initiatives. This phase, lasting from 1970 to the early 1980s when it ended abruptly
under debt-crisis austerity, was characterized by massive government intervention in peasant production via controlled collectivization, credit societies,
large-scale development projects, infrastructural investment, and a variety of
incentive programs and subsidies.[10] The cumulative effect of these agricultural
policies has been the progressive loss of peasant production autonomy and the
consolidation of the ejido at the base of the ruling-party pyramid through effective bureaucratization of agriculture right down to the grassroots level.

The net result of this statist rural development strategy in a rapidly changing global economic context has been two decades of intensifying agricultural
crisis. In particular, the internationalization of the Mexican economy as exhib-
ited in agriculture, reflected in the increasing emphasis on exports, domestic
agribusiness, and cattle rearing, has displaced basic foods production commer-
cially and increased pressures on staple crop land (Barkin and Suárez, 1982;
Sanderson, 1986). For ejidatarios, this has often meant either designation as
cheap part-time laborers for capital-intensive cash crop production or relega-
tion to low-value staple producer status through a succession of policies and
programs designed to stimulate basic food production. The overall outcome
was the creation of a quasi-modernized sector of heavily subsidized yet marginal peasants dependent on poorly planned state initiatives—a contradiction
in terms both with respect to economic efficiency and social justice, as the latter has been redefined in terms of production tons instead of rights to land.[11]

Despite this high cost-benefit ratio, extensive government spending on agricultural modernization programs for the ejidal sector has served the interests
of both the state and the private sector by keeping at least some peasants tied
to otherwise infrasubsistence holdings, where they need to remain until the
formal economy is able to absorb them fully.[12] A relatively stable and semi-
skilled pool of cheap labor has been created, functionalized to the requirements of commercial agriculture but still dependent on traditional subsistence
activities because of the limited remuneration accruing from state projects and
temporary wage work. In other words, a rural semiproletariat has been consolidated as the peasantry has been reshaped through articulation by the labor

market as part of an evolving relationship of asymmetrical complementarity between commercial and peasant agriculture (Kearney, 1980; Bartra and Otero, 1987; Bartra, 1993).

From 1940 until 1970, this implicit subsidy of commercial agriculture by the peasantry was paralleled by a net transfer of value from the agricultural sector to industry through production of cheap food for urban areas where low wages could also be sustained. This direct transfer was reversed after 1970 with the injection of state funds and other agricultural supports, but the continued repression of crop prices together with the inefficiencies and discontinuities of state programs have acted as a disincentive to both private- and social-sector investment and fostered an ongoing outflow of resources from the countryside. This long-term rural decapitalization has been further accentuated under debt-crisis austerity by the sharp reduction in government agricultural subsidies, and the official crop-pricing policy became, once again, a primary device for masking inflation. The wage and price control pacts have underscored the state's implicit antiagrarian bias by excluding the majority of agricultural inputs from regulation. These policies of price and wage controls have continued in the administration of Ernesto Zedillo.

At this juncture, the ongoing agricultural crisis, the continuing need for firm restraint in public-sector spending, and the rapid transition to a free market economy are transforming the previous modus vivendi among the state, the private sector, and the peasantry. Since the mid-1980s, Mexican agricultural policy has developed an even more emphatic stress on *política agrícola* but with a major reversal of the previous state interventionism as far as peasant agriculture is concerned, in keeping with the dramatic opening of the economy overall.

However, reform in agriculture is much more difficult than in other sectors of the economy, given the depth of the thirty-year-old crisis, the extent and complexity of the structural imbalances, the existence of politically sensitive areas such as the ejido and food subsidies, and problems with reconciling comparative advantage in this sector, both internally and externally. Mexicans at large have yet to enjoy the tangible fruits of economic liberalization. The peasantry in particular has seen little evidence so far that market forces per se will be directly equated with improved social conditions, particularly given the uncompetitive position of much of Mexico's agricultural production in the world arena.

Consequently, the main agricultural question for the Mexican government at this time would seem to be this: Even if the nation can be returned to export-crop vitality and self-sufficiency in basic foods, can the correlative processes that have impoverished the peasantry be reversed? More specifically, because increasing state intervention has been one of the main causes of the agricultural crisis and the intensification of peasant marginality, is the state likely to be able to legislate—or rather, create through deregulation—a productive base that is both economically viable and socially and politically just?

The Salinas administration seemed confident that it could achieve this goal and initiated a number of bold reforms and innovative programs during its term of office. The task of reestablishing economic dynamism in Mexican agriculture is huge, however, and the obstacles are enormous. The value of U.S.-Mexican bilateral agricultural trade increased to $3.9 billion in the six months following the implementation of NAFTA (January–June 1994), 9 percent higher than during the same period in 1993, yet this still resulted in a net agricultural surplus of $875 million in favor of the United States. During that period, U.S. agricultural exports to Mexico rose 11 percent over the previous year; Mexican agricultural exports to the United States increased 6 percent (U.S. Embassy, 1994).

Adjustment problems associated with the transition to a free market economy have led to a sharp decline in agricultural productivity in some sectors, and this has been compounded by continuing high interest rates for agricultural loans, rising input costs, and decreasing commodity prices. Meanwhile, erratic weather conditions make harvests uncertain in many regions. In sum, it will take much more than the mere fact of a free market economy and a handful of new programs to reverse the effects of fifty years of favoring the city over the countryside, a policy resulting in decapitalization that has reached critical levels under the debt crisis.

The agricultural policies of the Salinas administration can be expected to be continued under the Zedillo regime. To date, it appears that the outcome is likely to be further socioeconomic differentiation among the already divided peasantry, a situation that mediates against reversal of the ethos of failure for the majority, who are severely decapitalized in social as well as material terms. Specifically, the opening up of the ejido to associations with agribusiness seems likely to promote increased de facto proletarianization, as ejidatarios become the servants of the private sector rather than the wards of the state, probably enjoying more prosperity than before but still functioning as peones (laborers) on their own land for a new breed of patrones (masters). On the other hand, programs such as PRONASOL and PROCAMPO for the most marginal peasants are unlikely to fortify low-value staple crop producers against the forces of international competition. Rather, contrary to the government's proclaimed intent, the net result of this type of individual incentive program is likely to be the inadvertent repeasantization, in the short term at least, of a sizable segment of the ejidal sector. It will likely return those ejidatarios who had failed to perform adequately under state-directed agricultural modernization programs to household subsistence units producing little or no economic surplus. In the long term, given the uncertainties of staple production on the subsistence margins, this strategy seems likely to further accelerate the proletarianization process, whether or not free trade produces the promised increased employment opportunities and better wages. In the interim, however, some ejidatarios have been able to profit simply from the increased farming flexibility with respect to local conditions and opportunities permitted by the dwindling state presence. Nevertheless, from the peasant perspective overall, the winds of neoliberal change mean increased uncertainty and stress, as they wait to see if the new era of free market forces means life after debt, fulfillment of the Mexican government's constitutional commitment to improve their social condition, or de facto abrogation of any state responsibility for their destiny. One peasant put it this way during the Salinas era:

> Agriculture today is like a waiting room where we guess what will be the outcome of this sudden outburst of energy Salinas is turning on the countryside. This is quite a shock after years of tortoise-like bureaucracy. Is it real reform? We don't know. If it is, can he get away with it, and what will happen to Mexican peasants after the free trade tornado (Mexican peasant, Bonfil, Campeche, February 1990)?

Notes

1. Parts of this chapter are revised and updated versions from a text that appeared originally in Gates, 1993.

2. The Mexican ejido is a unique form of peasant land tenure combining communal title vested in the state with usufruct rights to land worked individually or collectively; the system originated in the breakdown of large estates during the postrevolutionary land reform after 1917. The beneficiaries of this land reform are known as ejidatarios. Despite the low productivity of many ejidos (attributed to the small size of individual plots, the contradictions of collective production, the insecurity of corporate tenure, poor land, or inappropriate state policies, depending on the perspective of the critic), the institution has persisted as a visible symbol of revolutionary reform via land redistribution to dispossessed peasants. However, agricultural policy shifts over the past decade contain a number of components that appear to undermine the ejido's foundation by threatening the termination of redistribution or by opening it up to private investment (Bailey, 1981; Bartra and Otero, 1987; Gates, 1988; Wessman, 1984). The new Agrarian Law of 1992 formally ended the state's responsibility for redistributing land and opened the possibility of privatizing the ejido while promoting the association between ejidatarios and private capitalists (Cornelius 1992; DeWalt et al., 1994).

3. Agriculture increased its contribution to GDP from 8.8 percent in 1982 to 9.7 percent in 1986 (*Excelsior*, 29 January 1987).

4. Maize production suffered a particularly severe decline under the debt crisis, with total yields falling from 13.18 million tons in 1983 to 10.6 million tons in 1988 (Gordillo de Anda, 1990).

5. Mexico's population grew from 66.8 million in 1980 to 81 million in 1990, an increment of some 4 million less than had been estimated from decade census trends (*Excelsior*, 5 September 1990).

6. By the end of 1993, the number of state-owned enterprises was down to 217 from approximately 1,100 in the early 1980s. Income from the sales of these enterprises totaled over US$21 billion, of which 91 percent was used to amortize public-sector debt (U.S. Embassy, 1994).

7. Mexican agriculture experienced another disastrous year in 1989. As a result, basic grain imports reached 10.3 million tons at a cost of over $4 billion and represented 30 percent of national consumption (*Excelsior,* 20 May 1990).

8. Other Mexican agricultural products estimated to have considerable sales potential in the United States include feed grains and balanced feeds, oilseeds and products, dairy products, and alcoholic beverages. U.S. agricultural sectors likely to face increasing pressure from Mexican competition under NAFTA include fresh and processed tomato products, asparagus, frozen vegetables, citrus, strawberries, and fresh-cut flowers. The Mexican government hopes that increased export earnings from such sectors will be able to cover the costs of importing products in which the country is not competitive, such as maize and other grains (U.S. Embassy, 1994).

9. Some investors, however, have been encouraged by the changes in Article 27. For example, both foreign and domestic companies are engaging in partnerships with ejidos in the southeastern lowlands to expand forest products (U.S. Embassy, 1994), and Trasgo, the big Mexican chicken producer, has greatly increased its ejidal collaborative ventures since the legitimization of its previous activities in this area (*Wall Street Journal,* 10 June 1993).

10. It has been estimated that approximately half of Mexico's ejidos are involved in some kind of production association on an inter- or intraejidal basis or in collaboration with private property owners and agribusiness (Gordillo de Anda, 1990).

11. The overall record of minimal productivity increases achieved by state agricultural programs for the ejidal sector (at high investment, opportunity, environmental, and social cost) overshadows some notable exceptions wherein planned development resulted in greatly improved economic dynamism or a significant rise in producer initiative. Some relative success stories include the Edzná-Bonfil project in Campeche and Plan Chontalpa in Tabasco, where, for a time in the 1970s, substantially increased income levels were matched by notable gains in peasant management autonomy. More sustained success in terms of increased crop yields, self-management, and democratic organization has been achieved by semiproletarian direct producers in the Coalición de Ejidos Colectivos de los Valles del Yaqui y el Mayo (Coalition of Collective Ejidos of the Yaqui and Mayo Valleys) as a result of conscious efforts to achieve a degree of independence from both the state and the private sector (Otero, 1989). However, these achievements have been under increasing stress since the onset of the debt crisis.

12. At the beginning of the 1980s, it was calculated that 52 percent of Mexico's ejidatarios and 63 percent of private property owners operated infrasubsistence-level units of less than four hectares of nonirrigated land (Gordillo de Anda, 1990).

Bibliography

Bailey, John J. 1981. "Agrarian Reform in Mexico." *Current History,* 80(469):357–360.
Barkin, David, and Blanca Suárez. 1982. *El fin de la autosuficiencia alimentaria.* Mexico City: Nueva Imagen.
Bartra, Roger. 1993. *Agrarian Structure and Political Power in Mexico.* Baltimore, Md.: Johns Hopkins University.

Bartra, Roger, and Gerardo Otero. 1987. "Agrarian Crisis and Social Differentiation in Mexico." *Journal of Peasant Studies*, 14(13):334–362.

Calva, José Luis. 1988. *Crisis agrícola y alimentaria en México, 1982–1988.* Mexico City: Fontamara.

Centro de Estudios Económicos del Sector Privado. 1987. *La economía subterranea en México.* Mexico, D.F.: Diana.

Collier, David. 1995. "Trajectory of a Concept: 'Corporatism' in the Study of Latin American Politics." Pp. 135–162 in Peter H. Smith, ed., *Latin America in Comparative Perspective: New Approaches to Methods and Analysis.* Boulder, Colo.: Westview.

Cornelius, Wayne A. 1992. "The Politics and Economics of Reforming the *Ejido* Sector in Mexico: An Overview and Research Agenda." *LASA Forum*, 23(3):3–10.

Cornelius, Wayne A., Ann L. Craig, and Jonathon Fox. 1994. *Transforming State-Society Relations in Mexico: The National Solidarity Strategy.* U.S.-Mexico Contemporary Perspectives Series, 6. San Diego: Center for U.S.-Mexican Studies, University of California, San Diego.

DeWalt, Billie R., Martha W. Rees, and Arthur D. Murphy. 1994. *The End of Agrarian Reform in Mexico: Past Lessons, Future Prospects.* Transformation of Rural Mexico Series, no. 3. San Diego: Ejido Reform Research Project, Center for U.S.-Mexican Studies, University of California, San Diego.

Economist, The. 1991. "Mexico: Not so Sweetcorn." 2 March, p. 44.

———. 1994. "Foreign Investment in Mexico." 15 October, p. 91.

Gates, Marilyn. 1988. "Codifying Marginality: The Evolution of Mexican Agricultural Policy and Its Impact on the Peasantry." *Journal of Latin American Studies*, 20 (November):277–311.

———. 1993. *In Default: Peasants, the Debt Crisis, and the Agricultural Challenge in Mexico.* Boulder: Westview Press.

Gobierno del Estado de Campeche. 1990. "Programa Nacional de Solidaridad." Campeche. March.

Gordillo de Anda, Gustavo. 1990. "Policies for Modernizing the Agricultural Sector: Financial and Technical Support." Pp. 32–40 in *The Development of Agriculture in Mexico: Current Prospects and Policies*, Texas Papers on Mexico, Conference Publications Series, no. 90–02. Austin: The Mexican Center, Institute of Latin American Studies, University of Texas.

IMF Survey. 1989. 10 July.

Kearney, Michael. 1980. "Agribusiness and the Demise or the Rise of the Peasantry." *Latin American Perspectives*, 7(4):115–124.

Ostler, Patrick. 1989. *The Mexicans: A Personal Portrait of a People.* New York: Harper & Row.

Otero, Gerardo. 1989. "The New Agrarian Movement: Self-Managed, Democratic Production." *Latin American Perspectives*, 16(4):28–59.

Salinas de Gortari, Carlos. 1990. *Segundo informe presidencial, 1990.* México D.F.: Secretaría de Programación y Presupuesto.

Sanderson, Steven E. 1986. *The Transformation of Mexican Agriculture: International Structure and the Politics of Rural Change.* Princeton: Princeton University Press.

Santos de Hoyos, Alberto. 1990. "Partnership in Production: An Option for Modernizing the Agricultural Sector." Pp. 45–51 in *The Development of Agriculture in Mexico:*

Current Prospects and Policies, Texas Papers on Mexico, Conference Publications Series, no. 90–02. Austin: The Mexican Center, Institute of Latin American Studies, University of Texas.

SARH (Secretaría de Agricultura y Recursos Hidráulicos). 1990. "Programa Nacional de Modernización del Campo: Informe General." Campeche.

———. 1993. PROCAMPO. México, D.F.

Singelmann, Peter, and Gerardo Otero. 1995. "Peasants, Sugar, and the Mexican State: From Social Guarantees to Neoliberalism." In Peter Singelmann, ed., *Mexican Cane Growers and the Sugar Industry in Mexico,* Transformation of Rural Mexico Series, no. 7. San Diego: Ejido Reform Research Project, Center for U.S.-Mexican Studies, University of California, San Diego.

U.S. Embassy. 1994. *1994 Agricultural Situation Report.* México, D.F.

Warman, Arturo. 1978. "Frente a la crisis: Política agraria o política agrícola?" *Comercio Exterior* 28(6):681–687.

Wessman, James W. 1984. "The Agrarian Question in Mexico." *Latin American Research Review,* 19(2):243–259.

4

From Export-Oriented to Import-Oriented Industrialization: Changes in Mexico's Manufacturing Sector, 1988–1994

Enrique Dussel Peters

In the context of the tendency to liberalize economies in Latin America in particular and in the capitalist periphery in general, the structural change of Mexico's economy is of utmost interest. Mexico has been regarded as one of the first and most successful cases of liberalization and has taken a leading role among Latin American nations. Furthermore, the Mexican case has extended over a period sufficiently long to allow analysts to evaluate the impact of that liberalization. In this sense the results should be of interest to other nations following the "path of liberalization."

Mexico's manufacturing sector was at the center of the development strategy during the import-substitution period and has continued to play a significant role since liberalization. This chapter focuses on the conditions of Mexico's manufacturing sector in order to assess structural changes since 1988. One of the central tasks is to examine, through the study of production and trade patterns, how certain branches of manufacturing either benefited from or were hurt by liberalization.

This chapter is divided into three main sections. In the first key macroeconomic issues are addressed that characterize the period since 1988 in terms of their impact on manufacturing. In the second section industrial policy since 1988 is examined; while the third focuses on the structural change that has occurred in this sector. Furthermore, the analysis of the evolution of employment proves to be of critical importance for both macroeconomic development and for sociopolitical aspects examined in other chapters of this book.

Structural Change
in Mexico's Macroeconomy Since 1988

During the 1980s new international tendencies had a significant impact on Mexico's economy. On the one hand, after 1982 the United States shifted from being a net capital exporter to a net capital importer in order to finance its trade and fiscal deficits with external credits, a shift that caused increasing real interest rates and a relative "illiquidity" in international capital markets. This process meant that nations like Mexico, among others, were unable to service their external debt in 1982. Moreover, it showed that massive external debt would no longer be available in international markets, as had been the case since the mid-1960s (Dussel Peters, 1993). On the other hand, the collapse of oil prices during the 1980s resulted in a rapid decline of oil revenues, from $16.6 billion in 1982 to $6.5 billion in 1994. Nevertheless, it is important to stress that Mexico benefited significantly under the new selective approach of the United States and multilateral agencies from the beginning of the 1980s. Mexico was granted preferential treatment regarding its external debt through the Baker and Brady initiatives in 1985 and 1989 as well as through bilateral trade agreements with the United States and the Enterprise Initiative for the Americas, announced in 1990. A central piece of the latter, the North American Free Trade Agreement (NAFTA), integrates Mexico into the North American economy as an initial step toward hemispheric integration.

Within this international context and after the crisis of the import-substitution strategy by 1982, the de la Madrid administration (1982–1988) began gradually to liberalize the economy. However, it is generally accepted that the government's initial gradual approach to the crisis for the period 1982–1987 failed. The "socialization of losses" was high. Real wages fell drastically, as did overall public expenditures, and the distribution of income deteriorated. Moreover, the implemented gradual approach became economically unsustainable: High foreign debt service and inflation rates as well as low rates of investment and overall economic growth in GDP did not allow for a continuation of this strategy (see Table 4.1; Dussel Peters and Kim, 1993; López G., 1994; Ros, 1990).

Several economic pacts (or shock programs), the first established in December 1987, were imposed in an agreement among the government, the official unions, and the private sector. They became the centerpiece of the new liberalization strategy. Control over inflation, financial deficit, and foreign investment were the main priorities of the government. The crucial elements for macroeconomic liberalization included significant tariff reductions, privatization of state-owned enterprises, and an overall shift toward "flexible specialization" in industrial relations. The latter involved the continued prevalence of authoritarian political structures and nondemocratic official unions to guarantee an abundant supply of cheap labor power.

Various new policies and institutions differentiate the macroeconomic conditions of the period since 1988 (Aspe Armella, 1993; Córdoba, 1991). First, the reduction of inflation rates and of the financial deficit as well as the attraction of foreign investment became the main "exogenous" variables (or priorities) of liberalization.

Second, the government expected that a change in the "macroeconomic environment"[1]—that is, a reduction of inflation rates and of the financial deficit—would induce a sectoral and microeconomic structural change. Sectoral policies were thus not to be implemented because they could distort and revert the macroeconomic strategy.

Third, the private manufacturing sector was placed at the center of the export-oriented and modernization strategy. Structural change was primarily understood as the process of privatization or reduction of state activities, which would reallocate factors of production efficiently. The privatization of state-owned enterprises, which began in 1983, was agressively reinforced after 1989. Privatization was not only important to increase the role of the private sector in the economy, but it also became a strong source of revenue for the government, which accumulated $23.7 billion for the period 1989–1993. The number of state-owned enterprises fell drastically—from 1,155 in 1982 to 210 by the end of 1993—and the privatization of commercial banks and Teléfonos de México accounted for 78.1 percent of total revenue from privatization in this period.

Fourth, import liberalization became a crucial aspect of this new strategy, since it would allow an export orientation of the economy, particularly of manufacturing, through cheap imported inputs and the adjustment of domestic relative prices and the economy in general. By the end of 1985 import licenses were replaced by tariffs. In order to join GATT in 1986, Mexico continued unilateral import liberalization in 1986 by the elimination of official import prices. The pace of liberalization was accelerated in 1987 and achieved a definitive status, reducing tariffs to a maximum of 20 percent ad valorem. As a result, five tariff levels accounted for five categories (ranging from 0 percent to 20 percent), and the weighted average tariffs declined from 28.5 percent in 1985 to 12.5 percent in 1992. Moreover, NAFTA reduced even further the tariff levels with Canada and the United States. Most of these reductions are at the product level (SECOFI, 1993).

Fifth, in addition to cheap labor power and energy, foreign investment became the main financing source of the new export-oriented model. Up to 1972, the Law to Promote Mexican Investment and to Regulate Foreign Investment gave the government the discretionary power to determine in which activities and sectors up to 51 percent of ownership had to be national. These conditions were substantially changed in 1989, and the reform primarily addressed small- and medium-sized firms because it permitted an automatic 100 percent share of foreign capital if foreign investments (FI) could show a positive balance in

TABLE 4.1
Main Macroeconomic Indicators, 1980–1994[a]

	1980	1981	1982	1983	1984
GDP	8.2	8.8	−0.6	−4.2	3.6
GDP per capita	5.4	6.1	−3.0	−6.5	1.2
Employment	14.7	6.2	−0.3	−2.3	2.3
Real wages					
(1980 = 100)	100.0	106.4	99.7	81.5	80.5
Gross fixed investment/GDP	24.8	26.4	23.0	17.5	17.9
Private	14.1	14.3	12.3	11.0	11.3
Public	10.7	12.1	10.2	6.6	6.6
Gross investments/GDP	27.2	27.4	23.0	20.7	19.9
Domestic	13.6	12.8	12.6	12.5	11.1
External	5.0	6.0	0.5	−3.9	−2.6
Depreciation	8.6	8.6	9.8	12.2	11.4
Inflation	29.8	28.7	98.8	80.8	59.2
Financial deficit/GDP	7.5	14.1	16.9	8.6	8.5
Exports	35.2	18.8	23.8	12.3	7.3
Imports	34.8	16.9	−40.2	−35.4	20.5
Trade balance (US$ billion)	−4.7	−5.7	8.7	12.6	11.9
Current account (US$ billion)	−10.7	−16.1	−6.2	5.4	4.2
Capital account (US$ billion)	11.4	26.4	9.8	−1.4	0.0
International reserves					
(US$ billion)	4.2	5.0	1.8	4.7	8.0
Foreign investments					
(US$ billion)	1.6	1.7	0.6	0.7	1.4
Total foreign debt including					
"internal" debt held by foreigners					
(US$ billion)	57.5	78.3	86.1	93.1	94.9
Total foreign debt (US$ billion)	57.5	78.3	86.1	93.1	94.9
Public foreign debt					
(US$ billion)	34.0	43.1	51.6	66.9	69.8
Including "internal" debt held					
by foreigners (US$ billion)	34.0	43.1	51.6	66.9	69.8
Private foreign debt (US$ billion)	7.3	10.2	8.1	14.8	16.3
External debt service					
(US$ billion)	9.4	10.6	12.3	13.0	15.9
Interest payments					
(US$ billion)	4.6	6.1	7.8	8.2	10.3
Principal payments					
(US$ billion)	4.8	4.5	4.5	4.8	5.7
Real exchange rate					
(March 1988 = 100)	66.4	61.1	92.7	130.1	99.7

[a] All data refer to growth rates unless otherwise specified. Does not include maquiladora activites.
[b] Preliminary estimations.

Sources: Own estimations based on data from Instituto Nacional de Estadística, Geografía e Informática and Banco de México; Abud, n.d.

1985	1986	1987	1988	1989	1990	1991	1992	1993[b]	1994[b]
2.6	−3.8	1.7	1.2	3.5	4.4	3.6	2.8	0.4	2.0
0.5	−5.5	0.0	−0.2	1.9	3.2	2.4	1.5		
2.2	−1.4	1.1	0.9	1.3	0.9	2.6	0.4	−1.9	−0.2
80.9	78.6	73.9	72.1	73.1	73.5	76.7	83.2	87.0	
19.1	19.4	18.4	19.3	18.2	18.6	19.5	20.8	20.7	
12.5	12.9	13.2	14.2	13.3	13.7	14.9	16.6	16.6	
6.6	6.5	5.2	5.0	4.8	4.9	4.6	4.2	3.3	3.5
21.2	18.5	19.3	20.4	21.4	21.9	22.4	23.3	21.6	
11.2	4.4	8.9	7.3	8.2	9.6	8.3	7.0	5.5	
−1.3	0.4	−2.7	1.1	2.6	2.7	4.6	6.7	6.5	
11.2	13.7	13.1	12.0	10.6	9.6	9.6	9.6	9.6	
63.7	105.7	159.2	51.7	19.7	29.9	18.8	11.9	8.0	7.3
9.6	16.0	16.1	12.5	5.6	3.9	−1.8	0.5	0.7	−1.0
−6.1	2.2	8.8	6.4	−0.1	3.8	6.5	1.5	3.0	2.8
14.5	−8.3	6.8	44.2	21.6	19.9	20.0	24.0	5.2	6.0
7.7	3.3	5.9	−0.9	−4.1	−6.3	−13.4	−23.0	−23.4	−29.0
1.2	−1.7	4.0	−2.4	−5.8	−7.5	−14.9	−24.8	−23.4	−26.5
−1.5	1.8	−0.6	−1.4	3.1	9.7	20.2	26.5	30.9	10.8
5.7	6.7	13.7	6.6	6.9	10.3	18.1	19.3	24.3	15.8
1.9	2.4	3.9	3.2	2.9	5.0	9.9	8.3	15.6	16.1
96.9	100.9	109.5	99.2	93.8	106.0	121.7	131.1	142.9	
96.9	100.9	109.5	99.2	93.8	106.0	115.3	113.4	120.8	
72.7	75.8	84.3	80.6	76.1	77.5	79.0	72.2	78.7	83.6
72.7	75.8	84.3	80.6	76.1	77.5	85.5	90.0	100.8	107.1
15.7	15.1	14.1	5.9	4.0	5.8	7.6	10.7		
15.3	12.9	12.1	15.5	15.6	11.5	13.7	20.7		
10.2	8.4	8.3	8.7	9.3	7.4	8.4	7.6	10.5	12.7
5.1	4.6	3.8	6.8	6.3	4.0	5.3	13.1		
107.1	122.0	121.6	96.2	90.7	86.4	78.0	71.3	68.4	

their current account for the first three years and could guarantee employment and abide by environmental protection laws. The decree of December 1993 further increased the range of activities for FI in Mexico. Only thirteen activities are exclusively reserved to the state and six to Mexican investors; a range of sectors—such as cooperatives in agriculture, national airports, insurance companies and credit unions, and harbor services—allow an FI share between 10 percent and 30 percent and have to be approved by the National Commission of Foreign Investment.

Finally, NAFTA significantly changed investment-related issues. Each nation has to treat investors and their investments no less favorably than national investors. More important, new performance requirements, such as export levels and trade balancing, will have to be phased out over the next ten years (Hufbauer and Schott, 1993; SECOFI, 1994).

As shown in Table 4.1, FI flows to Mexico were one of the most outstanding successes of the Salinas administration. Adding up the figures for 1988–1994, FI accumulated a total of $61 billion and evolved as the main source to finance Mexico's current account deficit. However, the share of manufacturing's foreign direct investment (FDI) on FI declined from 54.4 percent in 1988 to levels below 30 percent in 1993. From this perspective, and in spite of the high absolute values of FDI and FI, the high share of portfolio investments in FI have become one of the most important sources of financial and macroeconomic instability in Mexico. This was dramatically demonstrated in the currency crisis set off in December 1994, which sent shock waves through the entire world's financial system, especially in the so-called emerging markets.

What are the dynamics and some of the outcomes of the model followed after 1988? Because the control of inflation rates and fiscal deficits as well as the attraction of FI are exogenous variables imposed by the government, the initial export-oriented industrialization (EOI) proposal became substantially modified and reversed in a short period of time. In order to sustain low inflation rates and the attraction of FI, the government resorted to two policy instruments. On the one hand, it allowed for a fixed exchange rate from December 1987 to January 1989 and began a preannounced currency depreciation of 1 peso per day. Such depreciation, however, was lower than the difference between internal and external relative prices, which eventually led to overvaluation of the exchange rate. On the other hand, attracting FI was imperative to continue servicing the external debt and to offset the private sector's trade deficit. The latter could only be achieved with a stable macroeconomic environment (Abud, n.d.; Huerta, 1994; Ros, forthcoming).

Thus, the model shows at least five critical aspects of the macroeconomic dynamism for the 1988–1994 period. First, given the structure of Mexico's economy, particularly of its manufacturing sector's historically high trade deficit exacerbated by import liberalization, an appreciation of the exchange rate became an unavoidable outcome of the strategy pursued. In Table 4.1, the real exchange rate is overvalued when the figure is below 100, and undervalued when it is above 100, as in 1985–1987. For 1994 the exchange rate was estimated to be overvalued by over 30 percent.

Second, high absolute and real interest rates have been able to attract FI,[2] but they also reflect the inefficiency of the financial system (Glaessner and Oks, 1992). They exacerbated the declining domestic propensity to invest after 1982. Table 4.1 shows that the coefficient of investments to GDP has remained relatively stable since 1988 and well below the levels of the beginning of the 1980s. However, domestic investments have declined significantly, although external capital inflows have allowed for maintaining the coefficient at a relatively stable level.

Third, the structure of manufacturing and the investment coefficient led to a reversal of the initial intent of the strategy. Macroeconomic liberalization resulted in an increase in manufacturing's imports, the overvaluation of the exchange rate, and a fall in manufacturing's exports, all of which produced a widening trade balance deficit. This runs contrary to the initial strategy in which macroeconomic changes were expected to induce efficiency and microeconomic structural change. Tradables, particularly manufacturing, are affected by these new macroeconomic conditions, as we shall see. The impact of these policies has caused one of the most significant structural changes in Mexico's economy since 1988 and resulted in a shift from export-oriented industrialization to import-oriented industrialization. The economy's coefficient of trade balance to GDP increased from –0.51 percent in 1988 to –6.98 percent in 1992.

Two important developments stand out for Mexico's economy. On one hand, exports continued to increase during the 1988–1992 period at an average annual growth rate (AAGR) of 2.9 percent. However, the export dynamism was well below the 1982–1987 performance of 4.7 percent AAGR. On the other hand, the economy's AAGR of imports was 21.3 percent for 1988–1992, which manifests one of the most significant negative features of liberalization with important effects on domestic value-added potential and employment, among other factors. The import structure reflects an increasing share of consumption and capital goods, in contrast to intermediate goods. They accounted, respectively, for 9.48 percent and 19.78 percent of total imports in 1988 and 15.7 percent and 22.48 percent in 1994. Hence, it is not accurate to argue that capital goods have caused most of the increase in imports. In fact, the AAGR in imports of capital goods for 1988–1994 was 21.9 percent, and for consumption goods it was 29 percent.

Fourth, trade and productive specialization patterns of manufacturing are strongly affected by macroeconomic adjustment. Rapid liberalization and the overvaluation of the exchange rate will cause a fall in domestic inputs, value-added potential, and backward linkages, whereas high real and absolute interest rates limit investments, technological upgrading, and forward linkages.

Last, the outcome of the model not only reversed the initial conditions of EOI but also produced an overkill of the economy in terms of GDP growth and subsequently of employment. As a result, cheap labor power and energy became the main domestic variables in which Mexico has an absolute and declining comparative advantage. However, whether specialization is in labor-intensive or capital-intensive production is not yet clear, since relatively cheap imported inputs would call for specialization in more capital-intensive production, whereas the absolute advantages of Mexico's cheap labor power and energy would call for specialization in labor-intensive activities.

From a macroeconomic perspective, what are the conditions for sustainability of the liberalization strategy? A "double squeeze" has occurred since 1988: on the one hand, declining backward linkages (given massive imports); on the other, declining forward linkages (given overall disincentives to invest). The continuation of the model could result in a deindustrialization process with a sharp negative impact on investments, the trade balance, value-added potential, backward and forward linkages; other variables such as employment and growth would also be directly and negatively affected. Finally, it was assumed that FI has a high elasticity and would be willing to enter Mexico under any circumstances, which was by no means guaranteed.

Interestingly, Mexico's liberalization strategy after the late 1980s increasingly relied on external debt, in addition to FI, to finance the current account deficit. The resulting surge of foreign debt was primarily the result of private borrowing and the new dollar-denominated government bonds, *tesobonos*. Total foreign debt including such "internal" debt held by foreigners increased from $99.2 billion in 1988 to $160 billion in 1994. Thus, the need to finance the current account deficit has been a structural condition of Mexico's economy since the 1940s. It has been exacerbated since liberalization, particularly in the manufacturing sector.

Industrial Policy in Mexico, 1988–1994

From the government's perspective, industrial policy after 1988 was to be primarily an outcome of the liberalization process itself—of the macroeconomic structural change. Industrial policy has thus generally focused on the import regime and import liberalization, and export restrictions have been eliminated since the mid-1980s. Most important since liberalization, traditional export promotion, particularly sector-oriented promotion and overall subsidies, has been dismantled and replaced by self-financing programs. Moreover, industrial policy after 1988 almost exclusively followed "horizontal" promotion policies— affecting manufacturing as a whole—in order not to conflict with liberalization's exogenous variables. Thus, various types of economic deregulation—such as modernization of customs measures, ports, and railroads as well as creation of information services regarding foreign markets and commercialization—are at the center of the new industrial strategy (Pérez Motta, 1991). This departure from prior conception of industrial policy has been very significant, since industrial policy has been subordinated to macroeconomic liberalization.

By 1988 and up to 1994, only two main export incentives and three sectoral programs had persisted. Only the automotive, computer, and pharmaceutical industries, all dominated by transnational corporations, were under specific policies. On the one hand, partial protection through the highest tariff levels continued to be essential, although the elimination of import licenses and duty drawbacks for imports to be exported were the main innovations in all three cases. In the case of the automotive industry—the most significant in terms of its economic share in GDP, imports, and exports—the 1989 decree did not allow for automobile imports higher than a 15 percent share of Mexico's market or imports of used cars. It also included guidelines on trade surplus and vertical integration to reach a minimum of 36 percent of domestic value added for each firm. However, most of these regulations have been eliminated through NAFTA. Tariff and nontariff barriers will be eliminated completely in 2003, particularly trade balance requirements (Moreno Brid, 1994).

The computer policy is less extensive than that for the automobile industry and has been significantly modified since 1981. After 1985, this sector was granted tax incentives (20 percent tax credit) and trade protection (20 percent tariffs for imports), and domestic content and foreign exchange requirements were phased out by the beginning of the 1990s (SECOFI, 1994).

The two main export promotion programs do not constitute a fiscal burden for the government and are an attempt to give broader information regarding foreign markets in order to reduce red tape. The Program of Temporary Imports to Produce Export Goods (PITEX), created in 1985 and regulated by a decree of May 1991, permits nonoil exporters to import duty-free inputs for goods to be exported. A maximum of 30 percent of imported value can be sold in the domestic market, and firms under PITEX are required to present a trade surplus. Firms under PITEX accounted for a 22.6 percent share in total exports in 1988 and 53.3 percent in 1993. The automobile and auto parts sectors were the main beneficiaries under PITEX, representing 50 percent of all exports under the program in 1993.

The Program for High-Export Firms (ALTEX) attempts to eliminate red tape through fast reimbursement of value-added tax (in a maximum of five days), customs clearance, access to trade information, and priority treatment with other ministries. Originated in 1986 and regulated by decrees of 1990 and 1991, ALTEX requires firms to display $2 million in annual export sales but does not require a trade surplus. Up to May 1993, 714 ALTEX programs were registered and represented 32.8 percent of total nonoil exports.

The conception of these "horizontal industrial policies"—they affect manufacturing as a whole—has been slightly reformulated since the end of 1992.

Multiple economic factors—overvaluation of the exchange rate, particularly since 1988, the growth of real interest rates, the high trade deficit of the manufacturing sector, the recession of Mexico's economy since 1992, which was manifested in a fall of manufacturing activity, increasing competition, and the failure of ALTEX and PITEX to promote exports significantly—have all raised serious questions about the compatibility of macroeconomic adjustment, particularly monetary and fiscal policies, with sectoral restructuring.

In response to the deterioration of manufacturing activities, SECOFI implemented several programs to promote industrial competitiveness in thirty-four activities of manufacturing from August 1992 to July 1994.[3] These programs do not offer direct funding by the government; rather, they seek to promote a "self-selection process" through business chambers. The respective business chambers have voluntarily committed to submit diagnosis on the problems of their branches and elaborate on agreements with SECOFI, which are continuously being revised.[4]

Three broad critical issues arise in a review of industrial policy in Mexico. First, it has become clear that imposed liberalization has thus far been unable to serve as a development strategy. From the government's perspective, the discussion of industrial policy (as has occurred with other apparently "sectoral" issues, such as agriculture, employment, poverty, and regional disparities) has been subordinated to macroeconomic priorities. Second, the period 1988–1994 shows that liberalization presents a lack of coherence and consistency between macroeconomic and sectoral policies. This is particularly important for manufacturing, since the latest attempts of industrial policy are more of a short-term and conjunctural nature. More surprisingly, this analysis reveals that initial cautious attempts to face the problems of manufacturing have been implemented with a time lag of at least five years and have thus lost many of the initial dynamic benefits of liberalization. This time lag is characteristic not only of manufacturing but also of agriculture (PROCAMPO), social issues and poverty (PRONASOL), and so on. Third, the liberalization approach suggests a strong incompatibility between liberalization and export-oriented industrialization. Given the structural conditions of Mexico's manufacturing sector, there is a historical trade-off between the three mentioned exogenous variables and manufacturing's exports and overall growth. However, so far macroeconomic variables have worked against manufacturing. Similarly, industrial policy and export promotion have not been able to offset even partially the negative impact of liberalization on manufacturing.

Structural Change in Mexico's Manufacturing Sector, 1988–1994

General developments within manufacturing after liberalization are summarized in Table 4.2. Liberalization has been associated with a relatively high growth of nonoil exports as well as rapid growth of labor and capital productivity. GDP growth has been significantly higher for manufacturing than for the rest of the economy after 1987, although it showed a tendency to decline after 1990 and became negative in 1993. Most impressive, in spite of the decreasing share of foreign direct investment in total investment, the former increased from $2.9 billion to $4.4 billion for the period 1988–1992. Thus, the postliberalization period 1988–1992 could be assessed as a relatively strong growth or boom period for manufacturing with an AAGR of 4.9 percent.

It is vital to have a clear understanding of the limited presence of the manufacturing sector in the Mexican economy, however. Since 1970 its share of GDP has been relatively constant at around 22 percent. Similarly, it accounted for only about 11 percent of total employment during the 1980–1992 period.

Furthermore, important difficulties and contradictions in the restructuring of the manufacturing sector's productive capacity have emerged since liberalization. On the one hand, a drastic divestment process occurred after 1983 and was only recovered by 1991. Moreover, capacity utilization has increased significantly, also because of a fall in investments and the more efficient use of existing capital stock. On the other hand, in spite of significant export dynamism, manufacturing has accounted for a decreasing export coefficient (exports/gross production) since 1989 and an explosive growth of the coefficient of the trade balance/GDP, which increased from –14.24 percent in 1988 to –42.42 percent in 1992, the highest level achieved since 1970. This process reflects the tendency toward an import-oriented industrialization that is incapable of producing increased value added and overall backward linkages and has significant negative effects on manufacturing's potential to spread technological improvements and increase growth and employment.

Thus, liberalization presents several nuances, achievements, and contradictions. Two apparent paradoxes arise from this general development since liberalization: (1) manufacturing's ability to account for significant GDP growth rates, although declining since 1990 and negative in 1993, while decreasing net capital stock as well as gross formation of capital; and (2) manufacturing's growth performance in terms of GDP and exports, although registering a substantial decline in backward linkages.

An important question that emerges from this analysis regards the diverse patterns found at the branch level of manufacturing.

A Typology of Mexico's Manufacturing Sector

In view of the heterogeneous performance of manufacturing since liberalization, it is necessary to break down the analysis at the branch level. This section classifies the sector and its forty-nine branches according to their level of economic activity. Branches have been classified into three groups based on their AAGR in terms of GDP for the boom and postliberalization period 1988–1992. Each branch in Group I accounts for an AAGR of GDP at least 2 percent higher

TABLE 4.2
General Indicators of Mexico's Manufacturing Sector, 1980–1994
(does not include the maquiladora section)

	1980	1981	1982	1983	1984	1985
GDP[a]	6.6	6.4	-2.7	-7.8	5.0	6.1
GDP[b]	22.12	21.65	21.19	20.38	20.66	21.36
Percentage of value-added[c]	41.46	42.07	42.34	42.84	42.49	42.79
Net capital stock[a]	4.6	10.2	13.3	2.4	-4.9	-2.9
Net capital stock[b]	40.89	41.31	43.48	44.15	42.47	41.32
Gross formation of capital[a]	-19.3	43.3	25.0	-39.0	-54.2	37.3
Gross formation of capital[b]	42.96	47.49	59.17	55.73	30.91	37.36
Labor productivity[a]	0.1	1.6	-0.7	-0.8	2.9	2.8
Capital productivity[a]	1.9	-3.4	-14.1	-10.0	10.4	9.2
Employment[a]	6.6	4.8	-2.0	-7.1	2.1	3.2
Employment[b]	12.04	11.87	11.66	11.08	11.05	11.16
Real wages[a]	-9.2	4.3	-4.3	-17.8	-2.3	1.0
Capital intensity	0.246	0.259	0.299	0.330	0.308	0.290
Capital utilization	—	—	58.22	52.39	57.86	63.19
Imports[a]	30.7	18.5	-39.5	-44.4	25.2	20.3
Imports[b]	87.94	89.07	90.90	79.78	82.86	87.37
Import coefficient	14.87	15.21	12.51	10.07	10.34	11.34
Exports[a]	-9.3	-0.6	-2.4	62.0	29.6	-4.0
Exports[b]	25.76	21.16	17.15	25.50	30.28	31.16
Export coefficient	3.75	3.20	4.32	7.68	7.76	6.65
Foreign direct investment[df]	1,549	1,964	1,340	1,388	990	1,386
Trade balance[d]	-13,540	-18,233	-7,961	-1,942	-2,671	-5,322
Trade balance/GDP	-31.49	-33.68	-22.09	-6.18	-6.77	-12.36

[a] Annual growth rate.
[b] Share of manufacturing over total economy.
[c] Absolute value
[d] Millions of US$.
[e] Estimation.
[f] Foreign direct investment exclusively in manufacturing.
[p] Preliminary.

Percentage of value-added = GDP/gross production
Labor productivity = GDP/employment
Capital productivity = GDP/net capital stock
Capital intensity = net capital stock/employment
Capital utilization = Capital productivity/maximal capital productivity. Two maximal
    values for 1982–1992 = 100
Import coefficient = imports/(gross prodcution – imports + exports)
Export coefficient = exports/gross production

Sources: Author's estimations based on data from INEGI and Banco de México.

1986	1987	1988	1989	1990	1991	1992	1993P	1994e
−5.3	3.0	3.2	7.2	6.1	4.0	2.3	−1.5	3.0
21.03	21.30	21.72	22.49	22.84	22.92	22.80	22.35	
42.91	43.41	43.24	42.84	42.77	43.06	43.58		
−4.7	−5.8	−6.5	−5.4	−7.3	1.5	3.7		
39.95	36.86	34.20	32.78	30.88	30.48	30.74		
−18.4	−14.5	−7.2	19.3	−22.1	83.7	12.8		
34.17	20.81	20.97	29.96	24.10	31.92	35.65		
−3.4	2.0	3.1	4.6	5.3	4.5	4.4		
−0.6	9.4	10.3	13.3	14.4	2.5	−1.4		
−1.9	1.1	0.1	2.5	0.7	−0.5	−2.1	−1.9	0.0
11.11	11.11	11.03	11.16	11.14	10.81	10.54		
−1.2	−4.0	6.8	1.6	1.3	6.2	9.4		
0.281	0.262	0.245	0.226	0.208	0.212	0.225		
62.79	68.70	75.81	85.39	98.26	100.71	99.29		
−4.0	5.0	46.5	23.5	21.6	21.2	23.6	5.7	
91.06	91.07	90.07	91.13	92.56	93.92	93.55		
15.08	15.00	16.54	18.81	20.95	22.20	24.82		
23.9	18.4	18.6	3.4	7.6	6.2	5.9	17.7	
53.87	52.20	61.04	58.57	56.10	62.45	63.98	67.00	
11.70	12.54	11.40	11.17	11.49	11.21	10.93		
1,748	1,827	1,741	1,997	2,154	3,087	3,433		
−2,948	−2,420	−6,668	−11,112	−15,538	−20,949	(29,576)		
−9.27	−6.67	−14.24	−21.97	−27.96	−32.78	−42.42		

TABLE 4.3
Typology of Mexico's Manufacturing Sector

	GDP Growth (1988–1992)	Capital Intensity (1988–1992)
Group I	10.4	0.26
Subgroup IA	14.7	0.69
56 Automobiles	22.8	0.68
34 Basic petrochemicals	9.6	2.11
21 Beer and malt	7.5	0.42
43 Glass and products	7.5	0.29
55 Electrical equipment	6.9	0.31
Subgroup IB	8.0	0.11
12 Fruits and vegetables	11.3	0.06
20 Alcoholic beverages	10.9	0.20
48 Metal furniture	9.0	0.09
49 Structural metal products	8.9	0.11
54 Electronic equipment	8.8	0.16
53 Household appliances	8.2	0.08
52 Machinery and electric equipment	7.6	0.09
39 Cleaning and toilet preparation	7.6	0.20
11 Meat and milk products	7.5	0.07
57 Motors and auto parts	7.2	0.12
19 Other food products	6.9	0.11
Group II	4.5	0.24
Subgroup IIA	4.0	0.92
38 Medicinal products	5.5	0.55
35 Basic inorganic chemicals	4.8	1.15
44 Cement	4.1	1.29
41 Rubber products	3.5	0.23
37 Plastic resins, synthetic fiber	3.2	0.57
33 Petroleum refining	2.9	1.84
Subgroup IIB	4.7	0.09
59 Other manufacturing industries	6.5	0.07
22 Soft drinks and flavorings	5.7	0.07
42 Plastic products	4.8	0.11
40 Other chemicals	4.6	0.20
32 Printing	4.5	0.08
27 Apparel	4.5	0.04
50 Other metal products	4.4	0.14
45 Ceramics	4.4	0.05
26 Other textile industries	4.1	0.04
51 Nonelectrical machinery	4.1	0.19
17 Fats and oils	4.0	0.18
18 Food for animals	3.3	0.04
Group III	–0.5	0.17
Subgroup IIIA	0.3	0.66
46 Steel and iron	2.3	1.15

(continues)

TABLE 4.3   continued

	GDP Growth (1988–1992)	Capital Intensity (1988–1992)
Subgroup IIIA (continued)		
31 Paper and paperboard	1.5	0.35
15 Coffee	−1.0	0.24
36 Pesticides and fertilizers	−7.4	0.42
25 Jute, rough textiles	−31.4	0.49
Subgroup IIIB	−1.0	0.07
23 Tobacco	1.9	0.11
14 Corn milling	1.3	0.02
30 Other wood products	0.8	0.02
16 Sugar	0.5	0.17
13 Wheat milling	0.3	0.05
47 Nonferrous metals	−0.3	0.19
28 Leather and footwear	−1.2	0.02
29 Lumber, plywood	−2.7	0.03
24 Cotton, wool, synthetic textiles	−4.6	0.13
58 Other transportation equipment	−9.0	0.08
Agriculture	0.9	—
Mining	1.2	0.35
Manufacturing	4.9	0.22
Services	3.7	0.11
Total	3.6	0.13

Sources: Author's estimations based on INEGI and Banco de México data.

than manufacturing's average (4.9 percent), while each branch in Group II accounts for an AAGR of GDP that falls between 2 percent of manufacturing's average and −2 percent of the overall average. Each branch in Group III shows an AAGR of GDP 2 percent below manufacturing's average (see Table 4.3).

Furthermore, subgroups within each of the groups have been established. Thus, the branches with a capital intensity (net capital stock/employment) higher than manufacturing's average during the period 1988–1992 (0.22) are in the respective Subgroups A, and the branches with a capital intensity lower than manufacturing are in Subgroups B.

This relatively arbitrary typology is useful for various reasons. Growth both in GDP and in capital intensity are crucial for capital accumulation. High and increasing capital intensity reflects the potential modernization of the respective activities and a higher potential for facing increasing competition as well as for realizing higher profit rates (Dussel Peters, 1994). From this perspective, it is anticipated that Group I with its sixteen branches, particularly the five branches of Subgroup IA, will represent the "leading" branches of the Mexican manufacturing sector with the highest growth potential and the highest probability for achieving successful modernization and integration into the world market.

Based on this methodology, then, the three groups display significant structural changes within the period 1988–1992. First, all five leading branches of Subgroup IA are related either to transnational corporations (automobiles and electrical equipment), monopolies (basic petrochemicals), or national oligopolies (beer and malt, glass). Second, there is a sharp contrast between the branches in Subgroup IA and the branches in Group III. The latter are characterized as "traditional industries," such as food, beverages, tobacco, textiles, and leather and shoes.

As may be expected, the sixteen branches of Group I, particularly those in Subgroup IA, accounted for the highest AAGR of GDP for the period and registered significantly higher percentages than manufacturing and the economy, 10.4 and 14.7, respectively. Moreover, the shares in GDP of Group I and Subgroup IA in total GDP were only 8.13 percent and 3.19 percent in 1992, respectively. It stands out that automobiles, the most dynamic branch in terms of AAGR of GDP, accounted for a share of only 1.71 percent of total GDP in 1992.

The heterogeneous dynamics of manufacturing for the 1988–1992 period is highlighted by the performance of the fifteen branches of Group III, in contrast to the development of Groups I and II, with an AAGR of –0.5 percent and a share of 5.85 in total GDP for 1992. Such heterogeneous dynamics have crucial implications for Mexico's trade balance.

Exports, Imports, and Trade Balance in Manufacturing

Manufacturing exports have increased their share in total exports since the mid-1980s and continued to do so after liberalization, from 61 percent of total exports in 1988 to 64 percent in 1992. In spite of the high AAGR of exports during the 1988–1992 period of 5.8 percent, the export performance was well below the 1982–1987 figure of 24.2 percent.

At the group level, several important issues have emerged since 1988. First, the slowdown in export performance is reflected in all groups and subgroups. Second, the most dynamic branches in terms of GDP and capital intensity, (the five branches of Subgroup IA) present the highest AAGR of exports since liberalization, and their share in total exports jumped from 11.9 percent in 1988 to 19.4 percent in 1992. Third, all the branches in Subgroups A (those with highest capital intensity) account for the highest AAGR in exports.

In addition to the highly heterogeneous specialization of exports in capital-intensive production, the evolution of exports since 1988 reflects an increasing concentration. Hence, for example, only two branches (automobiles and motors and auto parts, both in Group I) contributed with 41 percent of the growth in total manufacturing exports during the 1988–1992 period.

In general, import development since 1988 reflects one of the most relevant and structural changes in Mexico's manufacturing sector. Given the dramatic increase in imports, with an AAGR of 22.4 percent for the 1988–1992 period, the share of manufacturing imports achieved its highest historical level in 1992, with 93.6 percent. Interestingly, the branches of the respective Subgroups B (the ones with the lowest capital intensity) accounted for the highest growth in imports. Subgroups IB and IIB accounted for 70.5 percent of the change in total imports for the period. This high concentration is also manifested at the branch level, since only two branches (nonelectrical machinery and motors and auto parts) accounted for a share of 34.19 percent of manufacturing imports and contributed with 34 percent to manufacturing's import increase.

Given these trends in exports and imports, it is not surprising that the manufacturing trade balance has deteriorated drastically since liberalization, from –$6.7 billion in 1988 to –$29.6 billion in 1992. With the exception of Subgroup IA, all groups and subgroups accounted for increasing trade deficits after 1988. The performance of Subgroup IA has been strongly influenced by the automobile branch, which increased its trade surplus for the same period from $1.2 billion to $3.4 billion. However, if automobiles and motors and auto parts are combined—since the latter imports most of the inputs for automobiles—their accumulated trade balance accounts for –$7.7 billion for the 1988–1992 period.

An analysis of the coefficient of trade balance/GDP helps in understanding this process and highlights the net penetration of imports in the respective activities. As mentioned earlier, the coefficient tripled for manufacturing during the 1988–1992 period and increased most strikingly in the most dynamic groups. In fact, the coefficient for Group I increased from –15.34 percent in 1988 to –43.44 in 1992 and for Group II from –21.47 to –52.59 percent. This process shows the dramatic impact of import liberalization in Mexico's manufacturing sector and the potentially negative effects on backward linkages, employment, and economic growth, among other central economic issues.

Employment and Real Wages in Manufacturing

The annual growth rate of remunerated jobs in Mexico was significantly lower than the growth rate of the economically active population (EAP) during the 1970–1990 period. It has been estimated that the average annual difference was 385,000 jobs. This gap has widened recently, feeding unemployment, underemployment, and the informal sector.

The young population is weighted heavily in Mexico's demographic structure, and official sources estimate that 1.2 million persons enter the EAP annually. This figure amounts to 5 percent of total formal employment—that is, the economy should increase its remunerated employment by at least 5 percent annually to satisfy the minimum employment requirements of Mexican society. However, only 28 percent of the population entering the EAP was absorbed by the formal labor market during the 1990–1992 period (Dussel Peters, 1994).

When this 5 percent level is taken as the turning point for the generation of net employment during the 1988–1992 period, AAGR figures for employment in the domestic economy and in manufacturing were 1.3 percent and 0.2 percent, respectively. Moreover, it is important to remember that during the period 1970–1981 the manufacturing sector had accounted for an AAGR of employment of 3.6 percent, or thirteen times higher than for 1988–1992.

At the group level, none of the Groups achieved an AAGR of 5 percent for this period, and only three branches (automobiles, fruits and vegetables, other manufacturing) generated employment in net terms. Finally, it is critical to keep in mind that the most dynamic groups, subgroups, and branches have only a small share in total employment. In 1992 the shares in total employment of Group I, Subgroup IA, and automobiles were 2.86 percent, 0.73 percent, and 0.27 percent, respectively.

Thus, a central characteristic of liberalization has been the vast exclusion of the population attempting to enter the formal economy. Moreover, the decline or relative stability of employment in absolute terms explains the high growth in labor productivity (GDP/employment). From this perspective, the "perverse" increase of labor productivity was at the expense of employment.

After a drastic fall in manufacturing's real wages during the period 1982–1987, they improved significantly between 1988 and 1992. If real wages are standardized (1988 = 100), real wage levels for 1992 were 119.6 percent in manufacturing, 124.9 percent in Group I, and 125.6 percent in Subgroup IA. In spite of this significant recovery, it is important to stress that real wages for manufacturing, including for all of its groups and subgroups, are still below levels of the 1980s.

Conclusion

Economic structural change in manufacturing since liberalization has been most significant in Mexico. The macroeconomic liberalization strategy reversed the most important conditions of the intended export-oriented industrialization to an import-oriented industrialization. Import liberalization, the overvalued exchange rate, high absolute and real interest rates, and domestic divestment have generated disincentives for manufacturing. Yet this sector has been most successful in attracting FDI and increasing productivity and GDP. The boom period 1988–1992, however, also showed that the main features of structural change in manufacturing are its heterogeneity, concentration, and exclusion as well as a significant tendency to lose backward and forward linkages with the domestic economy.

Horizontal industrial policy in Mexico after liberalization has thus far been insufficient to offset the resulting negative macroeconomic environment for manufacturing. More important, industrial policy has been unable to present a development strategy for the economy as a whole. This is particularly the case for manufacturing. Rather, liberalization has been consummated as an instrument and as a goal in itself. One result has been incompatibility and time lag between macroeconomic policy and industrial policy, but this has also affected other sectoral issues in all but the three exogenous variables: control of inflation and financial deficit and attraction of foreign investment.

As shown with the typology of manufacturing branches, the most dynamic branches since liberalization are dominated by either transnational corporations, monopolies, or domestic oligopolies. The boom period 1988–1992 for manufacturing was also characterized by a significant rise in imports and a decline in value added for the most dynamic branches in Subgroup I. This reflects a relative decoupling of their activities from the rest of the economy and a decline in their ability to propagate technology, labor processes, industrial organization, and employment. For instance, in spite of the boom period, manufacturing was unable to generate employment according to the requirements of Mexico's population and has expelled labor power since 1992.

It is unlikely that further deregulation, privatization, and reliance on extremely volatile foreign capital will solve some of these economic challenges and contradictions that have emerged under liberalization. Deepening of import-oriented industrialization as a form of integrating into the capitalist world market will not provide a potential for manufacturing, either for Mexico or for other nations. The crisis set off by the December 1994 devaluation of the Mexican peso dramatically showed the limitations of such model.

Alternatives to the liberalization strategy and import-oriented industrialization might be found in an "endogenous" framework, in both an economic and political sense. On the one hand, an endogenous strategy, as opposed to an authoritarian one, would necessarily have to include real negotiations among independent worker unions, capitalists, and the government to generate the domestic conditions for economic and political sustainability. Based on this socioeconomic consensus, which is very difficult to envision given recent political and economic turmoil, an endogenous economic strategy would have to be designed. Such an economic package would have to limit the incompatibilities between macroeconomic adjustment and the performance of the rest of the sectoral activities. In some cases, macroeconomic aspects have to be dominated by sectoral objectives. Thus, for example, measures to generate sectoral growth conditions would have costs such as a higher level of inflation as well as a real exchange rate appreciation. Furthermore, in addition to the recognition of the strategic importance of the manufacturing sector—because of its high value-added potential, its backward and forward linkages with the rest of the economy, and its potential impact on employment—overall trade liberalization would have to be reconsidered because it has had a dramatic negative impact on industry's structure. Finally, it is the responsibility of the state to generate at the very least the conditions and incentives for economic growth, particularly regarding domestic savings and investments, exchange rates, and, if necessary, export promotion schemes.

Notes

1. The government's understanding of "macroeconomy" is very narrow, since it includes only the three exogenous variables and not other classical macroeconomic issues such as employment, domestic investments and savings, and growth, among others.

2. Since the beginning of 1994, government bonds issued in pesos, previously the main form of borrowing by the government, have been almost completely replaced by *tesobonos*, which are issued in U.S. dollars. The interest rate on the previous bonds included an extremely high risk premium for devaluation, which is not included in *tesobonos*. *Tesobonos* constitute a new form of "internal" debt held by foreigners (see Table 4.1).

3. These programs include, among others, the following activities: leather and shoes, pharmaceuticals, capital goods, forestry, chemistry, plastics and rubber, textiles and garments, toys, electrical manufacturing, aluminum, glass, chocolates, candy and chewing gum, and construction.

4. These agreements between SECOFI and business chambers refer to issues such as foreign trade and tariff barriers, funding, productive organization, hygiene, ecology, technology, and inputs, among others. By July 1994, 63 percent of 1,728 covenants were fulfilled; the rest were either late or dismissed.

Bibliography

Abud, Jairo. n.d. "External Debt, Trade Liberalization, and Capital Inflows Under Exchange Rate Appreciation: The Case of Mexico (1988–1994)." Dissertation for the Fundaçào Getulio Vargas.

Aspe Armella, Pedro. 1993. *El camino mexicano de la transformación económica*. Mexico: Fondo de Cultura Económica.

Córdoba, José. 1991. "Diez lecciones de la reforma económica en México." *Nexos* (Mexico), 158:31–48.

Dussel Peters, Enrique. 1993. "Quo Vadis Señor Brady? The Brady Initiative: A Way Out of the Global Debt Crisis?" *Review of Radical Political Economics*, 25(1):87–107.

———. 1994. "Cambio estructural y potencialidades de crecimiento del sector manufacturero en Mexico (1982–1991)." Pp. 147–229 in Julio López, coordinator, *Mexico: La nueva macroeconomía*. Mexico City: Centro de Estudios para un Proyecto Nacional/Nuevo Horizonte Editores.

Dussel Peters, Enrique, and Kwan S. Kim. 1993. "From Trade Liberalization to Economic Integration: The Case of Mexico." Working Paper 187, The Helen Kellogg Institute, University of Notre Dame.

Glaessner, Tom, and D. Oks. 1992. "NAFTA, Capital Mobility, and Mexico's Financial System."

Huerta, Arturo. 1994. *La política neoliberal de estabilización económica en México: Límites y alternativas*. Mexico: Diana.

Hufbauer, Gary C., and Jeffrey Schott. 1993. *NAFTA: An Assessment*. Washington, D.C.: Institute for International Economics.

López G., Julio. 1994. "El proceso de ajuste de la economía mexicana." Pp. 19–56 in J. López (coord.), *México: La nueva macroeconomía*. Mexico City: Centro de Estudios para un Proyecto National/Nuevo Horizonte Editores.

Moreno Brid, Juan Carlos. 1994. "La competitividad de la industria automotriz." Pp. 313–394 in Fernando Ciavijo and José I. Casar, coordinators, *La industria mexicana en el mercado mundial: Elementos para una política industrial.* Mexico City: El Trimestre Económico/Fondo de Cultura Económica.

Pérez Motta, Eduardo. 1991. "Updating Mexico's Strategic Export Promotion Instruments." *Comercio Internacional Banamex,* 3(4):113–117.

Ros, Jaime. 1990. "El debate sobre industrialización: El caso de México." *Cuadernos de la CEPAL,* 63:119–171.

————. Forthcoming. "Trade Liberalization with Real Appreciation and Slow Growth." In G.K. Helleiner, ed., *Manufacturing for Export in the Developing World: Problems and Possibilities.*

SECOFI (Secretaría de Comercio y Fomento Industrial). 1993. *Fracciones arancelarias y plazos de desgravación.* Mexico: SECOFI.

————. 1994. *Structure and Policy of Foreign Direct Investment.* Mexico: SECOFI.

5

Mexico's "Old" and "New" Maquiladora Industries: Contrasting Approaches to North American Integration

Gary Gereffi

The maquiladora program in Mexico is one of the world's largest and most controversial experiments in export-oriented industrialization. It has received both accolades and criticism, but it is never viewed with indifference. Government officials, business groups, labor unions, scholars, and others have evaluated the maquiladora program from vastly different vantage points and, not surprisingly, have arrived at conflicting interpretations of its accomplishments.

Since its inception in 1965 as the border industrialization program, the maquiladora program has been viewed by Mexican public officials as an attempt to alleviate unemployment in the northern border region. Maquiladora plants export labor services that are incorporated into products assembled in Mexico and consumed in foreign markets, mainly the United States, based on duty-free inputs from those markets. (In fact, maquiladora exports are included in the service category of Mexico's balance-of-payments accounts rather than as a merchandise export.) A frequently heard concern even in government circles, however, is that maquiladoras are primarily a foreign enclave. As such, they are not really integrated into Mexico's industrial structure, except to take advantage of Mexico's low-wage workers, and therefore questions are raised about whether the program should play a key role in Mexico's strategy for national development.

Foreign investors tend to view the export-oriented assembly plants along the U.S.-Mexican border as a partnership that improves the competitiveness of manufacturing firms by allowing them to shift labor-intensive operations from capital-abundant countries to a nation where labor is plentiful but capital is relatively scarce. Thus the maquiladora industry is considered a prime example of mutually beneficial comparative advantage in the international division of labor: Foreign companies enhance their productivity, and Mexican workers gain jobs.

Critics of the maquiladora plants raise a different set of issues. Organized labor focuses on the hiring practices of the maquiladora plants that target young women and sometimes even children as providers of cheap labor. In the debates over passage of the North American Free Trade Agreement (NAFTA), some environmentalists joined forces with U.S. labor in contending that Mexico's looser enforcement of environmental regulations, along with its low wages, would lure U.S. companies to move more operations there, costing U.S. workers jobs and inflicting new air and water pollution on Mexico. Proposals for reform included improving wage and work standards, tightening enforcement of strict occupational safety and environmental codes, and promoting a cross-national harmonization of labor rights.

Scholars tend to bring the biases of their disciplines to the study of the maquiladoras. Economists focus on the optimal pursuit of static and dynamic comparative advantages, political scientists examine the role of the state in export-oriented industrialization, and sociologists highlight the social costs and benefits of export assembly operations. Most have emphasized, however, the need for the maquiladora program to have a positive impact in creating jobs, raising standards of living, transferring technology, and generating multiplier effects at the local and regional levels.

My purpose in this chapter is to discuss Mexico's maquiladora industries from both a historical and a comparative perspective. During the past four decades, the maquiladora program has evolved in several new directions that have important consequences for national development in Mexico. Furthermore, it is useful to compare Mexico's maquiladoras with the broader process of export-oriented industrialization in East Asian countries because their experience offers an insight into how manufactured exports can promote dynamism, deepening, and diversification within domestic economies. Finally, the East Asian experience is used as a reference point to sketch several scenarios that could emerge in Mexico and the Caribbean Basin in the context of North American integration.

The "Old" and "New" Maquiladoras

There has been an explosion of research on the maquiladora plants in Mexico that highlights the phases of maquila expansion and significant changes in the structure and performance of the manufactured exports they help generate (Grunwald and Flamm, 1985; Carrillo-Huerta and Urquidi, 1989; González-

Aréchiga and Barajas Escamilla, 1989; Schoepfle and Pérez-López, 1989; Sklair, 1989; Shaiken, 1990; Weintraub, 1990). The main facts are well known, so only a cursory review is needed here.

Maquiladoras are assembly plants that import parts and supplies duty-free into Mexico and export their production, largely to the United States. The U.S. government supported the setting up of export assembly operations through tariff items 806.30 and 807.00, which assess import duties only on the value added of work done abroad when U.S.-origin components are sent overseas for assembly and then returned to the United States. The Mexican government also cooperated by permitting duty-free entry of all materials and equipment used in the maquiladoras, and it authorized 100 percent foreign ownership of the enterprise, provided that the entire output was exported.

The number of maquiladora plants in Mexico grew from 620 in 1980 to over 2,000 by 1992. The personnel employed in Mexican maquiladoras during this period expanded from 100,000 to 518,000 (BID, 1993), and according to forecasts, that figure will grow to 600,000 by the end of the century. Total maquiladora exports soared from almost $2.5 billion in 1980 to $10.1 billion in 1988. Imported inputs in the latter year were $7.8 billion, resulting in a net value-added figure for Mexico of $2.3 billion, which corresponds almost entirely to Mexican labor costs. This was equivalent to about one-third of the value added for all of Mexico's manufactured exports. To the direct employment of 450,000 in 1990, Weintraub (1990:1146) estimated that one must add a similar amount of indirect employment in related industries. Assuming an average family size of five, maquiladora jobs thus contributed to the income of more than 5 million Mexicans by 1995.

The maquiladoras are not an "industry" in the conventional sense but rather group together assembly processes from a range of industries. In terms of both employment and value added, the most important sectors are electronic components, transportation equipment, and electrical machinery. In 1989, the maquiladoras in electronic components employed 105,000 people; transportation equipment, 94,000; and electrical machinery, 67,000. The next largest sector was apparel and textiles, with 42,000 employees (Shaiken, 1990:11). The cities with the greatest number of maquiladora establishments are Tijuana, Ciudad Juárez, and Mexicali. However, there also are growing numbers of maquiladora plants in Mexico's large interior cities such as Monterrey and Guadalajara (Wilson, 1990) and even in the Yucatán, where forty plants have been established (Ramírez Carrillo, 1993).

An important new trend has been the bifurcation of the maquiladora program into two distinct types of production processes. The "old" maquiladoras are characterized by the use of labor-intensive operations that combine minimum wages with piecework and hire mostly women. This situation tends to prevail in garment production, basic semiconductor assembly, and other types of light manufacturing. In recent years, though, the program has attracted more sophisticated forms of production in automobile-related manufactures and advanced electronics assembly. Maquiladora plants in this second wave, some of which are Japanese, have made substantial investments in complex technology. They also are hiring growing numbers of skilled male workers. These "new" maquiladoras are significant because they demonstrate that sophisticated, high-quality exports can be produced in Mexican plants using advanced production technologies. Whereas the old maquiladoras typically are export enclaves that generate employment and foreign exchange but use few local material inputs and have limited spread effects on the rest of the country's industrial structure, the new maquiladoras open up the possibility that they could help Mexico move to a higher level of development by fostering greater technology transfer and the training of a skilled and well-educated workforce, thus enhancing Mexico's integration into the global economy in a more advantageous competitive position.

It is too early to tell whether the new maquiladoras will usher in a higher stage of development in Mexico. Certainly, the maquiladora program cannot solve Mexico's employment problems. Maquiladoras account for 11 percent of Mexico's total manufacturing employment, with a much higher job impact (26 percent) in the six border states. However, the more than 500,000 workers in the maquiladora sector represent only 1 percent of the economically active population in the country and less than half of the amount by which the Mexican labor force expands each year. The foreign exchange picture is brighter, with maquiladora exports generating more foreign exchange than any other sector in Mexico except for oil production.

The new maquiladora plants do seem to perform better than the old enclave operations in terms of domestic linkages. Overall, only about 6 percent of the value added in Mexico from maquiladora production comes from domestic material inputs and packaging, up from less than 4 percent in 1987. However, the auto and computer firms, propelled by the Mexican government's local content regulations, seem to have developed more extensive and sophisticated supplier networks, a trend that has led them to use a much higher degree of Mexican inputs—parts and raw materials—in their production. In his case study of a major foreign personal computer manufacturer in Mexico (presumably IBM), Shaiken (1990:112) found that 30 percent of the value of the parts used in the production process were sourced in Mexico. Another study placed the domestic content of Mexico's leading computer exports at closer to 10 percent, although in two computer companies domestic integration levels were 38 percent and 76 percent (Unger, 1990:1112–1113). In general, more Mexican inputs tend to be used in locations where supplier industries already are established, such as Guadalajara and Monterrey, than at the border (Wilson, 1990).

What Can Mexico Learn from East Asia's Success in Export-Oriented Industrialization?

Japan and the newly industrialized countries (NICs) of East Asia—South Korea, Taiwan, Hong Kong, and Singapore—have been at the core of striking changes in the structure and dynamics of the world economy during the past several decades. Industrialization today is the result of an integrated system of global trade and production. International trade has allowed nations to specialize in different branches of manufacturing and even in different stages of production within a specific industry. This process, fueled by an explosion of new products and new technologies since World War II, has led to the emergence of a "global manufacturing system" in which production capacity is dispersed to an unprecedented number of developing as well as industrialized countries (Gereffi, 1994a; 1994b).

National development strategies have played an important role in shaping these new productive relationships in the global manufacturing system. Conventional economic wisdom has it that the Latin American and East Asian NICs have followed one of two alternative development strategies: (1) the inward-oriented path of import-substitution industrialization (ISI) pursued by relatively large, resource-rich economies like Argentina, Brazil, and Mexico in which industrial production is geared to the needs of a sizable domestic market and (2) the outward-oriented approach of export-oriented industrialization (EOI) adopted by smaller, resource-poor nations like the East Asian NICs that depend on global markets to stimulate the rapid growth of their manufactured exports (Gereffi and Wyman, 1990).

The World Bank, the International Monetary Fund, and other development agencies have been quite clear in their preference for the latter approach. The World Bank (1987:85) claimed that "the economic performance of the outward-oriented economies has been broadly superior to that of the inward-oriented economies in almost all respects." The obvious implication is that policy reforms aimed at a greater outward orientation would lead to substantial improvements in exports, economic growth, and employment in countries that earlier had followed inward-oriented policies. The East Asian NICs thus are put forward as a model to be emulated by the rest of the developing world.

Mexico's policy reforms since the early 1980s clearly took this lesson in neoclassical economics to heart. The exchange rate has been devalued, imports have been liberalized, the role of state-owned enterprises has been curtailed, government influence over banks and credit has been lessened, and most of the restrictions on direct foreign investment (DFI) have been removed. One result of these changes has been a rise in the level of foreign investment in Mexico and a dramatic increase in nontraditional exports after Mexico's 1982 economic crisis. Manufactured exports in Mexico (excluding the maquiladora sector), for example, nearly doubled from $2.7 billion in 1980 to $5.3 billion in 1985 and then more than doubled again to $12.5 billion in 1989 (Székely, 1991:115). The auto and auto parts sector has been one of the most dynamic in the recent export surge. Exports of engines to the United States, which made up 85 percent of auto part exports in 1990, climbed from $23 million in 1980 to over $1 billion in 1990 (Mattar and Schattan, 1993:110).

A key factor in this export success has been the fall in Mexico's real wages. The Mexican peso, which was valued at 24.6 pesos to the U.S. dollar in 1982, dropped by over 80 percent in the next year and continued plummeting to over 3,000 pesos to the dollar by the end of 1993. Combined with inflation, the devaluation led to a dramatic decline in maquila wages. The average hourly compensation cost for maquila production workers skidded from $1.67 in 1981 to $0.81 in 1987 (Shaiken, 1990:10). During this same period, the number of maquiladora plants and employees and the total value of exports soared.

In this context, a major concern in Mexico has been how to push beyond the enclave model of EOI represented by the traditional, labor-intensive maquiladora plants in order to adopt a more dynamic, industrially upgraded development strategy that would generate higher income and skill levels for workers, and at the same time allow Mexican exports to be internationally competitive in technologically advanced industries. With this objective in mind, some scholars have tried to use East Asian export-processing zones (EPZs) as a model to understand and perhaps shape the future evolution of Mexico's maquiladora program (Estrada and Castillo, 1990; Castillo and Ramírez Acosta, 1991).

Although the comparison between the East Asian EPZs and Mexico's maquiladora program is important, it is also hazardous because of the different historical, structural, and cultural factors involved in this kind of cross-regional analysis. Several additional issues thus need to be taken into account before deriving any lessons from the East Asian experience for Mexico.

EPZs: The Initial Stage
in Export-Oriented Industrialization

Mexico's maquiladora program and the EPZs in the East Asian NICs share a basic similarity: They both started out as labor-intensive export enclaves that were set up in the 1960s to attract foreign investment, especially in the apparel and electronics industries. A number of important differences, however, quickly set these programs on divergent paths.

The first has to do with the primary economic objectives of these efforts. Whereas Mexico's maquiladora program initially was set up to provide jobs in the northern border region, the top priority of the East Asian EPZs was to generate the foreign exchange needed to sustain their economic growth. When the U.S. government announced in the late 1950s that it planned to phase out its massive official aid disbursements to Taiwan and South Korea, these countries were left with little choice but to try to promote manufactured exports because they had few raw materials and no other sources of foreign exchange. Similarly, Hong Kong, as a commercial entrepôt, had no industrial alternative to EOI because it possessed a small domestic market and no agricultural hinterland. Mexico, on the other hand, did not confront the same kind of foreign exchange constraint in the 1960s and 1970s because it had substantial mineral, agricultural, and oil exports that financed its ISI development strategy for several decades.

In addition, the sources of foreign capital and the destination of exports were quite different in the two regions (Stallings, 1990). From its inception, Mexico's maquiladora program has been overwhelmingly oriented to the United States, both as a source of investment capital and as virtually the sole destination for its exports. The EPZs in the East Asian NICs have been far more diversified on both accounts. U.S. DFI in Taiwan was about two-fifths of the total stock at the end of 1986, followed closely by Japanese investors who held 30 percent of DFI on the island. In South Korea, Japan was the leading foreign investor in 1986 with over one-half of all DFI; the United States had a minimal share (less than 5 percent) of the total. The United States is much more significant as the major market for Taiwan's and South Korea's booming manufactured exports, but at the end of the 1980s it still accounted for less than 40 percent of the overseas sales of these two NICs (Grosser and Bridges, 1990).

These contrasts in the origins, financing, and external orientation of the assembly-oriented maquiladoras and EPZs are important because they contribute to the different trajectories that EOI has followed in Mexico and East Asia. Until the last few years, Mexico's maquiladora plants were a low-wage export enclave with virtually no connection to the rest of the domestic economy via either material inputs or local sales. Mexico's maquiladora plants thus were relegated to an export-processing role in the world economy. In the late 1980s, the new wave of maquiladora plants began to push beyond the enclave model to the more sophisticated type of export production associated with a component-supplier role, which refers to the manufacture and export of component parts in technologically advanced industries in the NICs, with final assembly usually carried out in the developed countries (Gereffi, 1995). Both of these types of industrial subcontracting in Mexico relied on high levels of DFI by U.S. manufacturers and a close bilateral trading relationship (including extensive intrafirm trade) with the United States.

In the East Asian NICs, on the other hand, access to the U.S. market for their manufactured exports was far from assured. Rising wages in the East Asian nations, intense competition from lower-cost neighboring countries (such as the Philippines, Malaysia, Thailand, Indonesia, and the People's Republic of China), and growing protectionism in the United States all combined in the 1970s to force the East Asian NICs out of the export-processing role toward a specification-contracting role (Gereffi, 1995). "Specification contracting" refers to the production of finished consumer goods by local firms, where the output is distributed and marketed abroad by large trading companies, retail chains, or their agents. Also known as "original equipment manufacturing," this is the major export niche filled by the East Asian NICs in the world economy. In 1980, for example, Hong Kong, Taiwan, and South Korea accounted for nearly three-quarters of all finished consumer goods exported by the Third World to the advanced industrial nations (Keesing, 1983:338–339).

Foreign capital is primarily important as "buyer" rather than as "manufacturer" in the commercial subcontracting relationship. Unlike in Mexico where foreign firms did most of the exporting, local companies in the East Asian NICs developed extensive subcontracting networks with significant backward linkages to the domestic economy. Also, the need to escape U.S. import quotas fostered a process of continuous industrial upgrading that led to higher levels of productivity and international competitiveness in the East Asian nations.

Given this situation, it is easy to see why the comparison between the EPZs and Mexico's maquiladora plants often is misguided. The EPZs in Taiwan and South Korea were only the first organizational stage in a diverse sequence of export activities. Rather quickly, the geographically restricted EPZs gave way to "bonded factories" that qualified for the same export incentives as the EPZs but could be located anywhere in the exporting country as long as the vast majority (usually more than 70 percent) of their production was destined for overseas markets. The central feature that set EPZs and bonded factories apart from other export assembly operations was their restriction-free, tax-free access to imported inputs (Keesing, 1990; Healey, 1990). Other Taiwanese and Korean firms engaged in exporting also could secure their imported inputs free of duty but only after initially paying the duty and then applying for a "customs drawback" that was administratively cumbersome and time-consuming. (Major export manufacturers in Taiwan and South Korea who were reliably identified in advance sometimes could avoid this procedure through direct exemptions or waivers of duties.)

One of the main results of this effort by the East Asian NICs to incorporate EPZs into a nationwide export-oriented development strategy was a rapid decline in the relative attractiveness of EPZs to foreign investors. South Korea's first EPZ, Masan, was established in 1970, and a second EPZ was set up in Iri in 1974. The peak level of foreign investment in South Korea's EPZs occurred in 1972 and 1973, amounting to about 30 percent of the country's total annual flows of DFI. In 1975, a mere two years later, only 2 percent of the DFI coming into South Korea went into the EPZs, and by 1985 there was a net disinvestment (i.e., withdrawal of funds) of $3 million in South Korea's EPZs (Healey, 1990:55).

The same sharp downturn in the significance of the EPZs is evident in export sales from the zones. In 1980, for example, 18 percent of the exports of foreign firms in Taiwan came from the EPZs, and 32 percent came from bonded factories, many of which were located in the northern end of the island near Taipei. The remaining one-half of the exports of foreign firms in Taiwan came from plants that did not qualify for special export incentives, either because they sold too much of their output to the domestic market or because many of the smaller firms were not registered with the government (Schive et al., 1986:36). By 1988, only 6.5 percent of Taiwan's export total of $56.4 billion came from its three EPZs (Keesing, 1990:31–32). In South Korea, the proportion of exports coming from EPZs was even smaller—2.8 percent in 1986 (Healey, 1990:84, fn. 25).

Science-based industrial parks like the one that opened in Hsinchu, Taiwan, in 1980 are an institutional innovation to promote high-quality, internationally competitive exports from the East Asian NICs (Hofheinz and Calder, 1982:141, 190–191). These high-technology research and development parks were explicitly conceived of by East Asian governments as successors to the EPZs. They are located close to science-oriented universities and good public infrastructure in order to encourage domestic as well as foreign computer, telecommunications, advanced electronics, and precision-machinery firms to invest in research and production facilities on or near their premises.

This expansion is part of a conscious effort by East Asian NICs to upgrade continually their national portfolio of industries. Such a strategy is geared to creating international competitiveness in dynamic knowledge-intensive industries rather than relying on the static comparative advantage of cheap labor in the EPZs. This gives the East Asian NICs an edge over poorer, less sophisticated economies and also enables them to compete effectively with the industrial West.

Transnational Corporations and Manufactured Exports: Help or Hindrance?

Transnational corporations (TNCs) have been an integral part of the industrialization process in Mexico and Brazil, especially since the phase of "ISI deepening" that began in the 1950s. During Mexico's turn to diversified EOI in the 1980s, TNCs facilitated the process of transnational integration (often at the behest of the Mexican government) by linking Mexico to the United States and other global markets through their exports of manufactures (Gereffi, 1994b).

The most dynamic export items in Mexico—the technologically sophisticated new-modern products as well as the more standardized mature products—are characterized by two variants of intrafirm trading strategies employed by TNCs. The first approach is a vertically integrated bilateral trading strategy whereby certain products, such as automobiles and auto parts, are exported from Mexican subsidiaries to their TNC parent companies in the United States, Germany, and Japan, although some auto parts shipments also are destined for Canada or other subsidiaries in Latin America.

The second approach is a horizontally integrated global export strategy that is followed in Mexico for products such as computers, typewriters, and radio and television components. Transnational corporations like Olivetti, Olympia, IBM, and Xerox have opted to split or partition their product lines among various countries. Olivetti, for example, has allocated the production of light non-electrical typewriters to Mexico, with the largest portion of these exports going to western Europe in recent years. Similarly, IBM exports microcomputers from its new plant in Mexico to the United States, Canada, Japan, and Australia in order to substitute for the output from IBM's more costly operations in Boca Raton, Florida (Unger, 1990:1101–1102). These bilateral and global trading strategies are driven by different ownership, locational, and internalization advantages possessed by TNCs that help to explain their success in international markets (Eden, 1991).

Resource-based products in Mexico, unlike most manufactures, usually involve trade between independent parties. These exports are shaped more by immobile comparative advantage factors such as the geographical location of natural resources than by the strategic considerations of TNCs. Mexican producers are relatively prominent in mature or resource-based industries as well as in products that are subject to protectionist trade restrictions or strong competition from independent manufacturers in other developing countries (Unger, 1990:1107). The situation is very different in Canada, where many of the natural resource industries are controlled by U.S. TNCs and vertically integrated intrafirm trade prevails.

The centrality of TNCs in Mexico's most dynamic export industries is a striking contrast to the situation in Taiwan and South Korea. A look at big business in the Latin American and East Asian NICs shows remarkable cross-regional differences in the industrial structures of these countries (Gereffi, 1990). Whereas the largest industrial firms in Mexico and Brazil tend to be either state-owned enterprises or TNC subsidiaries, local private companies are without question the dominant firms in South Korea, and together with state enterprises they share industrial leadership in Taiwan. Nine of the ten largest companies in South Korea are privately held industrial conglomerates, each involved in a wide range of industries with a staggering number of affiliates. In Taiwan, as in South Korea, there are no TNCs among the top ten companies, and only three foreign-owned firms are in the top twenty-five.

In Defense of State Policy

The key position of TNCs in Mexico's export industries poses serious potential constraints to the formulation of national industrial policies, since foreign firms operate with a global rather than a domestic frame of reference. This has not been a problem for South Korea and Taiwan because the governments were able to use a variety of financial and other controls to exercise leverage over the locally owned firms that were the major exporters. Thus it was relatively easy for the East Asian NICs to get national firms to follow the export imperative that has prevailed for the past three decades.

Scholars who have studied the export performance of Mexico's high-technology industries make a strong case for the positive role of certain state policies in fostering these export efforts. With reference to the surge of exports seen in the 1980s from the new generation of capital-intensive plants built by the automotive TNCs, Shaiken noted: "The construction of these facilities was initially spurred by Mexican local content decrees which mandated that auto-makers domestically manufacture a percentage of every vehicle sold—60 per-cent according to the 1983 decrees—and balance imports of auto parts with a required level of exports" (1990:14).

The Mexican government also won significant concessions after allowing the U.S. computer giant, IBM, to have 100 percent ownership of its Mexican com-puter operations, including the guarantee of a continuing flow of new products and additional technology transfer by the company; a commitment to export $600 million worth of its output over a five-year period; and research support to Mexican universities (Shaiken, 1990:108). Unger advocated that explicit government policies may be needed to get TNCs to export but added a cau-tionary note: "[TNC] exports are best explained by export performance re-quirements that TNCs use to secure a solid domestic position. Once that position is attained, additional exports beyond bare requirements may not be forthcoming" (1990:115).

The role of the state in the East Asian NICs from the 1960s through the 1980s also was significant. State policies were oriented toward promoting ex-ports, encouraging industrial upgrading, sponsoring research and development to help produce new materials and products in high-technology fields, and en-suring that foreign firms contributed to this effort without displacing local companies. As Keesing said, "Learning by local firms is a central feature of manufactured export-led growth in East Asia and elsewhere. In an EPZ, in order to benefit from such learning, what is desirable is that a large majority of firms are locally owned" (1990:38). The biggest difference between government efforts in the East Asian and the Latin American NICs is that in the latter the dominant role of TNCs means that exports will occur only to the extent that they serve the global interests of the foreign companies or if they are a condi-tion for the TNCs to have access to sales in sizable domestic markets.

The Role of Maquiladoras
in North American Integration

How will NAFTA affect the maquiladora sector in Mexico? What will be the role of these export-oriented assembly plants in the broader process of North American and Caribbean integration? Will the transnational production networks already established in the region diminish in importance or be strengthened?

One must take a dynamic approach to examining these issues. As previously noted, a new wave of maquiladoras is emerging in Mexico that has made substantial capital investments in complex technologies in the automotive and advanced electronics sectors, among others, and that has enhanced the possibilities for technology transfer and backward and forward linkages with domestic industry. Further, a comparison of Mexico's maquiladora operations with the EPZs in the East Asian NICs shows that within a decade or so the East Asian nations moved away from the EPZ concept per se and began emphasizing higher-value-added exports from bonded factories and other export plants diffused throughout their economies. This increased the likelihood of optimal production locations and facilitated spread effects across a wide range of local subcontracting networks.

From a regional perspective, East Asia has developed a distinctive international division of labor. Japan is the technologically advanced core country of the East Asian region, with the East Asian NICs (South Korea, Taiwan, Hong Kong, and Singapore) playing the role of a semiperiphery with continuous industrial upgrading pushing them toward more technology-intensive, high-value-added exports. The periphery in East Asia is represented by the resource-rich, lower-wage countries such as the Philippines, Malaysia, Thailand, Indonesia, and China. They not only supply the region with raw materials but also specialize in the labor-intensive manufacturing industries that were the export success stories of the East Asian NICs in the first stage of their EOI in the 1960s (Cumings, 1984; Henderson, 1989).

A similar regional division of labor is emerging in North America. The United States is the core country in the region, both as a production center and as a market. It has established tight transnational linkages with Canada and now also Mexico in a range of capital-intensive, high-technology industries such as automobiles and electrical and nonelectrical machinery. Unlike in the East Asian situation, however, all three of the main economies in North America also possess abundant natural resources. Although Mexico traditionally has been the site for labor-intensive exports from its old maquiladora plants, many of these same export-oriented assembly operations are now springing up in a variety of Caribbean nations that may become the favored locales for these low-wage economic activities in the future. One additional element in the North American situation is the growing importance of Asian investments in the region, with Japanese firms concentrating on the new technology-intensive export industries and Korean and Taiwanese companies investing in the old labor-intensive assembly operations.

This cross-penetration of regional blocs is fast making nations in the Caribbean Basin a preferred source of manufactured exports destined for the U.S. market. This trend is most readily apparent in the garment industry.

Caribbean apparel exports to the United States more than quadrupled to nearly $1 billion in the four years following the passage of President Reagan's Caribbean Basin Initiative (CBI) in 1983, creating upward of 100,000 jobs in the Caribbean (Finn, 1988:56). The CBI allows U.S. apparel manufacturers to ship fabric for sewing to low-wage factories in the islands and reimport the finished goods with substantial tax breaks. The maquiladora factories in Mexico have had a similar preferred status (Schoepfle and Pérez-López, 1989).

A more general analysis of garment exports into the United States that enjoy duty-free content under the Harmonized Tariff Schedule (HTS) subheading 9802.00.80 (formerly item 807 under the U.S. tariff schedules in effect prior to 1 January 1989) shows that most of the foreign sewing operations are located in Mexico and five Caribbean countries: the Dominican Republic, Costa Rica, Jamaica, Honduras, and Guatemala (see Table 5.1). These nations have an abundant supply of low-cost labor, and their proximity to the United States provides U.S. and other foreign firms with greater control over production and shorter delivery lead-times than goods shipped from East Asia. In addition, Section 936 of the U.S. Internal Revenue Code provides a tax break to U.S. companies operating "twin" or complementary plants in Puerto Rico and CBI beneficiary nations (USITC, 1989:6-5).

A study that compared the cost of producing four typical garments in three locales—the United States, the Caribbean in a sewing operation using the HTS subheading 9802.00.80, and Hong Kong, the major source of U.S. imported apparel—concluded that assembly costs in the Caribbean were only one-third of U.S. assembly costs and three-fourths of Hong Kong's costs. Even after duties

TABLE 5.1
Textiles, Apparel, and Footwear Exports into the United States
Under the Harmonized Tariff Schedule (HTS), 1990–1993

Source	1990	1991	1992	1993
Mexico	594	725	905	1,075
Dominican Republic	407	547	750	896
Costa Rica	205	254	339	374
Jamaica	119	131	168	251
Honduras	67	107	181	236
Guatemala	60	117	160	218
Colombia	63	82	107	113
El Salvador	25	44	80	103
Haiti	110	101	48	65
China	9	14	18	24
All other	103	115	114	126
Total	1,761	2,236	2,871	3,482

Note: Because of rounding, figures may not add to the totals shown.

Source: U.S. International Trade Commission, 1995, p. 2-22.

and other expenses associated with importing were subtracted, the use of Caribbean assembled products still resulted in cost savings of between 15 and 30 percent (USITC, 1989:6-4). Transit time by sea for U.S. clothing imports coming from East Asia is at least four weeks, compared with a matter of hours for goods flown to the United States from the Caribbean.

By the early 1990s, EPZs had become a leading source of exports and manufacturing employment in various Caribbean nations. In the Dominican Republic, for example, EPZs employed 142,300 Dominicans (primarily in the garment industry) in 1992 and generated $1 billion in trade, netting $300 million toward the balance of payments. In terms of employment, the Dominican Republic was the fourth largest EPZ economy in the world (the fifth if China's special economic zones are included), and 11 percent of the more than 300 EPZ firms in the Dominican Republic were Asian (EIU, 1993/94:20; Kaplinsky, 1993; Portes et al., 1994). Furthermore, East Asian factories were found to contribute more jobs, bigger investments, higher levels of local value added, and a greater utilization of skilled labor than the assembly-oriented sewing operations by other foreign firms (USITC, 1989:6-5).

Despite these gains, one nonetheless should be skeptical of the role that labor-intensive EOI can play in a nation's development. Although export-processing activities such as those that have grown so rapidly in Mexico and the Caribbean Basin in recent years have undeniable benefits in terms of their positive impact on job creation, foreign exchange earnings, and the fostering of industrial experience, they do not constitute an appropriate basis for a long-term development strategy. Export-processing industries may offer a good opportunity for the present, but they are not a permanent solution for the countries of the region. They are best seen as a transitional phenomenon: the first stage in a process of moving to a higher level of industrial development, when better remunerated and more secure jobs will be available (Weintraub, 1990).

The major problems of labor-intensive export industries are that they typically have very shallow roots in the local economy and contribute very little to the technological progress of the nation. This is one reason Taiwan and South Korea moved very quickly to increase the levels of local integration by export industries in their economies by allowing bonded factories to be established anywhere in the countries as long as the majority of their output was destined for export. In addition, even very small exporting firms in the East Asian NICs have been encouraged to use modern technology in their factories in order to enhance their industrial competitiveness. Although it usually takes a generation for a country's skill base to advance from garment work to electronics, both U.S. and East Asian electronics companies are beginning to establish new plants in the Caribbean in order to export electronics goods duty-free into the United States (Finn, 1988:58). A favorable geographical location thus is a major positive factor that can help the Caribbean Basin nations spur their industrial development onward if accompanied by policies addressing the right domestic priorities.

The start of the NAFTA era in 1994 is unlikely to diminish the substantial transnational integration between North America and the Caribbean. NAFTA explicitly focuses on trade, but the ongoing globalization of production in the world economy has produced a "silent integration" in North America that makes the strategic investment decisions by TNCs the prime determinant of new intraregional and interregional trading patterns.

In a formal sense, maquiladora industries will cease to exist in Mexico as a legal category with a zero-tariff now put into place with NAFTA. The only restriction remaining is the so-called rules of origin, which require a minimum 60 percent of North American content in the value of final products, higher than that existing in the previous U.S.-Canada Free Trade Agreement of 1989, which places its minimum at 50 percent. Historically, the main reason maquiladoras were set up was to take advantage of the U.S. tariff provisions (806 and 807) that allowed participating firms to receive duty-free inputs from the United States and thereby to pay tax only on the value added in Mexico. With no tariffs, maquiladora plants are an anachronism.

In reality, however, labor-intensive assembly industries tend to be established wherever low wages, adequate infrastructure, and political stability are to be found. Mexico remains a very attractive site for these investments, although there also is likely to be a sharp growth of old-style maquiladoras in the Caribbean and Central America where labor costs are as low as in Mexico and the rules-of-origin restrictions of NAFTA do not apply. If Mexico follows the example of the East Asian NICs, it will try to promote the new maquiladoras because of their added contributions to national development objectives and allow many of the old maquiladoras to migrate to other sites in the region.

It is important to note in this context, however, that there has been a proliferation of labor-intensive subcontracting plants on the U.S. side of the border as well. Industries like garments and electronics are burgeoning in large cities such as Los Angeles, Miami, and New York City that can draw on vast pools of low-wage and in many cases undocumented immigrant workers from Mexico, Central America, the Caribbean, and Asia. Many of these plants have been set up by East Asian entrepreneurs to avoid U.S. trade barriers and to exploit low-cost labor, with the added advantage of direct access to the design and marketing centers in the United States. Thus there are new social and economic networks that connect investment, trade, and migration flows among the countries at all levels of development in North America, with "reverse investments" from East Asian exporters into the region as well.

Mexico's new maquiladora plants in the automotive, computer, and advanced electronics industries should continue to prosper under NAFTA. Labor-cost advantages still are important relative to the United States and Canada, even in the lean production, high-technology operations that are being established in Mexico. The new-style maquiladoras are strategic investments by U.S., Japanese, and European TNCs that are motivated by global sourcing criteria, with foreign firms seeking to capitalize on the advantages conferred by their intrafirm trading networks.

NAFTA already is fostering new growth areas in Mexico, especially in transborder service industries. Cheap Mexican medical services, for example, are beginning to flourish along the U.S. border, undercutting the far more expensive services to the north. The maquiladora zone is attracting business services too, such as software programming and bank and airline data processing functions. These changes move us beyond the Global Factory to the Global Office, where white-collar as well as blue-collar jobs will be networked from disparate sites around the world.

With North American integration, the very concept of "national development" is being redefined. Indeed, it already may be outmoded. Countries are trying to create dynamic sources of competitive advantage that allow for both increased productivity and a higher standard of living for their citizens. These goals are particularly difficult to attain in a region like North America where nations are at such different levels of development and where the strength of transnational capital is so pronounced. The challenge for development studies is to discover how to promote an enhanced quality of life, participatory institutions, and a strong sense of cultural identity while national borders are becoming ever more porous.

Alternative Scenarios

The foregoing discussion of Mexico's maquiladora sector and comparison of it with East Asia's dynamic manufactured export industries can be distilled into several scenarios or "alternative futures." These scenarios correspond to distinct stages in the evolution of an export-oriented economy. They entail the involvement of various kinds of economic actors, and they have quite different implications for national development and Mexico's role in an integrated North America.

Scenario 1: Export Processing

Mexico could perpetuate the dualistic structure embodied in its current maquiladora sector: The old low-skilled, labor-intensive assembly plants would continue to serve the apparel and basic electronics industries, and the new higher-skilled, more technology-intensive plants would make components and finished products for the automobile, computer, television, and machinery industries. With NAFTA, there could be some deepening of the old assembly complexes (in apparel, for example, cutting processes might shift from the United States to Mexico), but this scenario would intensify the disparities in labor markets of varying skill and wage levels within Mexico. The primary economic agents are the U.S.-based firms that supply the material inputs and the Mexican factories that provide the labor.

Scenario 2: Component-Supply Manufacturing

Mexico could make a conscious effort to attract investors in the high-technology, high-value-added industries associated with the new-style maquiladoras and allow investments in the simple, unskilled assembly operations of the old-style maquiladoras to migrate to lower-wage countries in Central America and the Caribbean. To a certain degree, this already is happening in Mexico, although East Asia is much further along in this process. The governments in South Korea, Singapore, and to a lesser degree Taiwan are actively discouraging investments in labor-intensive industries in order to promote the industrial upgrading of their economies.

Mexico is unlikely to dispense entirely with its low-wage export-processing activities because of its large unemployed and underemployed population. In this scenario, however, the Mexican government could tip the balance toward higher-value-added industries by actively soliciting new investments in technology-intensive fields and by enhancing the training opportunities for workers who would be employed in these sectors.

The main economic agents in this type of component-supply manufacturing are TNC subsidiaries in Mexico that export needed parts to their U.S. factories that make the finished products. Although Mexican-owned firms can contribute to increased levels of domestic content in this scenario, this trend is counterbalanced by the movement of U.S., Japanese, and European parts suppliers to Mexico in an effort to maintain the links already established with the TNCs in their home markets.

Scenario 3: Specification Contracting

The second scenario is most likely in the near future, but a third scenario offers the best possibility for new export growth in the Mexican economy. To date, Mexico has lagged far behind the East Asian NICs in manufacturing finished consumer goods for U.S. retailers and importers. Imported consumer goods in the United States are an enormous market. Today, more than one-half of the apparel and over three-fourths of the footwear purchased in the United States are made overseas. Orders placed by large U.S. retailers account for a sizable proportion of these consumer goods imports.

The commercial subcontracting carried out in East Asia requires the exporting firms to make an entire product according to the specifications of the buyer. The old-style and new-style maquiladoras in Mexico, by contrast, only do assembly or component-supply manufacturing; they do not produce finished consumer goods for export. Commercial subcontracting has the greatest benefits in terms of industrial deepening and local value-added in Mexico, but it requires an extensive network of high-quality services and intermediate goods industries that Mexico lacks. East Asian countries have been successful in this area because the vast majority of their exporting firms are domestically owned, and the vast distance from their main export markets (especially the United States) has required them to develop their own supporting industries.

Currently, the companies that produce high-quality consumer goods in Mexico tend to be licensees for foreign brand–named companies (like Florsheim, Hush Puppy, Nike, and Reebok in footwear). They manufacture for Mexico's domestic market, not for the U.S. export market. In order to make the shift to specification contracting of finished goods for U.S. buyers, the Mexican companies will have to learn to export by mastering the international standards for price, quality, standardized sizing, and delivery schedules. Although this process is under way in some of the best-practice Mexican firms, the most likely option in the short run is for Asian manufacturers with strong links to U.S. buyers to enter Mexico (and neighboring countries in the Caribbean Basin) as new supply points for the U.S. market.

Scenario 4: Domestic and Overseas Retailers of Local Brands of Consumer Goods

The final stage in the development of an export economy is to move beyond contract manufacturing for foreign buyers to the establishment of proprietary brand names that allow exporters to have their own presence in retail networks. South Korea is perhaps the most advanced of the Third World countries in this regard, with Korean brands of automobiles, computers, and household appliances being sold in North America, Europe, and Japan. (For a discussion of Hyundai's efforts to build its own marketing network for cars in the United States, see Kim and Lee, 1994, and Lee and Cason, 1994.) Taiwan also sells its own brands of computers, bicycles, tennis rackets, and shoes in overseas markets, and Hong Kong has been successful in developing apparel brand names and retail chains to sell its own brands of clothing in Western nations as well as in many Asian countries, including China. Mexican beer has been one of the few branded products in Mexico to develop a retail niche north of the border.

This brand-name and retailing option, although the most remote for Mexico at present, establishes a standard against which successful export industries must be evaluated (Gereffi, 1995). Domestic entrepreneurs that are internationally competitive in manufacturing and that can create a strong brand image are the main economic agents that have an incentive for forward integration into retailing. The stakes are high, however, since successful retailers will be battling one another for a foothold in growing niche markets in North America and beyond.

The Transition from Scenario 1 to Scenario 4

In summary, the evolution from Scenario 1 to Scenario 4 in Mexico corresponds to four distinct modes of integration with the international economy: export processing, component-supply manufacturing, specification contracting, and domestic and overseas retailing of local brands of consumer goods. Each mode of integration has a distinctive economic agent: Mexican branch plants integrated with foreign apparel and electronics companies located in the United States (Scenario 1); TNC subsidiaries and some Mexican parts suppliers (Scenario 2); Asian and eventually Mexican contract manufacturers of finished consumer goods exported directly to U.S. retailers and brand-named companies (Scenario 3); and domestic entrepreneurs with a vested interest in exporting local (rather than foreign) brands of products (Scenario 4).

Each level of exporting is progressively more difficult to establish because it implies a higher level of domestic integration and local entrepreneurship, but the benefits for national development and international competitiveness are correspondingly greater as countries move from the first to the fourth scenario. Mexico appears to be moving from Scenario 1 to Scenario 2, but it still has a long way to go before it matches the success of the East Asian NICs that are moving from Scenario 3 to Scenario 4.

Bibliography

BID (Banco Interamericano de Desarrollo). 1993. "América del Norte: Las maquiladoras en México en vísperas del TLC." *Comercio Exterior* (Mexico City), 43(2):159–161.

Carrillo, Jorge. 1989. "Transformaciones en la industria maquiladora de exportación." Pp. 37–54 in Bernardo González-Aréchiga and Rocío Barajas Escamilla, eds., *Las maquiladoras: Ajuste estructural y desarrollo regional.* Tijuana, Mexico: El Colegio de la Frontera Norte and Fundación Friedrich Ebert.

Carrillo-Huerta, Mario, and Victor L. Urquidi. 1989. "Trade Deriving from the International Division of Production: Maquila and Postmaquila in Mexico." *Journal of the Flagstaff Institute*, 13(1):14–47.

Castillo, Victor M., and Ramón de Jesús Ramírez Acosta. 1991. "East Asian Export Processing Zones and the Mexican Maquiladora Program: Comparisons and Lessons in Subcontracting and the Transfer of Technology." Paper presented at the international symposium on The Impact of the Maquiladora Export Processing Industry: Economic Transformation and Human Settlement in the U.S.-Mexico Border Region, 6–8 March, Arizona State University, Tempe.

Cumings, Bruce. 1984. "The Origins and Development of the Northeast Asian Political Economy: Industrial Sectors, Product Cycles, and Political Consequences." *International Organization*, 38(1):1–40.

Eden, Lorraine. 1991. "Bringing the Firm Back In: Multinationals in IPE." Centre for International Trade and Investment Policy Studies (CITIPS) Discussion Paper 91–01. Ottawa: Carleton University.

EIU (Economist Intelligence Unit). 1993/94. *Dominican Republic, Haiti, Puerto Rico: Country Profile*. London: EIU.

Estrada, Leobardo F., and Victor M. Castillo. 1990. "Asian Export Industries in the Northern Mexico Border: Implications for the Integration of Mexico–United States." Unpublished manuscript, University of California–Mexus on U.S.-Mexico Relations, 51 pp.

Finn, Edward A., Jr. 1988. "Who Made Your Underwear?" *Forbes*, 25 July, pp. 56–58.

Gereffi, Gary. 1990. "Big Business and the State." Pp. 90–109 in Gereffi and Wyman, 1990.

———. 1994a. "The International Economy and Economic Development." Pp. 206–233 in Neil J. Smelser and Richard Swedberg, eds., *The Handbook of Economic Sociology*. Princeton: Princeton University Press.

———. 1994b. "Rethinking Development Theory: Insights from East Asia and Latin America." Pp. 26–56 in Douglas Kincaid and Alejandro Portes, eds., *Comparative National Development: Society and Economy in the New Global Order*. Chapel Hill: University of North Carolina Press.

———. 1995. "Global Production Systems and Third World Development." Pp. 100–142 in Barbara Stallings, ed., *Global Change, Regional Response: The New International Context of Development*. New York: Cambridge University Press.

Gereffi, Gary, and Miguel Korzeniewicz, eds. 1994. *Commodity Chains and Global Capitalism*. Westport, Conn.: Praeger.

Gereffi, Gary, and Donald Wyman, eds. 1990. *Manufacturing Miracles: Paths of Industrialization in Latin America and East Asia*. Princeton: Princeton University Press.

González-Aréchiga, Bernardo, and Rocío Barajas Escamilla, eds. 1989. *Las maquiladoras: Ajuste estructural y desarrollo regional*. Tijuana, Mexico: El Colegio de la Frontera Norte and Fundación Friedrich Ebert.

Grosser, Kate, and Brian Bridges. 1990. "Economic Interdependence in East Asia: The Global Context." *Pacific Review*, 3(1):1–14.

Grunwald, Joseph, and Kenneth Flamm. 1985. *The Global Factory: Foreign Assembly in International Trade*. Washington, D.C.: Brookings Institution.

Healey, Derek T. 1990. "The Underlying Conditions for the Successful Generation of EPZ-Local Linkages: The Experience of the Republic of Korea." *Journal of the Flagstaff Institute*, 14(1):43–88.

Henderson, Jeffrey. 1989. *The Globalisation of High Technology Production: Society, Space, and Semiconductors in the Restructuring of the Modern World*. London: Routledge.

Hofheinz, Roy, Jr., and Kent E. Calder. 1982. *The Eastasia Edge*. New York: Basic Books.

Kaplinsky, Raphael. 1993. "Export Processing Zones in the Dominican Republic: Transforming Manufactures into Commodities." *World Development*, 21:1851–1865.

Keesing, Donald B. 1983. "Linking Up to Distant Markets: South to North Exports of Manufactured Consumer Goods." *American Economic Review*, 73:338–342.

———. 1990. "Which Export Processing Zones Make Most Sense in Light of the Spillover Benefits and Practical Needs of Manufactured Exports?" *Journal of the Flagstaff Institute*, 14(1):29–42.

Kim Hyung Kook and Su-Hoon Lee. 1994. "Commodity Chains and the Korean Automobile Industry." Pp. 281–296 in Gereffi and Korzeniewicz, 1994.

Lee, Naeyoung, and Jeffrey Cason. 1994. "Automobile Commodity Chains in the NICs: A Comparison of South Korea, Mexico, and Brazil." Pp. 223–243 in Gereffi and Korzeniewicz, 1994.

Mattar, Jorge, and Claudia Schattan. 1993. "El comercio intraindustrial e intrafirma México–Estados Unidos: Autopartes, electrónicos y petroquímicos." *Comercio Exterior* (Mexico City), 43(2):103–124.

Portes, Alejandro, José Itzigsohn, and Carlos Dore-Cabral. 1994. "Urbanization in the Caribbean Basin: Social Change During the Years of the Crisis." *Latin American Research Review,* 29(2):3–37.

Ramírez Carrillo, Luis Alfonso. 1993. "El escenario de la industrialización en Yucatán." *Comercio Exterior* (Mexico City), 43(2):171–177.

Schive, Chi, R. H. Liu, J. B. Jou, and M. S. Teng. 1986. *Evaluation of the Impact of Direct Foreign Investment on Our Economy* (in Chinese). Report sponsored by the Investment Commission, Ministry of Economic Affairs, Taipei, Taiwan.

Schoepfle, Gregory K., and Jorge F. Pérez-López. 1989. "Export Assembly Operations in Mexico and the Caribbean." *Journal of Interamerican Studies and World Affairs,* 31(4):131–161.

Shaiken, Harley. 1990. *Mexico in the Global Economy: High Technology and Work Organization in Export Industries.* Monograph Series, 33. La Jolla, Calif.: Center for U.S.-Mexican Studies, University of California, San Diego.

Sklair, Leslie. 1989. *Assembling for Development: The Maquila Industry in Mexico and the United States.* Boston: Unwin Hyman.

Stallings, Barbara. 1990. "The Role of Foreign Capital in Economic Development." Pp. 55–89 in Gereffi and Wyman, 1990.

Székely, Gabriel, ed. 1991. *Manufacturing Across Borders and Oceans: Japan, the United States, and Mexico.* Monograph Series, 36. La Jolla, Calif.: Center for U.S.-Mexican Studies, University of California, San Diego.

Unger, Kurt. 1990. "Mexican Manufactured Exports and U.S. Transnational Corporations: Industrial Structuring Strategies, Intrafirm Trade, and New Elements of Comparative Advantage." Pp. 1091–1120 in *Unauthorized Migration: Addressing the Root Causes,* Vol. 2, sponsored by the Commission for the Study of International Migration and Cooperative Economic Development. Washington, D.C.: U.S. Government Printing Office.

USITC (United States International Trade Commission). 1989. *Production Sharing: U.S. Imports Under Harmonized Tariff Schedule Subheadings 9802.00.60 and 9802.00.80, 1985–1988.* USITC Publication 2243. Washington, D.C.: USITC.

———. 1995. *Production Sharing: U.S. Imports Under Harmonized Tariff Schedule Provisions 9802.00.60 and 9802.0080, 1990–1993.* Washington, D.C.: USITC.

Weintraub, Sidney. 1990. "The Maquiladora Industry in Mexico: Its Transitional Role." Pp. 1143–1155 in *Unauthorized Migration: Addressing the Root Causes,* Vol. 2, sponsored by the Commission for the Study of International Migration and Cooperative Economic Development. Washington, D.C.: U.S. Government Printing Office.

Wilson, Patricia A. 1990. "Maquiladoras and Local Linkages: Building Transaction Networks in Guadalajara." Pp. 1183–1219 in *Unauthorized Migration: Addressing the Root Causes,* Vol. 2, sponsored by the Commission for the Study of International Migration and Cooperative Economic Development. Washington, D.C.: U.S. Government Printing Office.

World Bank. 1987. *World Development Report, 1987.* New York: Oxford University Press.

6

The Mexican
Political Pretransition
in Comparative Perspective

Ilán Semo

In 1996 Mexico's political system appears in the catalog of twentieth-century regimes as "a museum piece," to cite the words of one North American observer. Although Mexican society had been noted for more than four decades for the stability (if also for the occasional volatility) of its semiauthoritarian order (Meyer, 1991)—having not suffered a military dictatorship since that of Victoriano Huerta in 1913—today it is most notable as an anachronism. The process of transition toward political democracy, although foreseeable, has yet to be initiated. The fundamental relationships between state and civil society continue to be defined by the system established in 1946 with the formation of the Institutional Revolutionary Party (PRI).

Presidential corporatism, based on one-party control of the central powers of the state, has repeatedly demonstrated its adaptability, its capacity to respond to the challenges presented by various opposition forces. Combining the principle of a single-term presidency with corporatist control of social organizations and business groups, the system was able to marshal the powers and resources necessary to embark on the path of economic neoliberalism without altering the basic structures of national politics. The deep political and social changes that have transformed the country since the crisis of 1968 have not resulted in the one reform that could launch a real transition to democracy: the

Research for this chapter was made possible by the sponsorship of the Social Science Research Council, which I thankfully acknowledge. I would also like to thank Francisco Valdés Ugalde and Arturo Acuña for their valuable comments. The opinions expressed, however, are my sole responsibility.

PRI's abandonment of the use of extralegal means to preserve its executive power (Smith, 1990).

Nonetheless, some significant changes have occurred. Only a decade ago the prospect of Mexico following in the footsteps of southern Europe and the rest of Latin America would have been registered in public opinion as among the most implausible of utopias, but the results of the 1988 presidential elections brought the theme of democratic transition into the forefront of national attention. In 1988 the PRI lost something more than just its constitutional majority in parliament. That something was a certain subterranean power that signified its legitimacy in the political imaginary of Mexican society: the assurance of its infallibility. The outbreak of the Chiapas rebellion in January 1994 undermined its credibility further. Immobilized by internal discord, the PRI is beginning to show signs of having lost the necessary cohesion to govern the country. The assassinations of Luis Donaldo Colosio and José Francisco Ruiz Massieu—respectively, the presidential candidate and general secretary of the PRI—the investigation of which the party has obstructed in a suspicious fashion, point to deep contradictions cleaving the party in power. Accused of perpetrating a massive electoral fraud, the official apparatus has failed to parlay the triumph of Ernesto Zedillo, the replacement candidate chosen by the PRI following Colosio's murder, into renewed legitimacy for the electoral system as a whole. Before 1988 there was no question as to who would win elections. Today there is indeed a question that, at least as far as the more critical sectors of public opinion are concerned, has become an essentially practical one: How and when will political society find the path—suggested but also interrupted in 1988—toward some sort of civil democracy?

My purpose in this chapter is to analyze the events that have dominated Mexican politics during the last few years, as seen in the light of various experiences of the collapse of authoritarian order that history has recently provided. I do not pretend to offer a general comparative analysis but a study of the current Mexican pretransition process and its possible courses of evolution in terms of the paradigms suggested by other experiences of democratization. Since 1989 the social revolutions of the eastern bloc and of the former Soviet Union have been added to the processes of transition in the Mediterranean and Latin America. There has been a notable increase in the diversity and complexity of routes of transition. The unprecedented character of the reforms engendered by the implosion of authoritarian regimes obliges us to reflect again on the consistency and scope of transition theories. An analysis of the (failed) Mexican case may serve this purpose, provided that we situate it within the range of transition paths that have emerged during the last decade and a half.

The primary hypothesis to be derived from this exercise may be formulated as follows. Comparing the varied democratic experiences leads us to conclude that the transition process can follow either of two paths: toward a democracy of the elites or toward a societal democracy. The first alternative involves the constitution of a concentrated state, manifesting a pronounced demarcation between political society and civil society. The second generates a diffused state, whose forms of representation are based not only on universal suffrage but also on the representation of a multiplicity of particular interests. Although the Mexican regime remains in the pretransition phase—freely contested general elections have yet to be held—the direction of change that has prevailed to date suggests the emergence of an elite democracy. This does not mean, however, that once the actual transition is in progress the nature of the democratization process cannot be altered. The Chiapas uprising has already initiated radical changes in national politics. It has served not only to accelerate the erosion of the one-party system but, more significant, to legitimize the social forces struggling for a societal democracy.

This chapter is divided into five sections. Outlined in the first are the general problems attendant upon any democratic transition as well as the varieties of regimes that have resulted therefrom. The next three sections offer an analysis of the PRI's crisis of legitimacy and the various changes that have been set in motion. Last, through an analysis of developments in the recent past, the definitive moments of the Mexican pretransition process are studied, and its possible results are indicated.

Elite Democracy and Societal Democracy: General Considerations

A democratic transition process can be defined as the set of institutional and extrainstitutional transformations that lead from the old authoritarian regime to a new democratic one (O'Donnell and Schmitter, 1988). From a strictly political perspective, an established regime is an institutional arrangement that demarcates with relative precision (the principle of self-definition, or "self-referentiality") the boundaries between legitimate means of access to public power (the "system of representation") and those deemed illegitimate (the external environment, or "periphery" of the system of representation). In principle there is no such thing as a "pure" regime. Authoritarian regimes tend to situate plural forms of representation in their periphery, and vice versa. If a democratic regime is to establish its own principle of self-referentiality, it must relegate the authoritarian mechanisms of power to its periphery. In a sense, the transition from one to the other may be regarded as a process of inversion: Periphery becomes system, system periphery. The self-referentiality of the system is the basis of the regime's existence (Luhmann, 1991).

Every political transition is a process of open-ended change; the new regime is constituted in the midst of uncertainty. The construction of the self-referentiality principle is a novel phenomenon, singular and unprecedented, determined by the historical contingencies of the transition itself and the forces it sets in motion. It is possible, however, to distinguish in each case among three differentiated moments: the pretransition, the transition proper, and the consolidation of the new regime (Linz, 1978). The Spanish transition describes a parabola leading from the death of Franco to the consolidation of a constitutional (and monarchical) democracy in the early 1980s. The Chilean transition begins with the first free elections for the Congress and presidency and is still in search of its ultimate physiognomy. Mexico and the former Soviet Union still find themselves in the pretransition stage.

The origins of the pretransition process must perhaps be sought in the attainment of a certain level of legitimacy by the forces aiming to dismantle the authoritarian order. Three quite dissimilar situations may be mentioned in this regard. In the Soviet Union these forces arose at the very center of the authoritarian system. (Although very unlike the Soviet leadership, the officer corps of the Portuguese army played an equivalent role in that country). Conversely, in Chile and Spain they were located at the periphery of the authoritarian system, which is to say in the space of repressive tolerance. The third variant is exemplified by the form this "launching" assumed in Brazil and Greece: Early initiatives for reform came, indiscriminately, from the system and its periphery. Regardless of their origin, the tentativeness or gradualism that characterized the various pretransition movements was essentially the result of three factors.

First, when the protagonists of the transition were still too weak to impose a democratization pact, and when the authoritarian establishment found itself less and less capable of preventing the implosion of the old order, the latter invariably took the form of a fragile equilibrium. The central forces of the old regime installed themselves in the transformative process, aiming to direct and contain it.

Second, the reformers had "learned" the mechanics of winning small battles in the sphere of public opinion, in local and union elections, and in the defense of basic political rights. They had thereby succeeded in neutralizing the instrumentalities of repression, nullifying the forms of co-optation that had hitherto prevented the constitution of a national and popular will capable of splitting the country into two polarized factions—for and against change.

Third, from both the system and its periphery, complementary initiatives of transition emerged. Hence arose the possibility of a convergence based on the exclusion of those who fought for the "total defeat" of the adversary on both fronts.

The transition, properly speaking, commences with the announcement of general elections to form an assembly whose mandate is the promulgation of a new constitution. Civil liberties are decreed by the interim government. Society discovers previously unsuspected resources for doing politics. The "opening" of the political process begins and euphorias are multiplied: the euphoria of publishing the forbidden, the euphorias of legislating, of demonstrating, of calling strikes, of purging the apparatuses of repression. In search of its principle of democratic self-referentiality, society believes itself capable of any change. But this is an illusion. To judge from recent experience, the democratization process can follow only two fundamentally contrasting routes: that tending toward the constitution of an elite democracy or that leading to a societal democracy. The transition process is in large measure a contest to decide which of the two will prevail.

Elite democracy means founding the new regime on a pronounced separation of politics from civil society and creating a "concentrated state" based on the parties. It entails the growing autonomy of the professional technocracy and the legislative bodies as well as the formation of private lobbies to represent particular interests. It is a unidimensional form of democracy, whose periphery is expanded to the same extent as the space for legitimate democratic representation is reduced. Societal democracy implies a movement in the opposite direction: a process of state diffusion (a "diffused state") involving multiple forms of representation that arise not only from universal suffrage based on citizenship but from universal balloting for the representation of particular social interest groups within the state. The sanctioning of new forms of management of the economy and social conflicts—forms that transcend "private order," on the one hand, and state intervention, on the other—provides the social basis of societal democracy. It is a multidimensional form of democratic representation, whose periphery is reduced to the point of comprising only extreme and exceptional situations (Semo, 1992).

None of the democratic transitions in the Mediterranean or in Latin America, not to mention those in the eastern bloc countries, has arrived at the consolidation phase. It is likely that some of them may have surmounted the danger of a return to the past, but they are still deeply immersed in the problem of defining their future.

Metamorphosis of the PRI or Legitimacy Crisis?

Two phenomena may shed light on the "surface" of Mexico's current political system. The first is the decreasing proportion of the official vote received by the PRI in federal elections held during the last few decades (see Table 6.1). The second phenomenon is the increasing number of seats at various levels of legislative representation and government (from aldermen to governors) gained by opposition parties in the elections held in the last few years: from fewer than a hundred in 1963 to 4,000 (out of a total of 19,000 seats) by 1991, among them three governors from the National Action Party (PAN) (*La Jornada*, 9 October 1993). The official language encodes this historical trajectory as a movement from "a single party to a majority party" (Farías Mackey, 1990). From an electoral perspective, the formula seems implausible: We know which is the single party but not which is the majority party.

TABLE 6.1
Vote for PRI as Percent of Total Vote in Elections for Federal Deputies, 1961–1994

Year	Percent of Total Vote	Year	Percent of Total Vote
1961	90.2	1979	69.7
1964	86.3	1982	69.3
1967	83.3	1985	64.8
1970	80.1	1988	51.1
1973	69.7	1991	61.1
1976	80.1	1994	49.2

Sources: Data from Molinar Horcasitas, 1991:71,129; El Cotidiano, January 1992; and La Jornada, 28 August 1994.

From its foundation the PRI ensured its dominance over the system of representation by recourse to two self-referential mechanisms and one principle of exclusion. These were (1) the system of legal, technical, formal controls whereby the state (i.e., the party) administers the electoral process; (2) the informal networks of clientelist, corporatist, and extralegal connections whereby captive votes are exchanged for spheres of influence within the state (i.e., a system that nullifies any prospect of electoral accountability and, consequently, of freely contested elections); and (3) extraordinarily reactive instruments of repression and co-optation directed against the forces acting outside the logic of the self-referential system. The elections of 1988 crystallized a reality that existed in essence during the previous decade: the emergence of forces opposed to the one-party system that could neither be marginalized by traditional coercive mechanisms nor be neutralized by co-optation. Having to admit officially the unexpected loss of a significant portion of the party's "traditional vote" in 1988 amounted, in effect, to admitting the fallibility of the exclusion principle and therefore of the self-referential mechanisms supporting the legitimacy of the one-party state. This leads to another possible interpretation of the 1988 election results: rather than facing a simple adjustment of the old one-party system to the presence of a belligerent opposition, the regime was now at the beginning of the transformation of the electoral system as a whole; that is the beginning of the pretransition process.

What is actually in crisis when one talks about the legitimacy crisis of a presidential and corporatist system such as Mexico's? In the Spanish transition process, the legitimacy crisis put an end to the Franco regime but not to the monarchy. In Portugal it dissolved the internal structures of the colonial army, whereas in Chile it had no impact on the armed forces per se but on their relation to political society. The Argentine crisis of legitimacy affected the political regime as a whole; Brazil resembled Argentina in this regard more closely than any other Latin American state. If we conceptualize the Mexican political system as the ensemble of three interrelated elements—the presidential regime, the captive electoral system, and a corporatist order that mediates between the state and the particular interest groups—we may interpret the events of the past decade as follows. The legitimacy crisis has not essentially affected the hegemony of the presidency. It has instead dismantled some of the elements of the corporatist order, but its main effects have been concentrated in the captive electoral system (Molinar Horcasitas, 1991).

A crisis of legitimacy cannot go on forever. Nonetheless, the outcome of the present crisis is difficult to predict; one cannot readily foresee what impact the crisis in the electoral system will have on the other two components of the political system as a whole. But the growing presence of opposition parties in popular elections has resulted from a two-sided trend. On the one hand, we have witnessed a decade of civil and social conflicts, beginning in 1979, that have dismantled the regional bases of the PRI's monopoly of official power, leading to division in the party and its poor showing in the 1988 and 1994 elections. On the other hand, there has been a series of electoral reforms, beginning in 1977, destined to relegitimize the hegemonic party. The history of the creeping decomposition of the PRI is, to a large extent, the history of the dialectic between these two phenomena.

The Captive Reform

The advent of a pretransition process is signaled by the relaxation of authoritarian order. The Brezhnev of 1982 was no longer the Brezhnev of 1965: In the microcells of power, the Soviet society that Gorbachev would inherit had been dismantling the bureaucratic order. In similar circumstances, and under the pressure of social protest, Franco attempted a "managed opening" before his death. The policy of the Brazilian military was in this respect not unlike that of the Spanish generalissimo. In principle, there are two ways in which the relaxation of an authoritarian regime may be effected: The main push for democratization may come either from the state or from society. The extreme cases are represented in the eastern bloc by the Soviet Union and Poland, in Latin America by Argentina and Chile. Soviet reform was initiated at the top of the CPSU (Communist Party of the Soviet Union), Polish reform in the clandestine meetings of Solidarity. As a result, the Russian transformation is trapped in the logic of the strong men of the old regime: Boris Yeltsin and Mikhail Gorbachev. In Poland, by way of contrast, Lech Walesa has not so far succeeded in establishing the rules of the game vis-à-vis the new parliament; the fabric of Polish society is not conducive to the formation of charismatic figures. The probability of the Russian transition process yielding an elite democracy appears high—provided the country does not first sink into an internecine war among nations and nationalisms. In Poland there is at least the prospect of a road to societal democracy being opened. A similar contrast may be seen in the Southern Cone: Argentinean parliamentarism has only the most tenuous connections with civil society; in Chile the parties of the transition are already embedded in the everyday life of the citizenry.

By 1977 Mexican society found itself at some intermediate point between these two options. The electoral reform conceived by Jesús Reyes Heroles, then secretary of the interior, placed the political system in a situation where some self-initiatives could be produced to create an opening "from above" and thus restore its legitimacy. If in the 1970s civil society had taken into its own hands what the state had refused to concede to it in 1968—the dismantling of corporatist order—Reyes Heroles believed the regime had the necessary strength and initiative to respond to this challenge (Bartra, 1982).

What impelled the administration of José López Portillo to undertake the 1977 reform? The answer is far from self-evident. The major questioning of the party that took place after the 1968 crisis had already died down. The clouds of the 1973–1976 economic crisis were beginning to clear with news of the discovery of sizable oil reserves. As the country was on the verge of joining the select club of major oil producers, international finance circles became increasingly solicitous. The PRI had just registered another major electoral victory. All in all, there was no obvious reason to grant such an extravagant "concession." The reform did secure the control of the executive power over the electoral process as a whole and preserved the principle of noncompetitive elections, but it also permitted the registration of new political parties that were noted for their antigovernmental belligerence: the PCM (Communist Party of Mexico) and the PRT (Revolutionary Workers Party) to the left and the PDM (Mexican Democratic Party) to the right. Such an action had no precedent in the political history of the country: Before 1977 any stance of uncompromising opposition had invariably been punished and marginalized. Moreover, the new parties were ensured a place in the lower house (Chamber of Deputies) through the principle of proportional representation. They were accorded the status of "public entities" and granted access to the means of communication and to the official budget. Their existence was guaranteed by special laws. Another law declared an amnesty for former guerrillas in 1978 with a view to extinguishing the armed opposition that had arisen in the 1960s (Paoli, 1984).

More than a new electoral law, the LOPPE (Political Organizations and Electoral Processes Law) was the beginning of a global political reform designed to strengthen the legitimacy of the PRI in two ways: by opening the electoral space to political and social conflict, and by legalizing all the opposition forces as captive minorities, as in the case of the PAN since the 1960s (Semo, 1988).

The nature of the reform of 1977 is perhaps best explained through the interaction of several factors. For the PRI the 1976 elections ended in the paradigm it had tried to avoid for over three decades. Since the Left was semiillegal and the PAN was almost paralyzed as a result of its internal crisis—it had not fielded a presidential candidate—José López Portillo appeared in fact as the single candidate of the single party for the presidency of the republic. The electoral collapse of the opposition resulted in an overwhelming majority for the PRI and brought back the specter of 1968 and 1971: If the system could not find a new mechanism to solve the conflicts between the state and the emerging civil society, the regime might revert to the cycle of maximalist politics. The elections appeared to demonstrate that neither the Left nor the Right could advance beyond the margins of proportional representation, as was evident from the PAN's traditional vote, on the one hand, and the poor showing of Valentín Campa, the PCM's unregistered presidential candidate, on the other. This confirmed the widespread conviction that the opposition would never transgress the limits of captive minorities. Last but not least, if López Portillo wanted to free himself from the legacy of his predecessor, President Luis Echeverría, he had to open a space within the very bosom of the system for the oppositional forces that until then had languished on the periphery, since they alone were sufficiently militant to be capable of containing the authoritarian apparatus that had presided over the electoral charade of 1976. Reyes Heroles defined this balancing act in the following epigram: "Whatever resists, supports."

The year of the reform—1977—is also significant. It coincided with the beginning of the Spanish transition, which surprised and engaged politicians and political scientists of the Ibero-American world. Jesús Reyes Heroles was familiar with that experience and was inspired by it. The differences, however, did not escape his attention either. The Spanish reform had as its object the demolition of the Francoist regime; the Mexican reform was merely intended to reaffirm the position of the hegemonic party. In contrast to the initiatives of 1963, the LOPPE achieved the results desired by the secretary of the interior. It became clear that the opposition parties campaigning for a radical change in the system lacked the necessary legitimacy to effect such a change. In the 1979 congressional election the PCM obtained 4.9 percent and the Left as a whole 9.6 percent of the total votes. The PAN received 10.8 percent (*Diarios*, 1986:218–221). In the following years these percentages increased only slightly.

Incapable of accessing the informal network of the captive vote, the opposition was confined to limited spaces in public opinion and the electoral system, legitimized as a captive minority. Its chance of fragmenting the corporatist basis of the political apparatus was thus visibly reduced. If in the 1970s the limited electoral options meant that the main thrust of democratization would be engaged in the process of dismantling the corporatist structures—the social base of the PRI—this situation was reversed after 1979. Electoral conflicts gradually came to the fore in the confrontation between the system and its periphery. The opposition was reduced to a combative yet captive minority; Mexico's governability had been restored. The presidential election of 1982 seemed to confirm Reyes Heroles's conviction: The transition process in Mexico would not resemble the processes in Poland and Czechoslovakia, where Solidarity and the Civic Forum had occupied the center stage of democratization. Neither would it be like those in Brazil or Spain, where Ignacio "Lula" da Silva and the unions or the Spanish civil movement had been key players in the erosion of the old regime (Moreira Alves, 1984). Yet the time had come in Mexico for a reform "from below."

From the Politics of Confrontation to Selective Tolerance

When the International Monetary Fund (IMF) allowed the nationalization of the banks in 1982 as a last resort to maintain the solvency of Mexico's foreign debt, the message did not get through to foreign or national capital. Once again the Mexican state had lost the trust of Mexican entrepreneurs and international financiers. Accelerated capital flight, a significant reduction in foreign investment, and a halt on loans from the IMF itself in 1982 and 1983 are testimony of this impasse (Valdés, 1984). The three "hypers" of contemporary depression plagued economic policy during the second half of Miguel de la Madrid's presidency: hyperinflation, hyperdeficit, and hyperunemployment. The conjunction of a devalued currency and unprecedented freedom for private and public speculation inflated the stock market—and with it all other markets subject to speculation. The head of a lower-middle-class household selling his or her mortgage from INFONAVIT (the state agency that provides housing loans at very low, subsidized interest rates) in order to buy shares in the stock market—this is the image that best captures a period that will go down in economic history as Mexico's Great Depression. Toward 1986 the middle class could be found "playing the lottery" with the meager goods and resources it still possessed. The worldwide market crash of 1987 was yet another blow for Mexico. Without the benefit of prior experience, laws, or special tribunals, hundreds of thousands of small investors lost the goods, savings, and resources they had accumulated during more prosperous times (Brailovsky et al., 1989).

If it was speculation that expropriated the savings of the middle class, hyperinflation had the same effect on the incomes of rural and urban workers. Exact figures are hard to obtain, but there is no doubt that the depression severely affected the social base of the PRI in the most modern sectors of production: employees of the state and its many firms, teachers, university instructors, media workers, the tertiary sector, the best-established unions, agroindustrial ejidos, and livestock ranchers supplying the national market. In other words, the losers were all those social groups for whom a retreat to the informal economy or to subsistence agriculture was particularly difficult, if not impossible. It should be noted here that the oil-boom years (1978–1982) brought the most substantial increase in real income since the heyday of Cardenismo (1934–1940). The absolute fall in wages during the 1980s was dramatic, but the relative decline, measured against long-term structural tendencies, was less so. Some groups found new options. The maquiladora sector expanded rapidly; frequent devaluations multiplied the demand for agricultural exports; the number of workers emigrating to the United States and sending part of their income to their impoverished peasant families increased. Another variety of accelerated migration was internal: Low-income sectors entered the informal economy or went back to subsistence production in the countryside (Brailovsky et al., 1989).

It is surprising, however, that the only protest movements of any lasting relevance during the presidency of Miguel de la Madrid (1982–1988) were those of the teachers and the social mobilization engendered in response to the earthquake that hit Mexico City in 1985 (Foweraker and Craig, 1990). All other attempts invariably failed. From the perspective of the corporatist system, the Reyes Heroles political reform was bearing fruit. In contrast with former periods, none of the social conflicts of the 1980s became a political dilemma for the regime, as had happened with the railway workers in the 1950s, the students in the 1960s, and the electricity workers in the 1970s. Jails did not lack political prisoners, but they were old guerrillas and not labor leaders such as Demetrio Vallejo or Valentín Campa in 1958. Massacres of demonstrators in broad daylight, such as occurred in 1968 and 1971, were not repeated. Although repressed in certain instances, strikes were generally tolerated. If one of the intentions of the 1977 legislation was to relocate the political center of social conflict to the electoral sphere, it met with considerable success. Regional electoral contests were the focus of political attention during the 1980s. To the neoliberal elites of the PRI, this suggested a two-pronged strategy whereby they might establish their hegemony in a quiet, incremental manner. On the one hand, they would tolerate and oversee the gradual emergence of the PAN in a subordinate role—that is, its metamorphosis into a party of government acceptable to the centrist tendencies of the PRI. On the other, they would interfere—frequently by resorting to violence—with any efforts on the part of the Left to acquire the legitimacy it had failed to secure with the 1977 reform (Nuncio, 1988).

To put it very schematically, the economic depression divided the country into three geographical units. The north sought to overcome the crisis by tying itself more closely to the U.S. economy, the center suffered the most dramatic collapse in production, and the south compensated its losses by recourse to the informal economy and subsistence production. The country's electoral geography evinced a parallel division between 1982 and 1987. The PAN achieved municipal electoral victories in Chihuahua, Sonora, Coahuila, Durango, Nuevo León, and other northern regions; although much more modest, the Left's advances in southern Mexico—in Guerrero, Oaxaca, Chiapas, Morelos, Highlands of Puebla, and Tabasco—were widely publicized; the central part of Mexico essentially remained in the hands of the PRI, which turned out to be the biggest loser on a national scale. Three states failed to conform to this pattern: San Luis Potosí, the home of navismo, the one movement that attracted the Left and the Right indiscriminately; Baja California, where the vote tended to swing unpredictably between the PAN and the PSUM (Unified Socialist Party of Mexico); and the Federal District, where elections were not held (Molinar Horcasitas, 1991).

The electoral advance of the opposition forces presupposed several simultaneous conditions: (1) the presence of a social and civic movement that could demolish or disable the machinery of the PRI's captive vote; (2) the emergence of a local civil society capable of defending its triumphs in the face of continuous harassment from the center; and (3) the division of the local PRI rank and file between those who accepted the verdict of the Electoral Commission and those who rejected it in an effort to make the locality ungovernable. Thus a municipal defeat for the PRI indicated the erosion of its traditional authority in the region rather than merely a change of opinion among the electorate.

It should be noted that elections, even federal elections, are always an ensemble of local events. The PRI's gradual loss of regional infallibility was the prelude to its collapse in 1988. What brought on the sudden decay of the ruling party's regional power between 1985 and 1988?

If the traditional centralism of the Mexican economy and polity had kept secular tensions between the regions and the federal government at bay, the economic depression sharpened them considerably. The metropolitan area of Mexico City continued to receive subsidies, but direct and indirect taxation increased in the states, the latter in the form of public utilities such as water, electricity, and telephone service. The transfer of federal funds to the states was considerably reduced. The PRI's own regional administrations began to blame local shortages on the central government in order to gain legitimacy among their constituencies and, at the same time, negotiated with the center for budgetary concessions. Within regional communities, the political situation came to be perceived in polarized terms: The PRI and the central government became synonymous with interventionism, and the latter was blamed for the economic depression. The opposition capitalized on anticentralist resentment. Some state governors were not slow in discovering that it was advantageous to tolerate opposition victories (especially those of the PAN) at the municipal level, since this tended to improve their negotiating position vis-à-vis the national federation. Eventually the policy of selective tolerance was adopted by the center itself (*Proceso*, 15 May 1987, p. 49).

Mexico City, the country's largest market, which had regularly consumed the products and labor power of other regions, began to refuse them. Entire areas, such as the Bajío, descended into crisis because the center no longer had the capacity to absorb their output. Workers who had traditionally found employment in the Federal District, Mexico state, and Puebla were repeatedly turned away (Banco Nacional de México, 1989). The indignation of those who had to return to their towns and villages or migrate to the United States increased.

In small municipalities the political reform translated into opportunities for local leaders in the electoral arena. Between 1978 and 1988, José Ramírez "Chencho" García, with the support of his neighbors in a town in Hidalgo, ran the gamut of five different parties (the PRI, PARM, PPS, PMT, and PRD) "so as to see which of them would solve our water problem." He finally obtained the concession from the National Solidarity Program in 1990 but not before the reform had involuntarily penetrated to the core of electoral clientelism. The equation "votes for the PRI = concessions from the state" was no longer self-evident (Semo, 1989). It would be worthwhile to explore the national dimension of this phenomenon.

If the U.S. administration supported the PRI unconditionally in federal elections throughout the 1980s, it also made the "cleanness" of regional elections—especially in cases where the PAN was deprived of its victories by the PRI machine—a touchstone in negotiating other relations between the two nations. The U.S. press became a factor in its own right, influencing critical situations in local elections. Sonora and Chihuahua, where the PAN obtained victories, were notorious cases in point. The role of U.S. diplomacy in global negotiations is still not known, but it must have been influential in orienting the policy of selective toleration toward the PAN.

The decline in the regional power of the PRI was evident in the national congressional elections of 1985. The official party obtained the lowest vote in its history, 64.8 percent. The PAN again surpassed 15 percent; the fragmented Left obtained a combined total of more than 10 percent (*Diarios*, 1986:218). The executive power then opted for a substantial change: officially to abandon the policy of captive minorities in favor of that of selective tolerance. The victories of the PAN were recognized although not definitively; the Left frequently had to struggle in open confrontations in order to assure them. It was in arenas of civil protest that the PAN's emergence was observed; spaces that appeared following outbursts of violence indicated conflicts with the Left or with independent candidates such as Salvador Nava in San Luis de Potosí. The PRI's neoliberal elite extended its hand to Panismo; the PAN capitalized on this gesture. It moderated its discourse, opted for negotiation rather than pressure, preserved its unity, and, above all, maintained its role as opposition party (Loaeza and Segovia, 1987).

Miguel de la Madrid decided to place the policy of selective toleration in the context of a global reform. The electoral law of 1987 introduced two changes: It made alliances very difficult and increased proportional representation to 200 seats. The only strategy available to the Left whereby it might have become a substantial force was, because of its atomized nature, precisely the politics of alliances. If the electoral trends of 1979, 1982, and 1985 were projected forward to 1988, without allowing for Cuauhtémoc Cárdenas's arrival on the political scene, one might have predicted that the PAN would obtain approximately 150 seats and the PRI 300 from a total of 500—that is, a formally bipartisan Congress or something close to it (Garavilla Moreno, 1991).

Toward 1987 the regional victories of the opposition had affected public opinion but not the nation as a whole. They were still not sufficiently numerous or significant to threaten PRI hegemony. On the contrary, in 1987 the political situation appeared to favor the official party. The opposition's likely presidential candidates, Heberto Castillo for the PSUM and Manuel Clouthier for the PAN, could at best hope to add a few points to their respective tallies. Consensus and confidence encouraged Miguel de la Madrid to announce two unheard-of, last-minute measures. First, instead of handpicking his successor in the traditional fashion, he decided to "unveil" six possible candidates who would compete in public view—thus adding a new component to the internal crisis of the PRI. Second, he chose to begin implementing a policy of economic "shock" (the Solidarity Pact) in advance of the national elections—thus adding new causes of indignation among salaried sectors. In the sphere of public opinion, the PRI was assured of its ritual of succession.

But the unexpected happened.

The System at the Crossroads?

As late as the mid-1980s, Cuauhtémoc Cárdenas, though a longtime member of the PRI, had attracted little national attention. He was, however, heir to a powerful myth—that of Cardenismo, the amalgam of agrarian reform, economic nationalism, and "socialist education" associated with the presidency of his father, Lázaro Cárdenas (1934–1940). It thus fell to his lot, upon leaving the party in 1987, to head the National Democratic Front (FDN), to assemble the social and political forces that would deprive the PRI of three of its dearest and most accustomed prerogatives: (1) an absolute majority in the presidential elections (according to the calculations of Juan Molinar Horcasitas, [1991], based on the official data, Carlos Salinas de Gortari obtained 48.7 percent of the valid votes cast in the 1988 election); (2) a constitutional majority in the Chamber of Deputies, which requires two-thirds of the seats (the official result was 51.7 percent in favor of the PRI); and (3) a monopoly of seats in the Senate. The PRI leaders discovered to their dismay that even an electoral system based on legislated noncompetition and the clientelism of captive votes was fallible.

The elections of 1988 marked the beginning of the Mexican pretransition process. As in the Soviet Union, it came about after the division of the dominant elite; as in Spain, it relied upon the support of a social movement without which the disablement of the state electoral apparatus would have been inconceivable. The impact of the FDN transcended its own organization. Had it not

touched sensitive nerves in the corporatist order and the local political machines, it could not have achieved the officially acknowledged 32 percent of the
vote; the true election results will probably never be known (Leal et al., 1988).
It is up to future historians to explain this unwonted phenomenon, but there is
no doubt that it affected the nodal principle of the Mexican political system:
the legitimacy of the president. Only the mass movement of 1968 had achieved
something similar, but its aim was not a gradual democratic transition. Miguel
de la Madrid's dream vanished when "the system came down."[1] The idea of
pursuing a controlled pretransition process involving a pact with the PAN—
which obtained 17 percent of the votes—evaporated in the tense atmosphere
that ensued after July 1988.

Carlos Salinas de Gortari assumed the presidency in a particularly precari-
ous situation. The country's economy continued to stagnate in the crisis that
started in the early 1980s. He was unable to convince the public that he had really won the elections—at any rate, not by the margins claimed in the official
computation—and his credibility within and outside the system fell to a lower
level than that of any former PRI president. The FDN as well as the PAN had
proved themselves forces to be reckoned with. Social militancy was on the increase throughout the country, ready to entertain proposals for more radical
action. For the first time in recent decades, international opinion, particularly
the U.S. press, questioned the "cleanliness" of federal elections.

Three years later, in 1991, the situation had changed. The economic crisis
had subsided. The corporatist system was once again brought under presidential discipline. Although less effective than in 1987, the captive electoral system
had been essentially restored. The PRI regained its constitutional majority in
the Chamber of Deputies, and the Cardenista FDN had split into a multitude
of irreconcilable factions. In 1991 the total vote of its former members was reduced to 16.5 percent. The president reclaimed the support of public opinion
and reestablished his role as the strong man in national politics (*Este País*, September 1991).

What made it possible for Salinas de Gortari to contain the process started
in 1988? His administration, unlike that of Miguel de la Madrid, managed with
relative ease to embark on a neoliberal shock policy based on strict compliance
with the recommendations of the IMF: fiscal discipline, privatization of public enterprises, a wage freeze, reduction of the deficit, free trade, and encouragement of foreign investment. Whereas the administration of Miguel de la
Madrid had reprivatized only 35 percent of the bank shares and a handful of
state enterprises, for fear of rupturing the political system, neo-Cardenismo
represented the anticipated rupture as an accomplished fact. Salinas could feel
confident about the future unity of the executive power and the corporatist
order; dissident elements had already positioned themselves outside the PRI.
As he warned in his first annual address (Salinas de Gortari, 1989), those who
opposed the neoliberal path knew where they could go. Fearing the further

destabilization of the hegemonic party, the IMF and the United States provided unqualified diplomatic support for the economic policies initiated in 1985, thereby facilitating their rapid implementation. Mexican investors now began repatriating capital they had exported during the 1980s, in order to purchase companies the state had put up for sale. The rise in oil prices during the Gulf War enhanced the revenues of the Ministry of Finance. The liquidation of unprofitable state enterprises and numerous government agencies enabled the administration to balance its books (Banco Nacional de México, 1991). In 1991 Salinas de Gortari was able to announce a surplus in the state treasury (*Excélsior*, 7 November 1991). The sense of impotence bequeathed by the de la Madrid administration gave way to a climate of government assurance and investor confidence. The end of the hyperinflation of the 1980s announced it; the increase in foreign and domestic investment confirmed it (Banco Nacional de México, 1991).

Worried by loss of consensus among industrial workers in 1988, Salinas made sure that the sale of state companies was not translated into massive layoffs. He proceeded to compensate those who did lose their jobs. The tensions provoked by privatization, though plainly evident in cases such as that of the Cananea mine, were thus diffused to a considerable degree. The unions, which traditionally controlled the captive electoral machines, along with teachers and oil workers, received wage raises and benefits that had been withheld for years. In order to facilitate the imposition of salary caps and derail union opposition to the process of privatization, the administration repressed the two union sectors that remained confrontational: the old official union leadership and union dissidents. From the beginning of Salinas's term, salaries and benefits were to be negotiated only at the summit level, within the newly established framework of the PECE (Economic Growth and Stabilization Pact). The old official union leadership was marginalized in the negotiations involving privatization.

Peasant regions that had supported Cuauhtémoc Cárdenas (mainly in Michoacán, Guerrero, Morelos, Mexico state, and La Laguna), figured in official policy as the main priority of the National Solidarity Program. The executive concentrated in its own hands a substantial part of the financial assistance that had formerly been distributed—or, more precisely, had not been distributed—by the bureaucracy. Although the numbers vary from author to author, it is agreed that more than 4 million campesinos benefited from new expenditures on agriculture and public works—funds they would scarcely have received had they been allocated through traditional channels. The results were immediately apparent. Agricultural production, stagnant since the early 1980s, resumed its growth. Food prices declined in urban areas, and the PRI recovered the captive vote in large rural zones. For the inhabitants of urban marginal zones, such as Chalco and Santa Fe in the Valley of Mexico, which had also supported the FDN in 1988, the government legalized 3 million informal housing lots and launched a sustained initiative for the construction of social housing. Rates of employment returned to 1982 levels in rural areas and in the construction industry, as did PRI votes.

Regional elections continued to occupy center stage in national politics. If Salinas intended to restore the pre-1988 political order, his efforts failed visibly at the regional level. One after another, regional conflicts provided the executive with a series of unpleasant surprises. The administration opted to resume its predecessor's policy of selective tolerance toward the PAN but applied it more vigorously and with a greater sense of urgency. Salinas's overall strategy aimed at reducing the neo-Cardenista opposition to the status traditionally reserved for the Left: that of a captive minority. The first step was to agree with the PAN on a new electoral law that would allow the government to regain the constitutional majority it required to legalize the neoliberal reforms. The new electoral law introduced a fundamental change: The party that obtained a majority of seats in the elections based on the plurality (or "first-past-the-post") principle was also allowed to participate in those based on proportional representation. In mathematical terms, this meant that 37 percent of the votes could theoretically suffice to provide 66 percent representation in the legislature. In exchange, the PAN was granted unhindered access to several spheres of political society: the first opposition governorship in national history, in Baja California (Guanajuato was the second, although in this case on an interim basis); respect for PAN's municipal victories; admission to the networks of communication linking the legislature with the executive; the right to lobby the state; and regular prime-time exposure on the mass media. For its part, the PAN reconciled itself to its convergence with Salinismo. The party forgot about its traditional anticonstitutional program and defined Salinas as the "Panista president." It abandoned extralegal activities, confining itself to tolerable mass demonstrations so as not to threaten the stability of the convergence. Its legislators voted with the government, at least on the main points of presidential policy. Under these circumstances, the fact that the PAN still manages to preserve its image as a party of opposition is quite remarkable.

The official attitude toward the FDN was radically different. In the weeks following the presidential election, Cuauhtémoç Cárdenas adopted a twofold strategy. He made a show of refusing to recognize the victory of Salinas de Gortari, but the actions he mounted against the new administration were noticeably moderate. Not only did he fail to call for a joining of forces against the PRI, which would have been a distinct possibility between July and November of 1988, but he also channeled the protest along the lines of a cautious civic movement that eschewed any form of forceful action. The response of the PRI and the president was, contrarily, severe and violent. Salinas probably feared that if he allowed the FDN to continue developing peacefully, the PRI would eventually disintegrate.

At this juncture, neo-Cardenismo elements decided to form their own party, the Democratic Revolution Party (PRD), based on an alliance with the old

PMS (Mexican Socialist Party). The forces making up this new formation were considerably smaller than those of the FDN. It was now Salinas's turn to pursue a double strategy: He adopted a conciliatory stance toward each of the groups composing the former FDN, negotiating the terms of its withdrawal from the coalition, and took up a confrontational posture against the PRD. The elections in Michoacán, Guerrero, and Morelos were virtually contested with "blood and fire" (*Proceso*, 8 May 1990). Entire municipalities lived in fear for months. The presence of the PRD seemed to entail a permanent state of emergency. Unable to secure new electoral successes or a relaxation of government policies, the PRD began to lose votes and supporters. By the end of 1990, its regional vote did not exceed 15 percent, even in areas where it had gained an absolute majority in 1988 (Trejo Delabre, 1991).

It was the successful economic policy of the Salinas administration, even more than its violent tactics, that ravaged the Left. The PRD stuck to its original policy of global opposition in both the legislature and the mass media: no to privatization of state enterprises, no to the North American Free Trade Agreement, no to the electoral reform, no to the proposed changes in the Agrarian Reform Law—and so forth and so on. Thus it maintained its image as an antisystem party, but in the face of the speedy results achieved by the government it criticized, its program took on the nature of a predictable protest, not the platform of a party that intended to form the next government. The political consensus attained in 1988 was considerably reduced. In the 1991 elections the PRD obtained 10.1 percent of the national vote—7 points less than the PAN. In three years neo-Cardenismo had lost, according to official numbers, 23 percent of its votes. However, this trend was reversed in the presidential elections of 1994, in which the PRD obtained 17.8 percent of the national vote. With these elections the PRD seems to have overcome the crisis of legitimacy that had brought it the poor results of 1991. But the question remains: Can it overcome its internal discord, its lack of unity and identity, in order to become a national force like the PAN?

Until 1 January 1994 the policy of Carlos Salinas de Gortari had been designed to arrest the process of democratization. The Chiapas insurrection, the assassinations of the PRI presidential candidate and its secretary general, and the multiplying forces of civil society have not managed to alter the authoritarian and extralegal nature of the electoral process. Although the triumph of Ernesto Zedillo was admitted by all political parties, the system has not convinced public opinion that the elections were free of fraud. Once again the PRI has imposed majorities of 64 percent in the houses of Congress, which bear no rational relation to the officially recorded vote.

The electoral reform of 1991, compared with that of 1977, has greatly enhanced the power of the executive to intervene in the electoral process. The fourteen years of history separating these reforms are marked by two tendencies and one question, inscribed like signposts along the winding road of the transition. The first tendency to note is that the PRI has never been inclined to surrender or renegotiate its constitutional majority in the lower house—the historical 65–70 percent that has already been recorded four times and that was only wrested from its grasp by a social movement of national scope. The PAN, however, converging with the neoliberal elites of the PRI, has meanwhile achieved a permanent vote of over 15 percent. The second tendency is the PRI's failure to arrest the erosion of its regional base; four PAN governors and the revolt in Chiapas—the most serious rural rebellion in decades—attest to this process in 1994 and 1995. The question is this: Was 1988 an accident in the electoral history of the country or the beginning of a generalized crisis of the one-party system?

The prospects for resolving the dispute between an elite democracy and a societal democracy in the Mexican pretransition process are unclear. A transition based on the survival and metamorphosis of PRI neoliberal elites and guaranteed by the convergence with the PAN would obviously favor the elitist option. A generalized crisis of the PRI, provoked by internal dissension, would enhance the possibility of a societal democracy. In the first case, elites of the old regime would dominate the process, as happened in the Soviet Union. In the second, avenues would be opened for the emergence of new social forces, perhaps along the lines of the Spanish example, that could redefine the relationship between civil society and the state. The fundamental condition for the development of a societal democracy in Mexico is the emergence of a social movement capable of dismantling the elitist bases of traditional political representation. The character assumed by the transition as it develops will be decisive in this regard.

Notes

1. *Editor's note:* This phrase refers to the official announcement after the elections of 6 July 1988 that the computing system at the Secretary of Interior, which was calculating electoral results, had collapsed. It took several days before the government was able to come up with the official results, and this was widely believed to have been an excuse to tinker with the figures. The reference in this context has a double meaning: It humorously depicts the excuse while also alluding to the beginning of the collapse of the corporatist system.

Bibliography

Banco Nacional de Mexico. 1986–1991. *Exámen de la situación económica de México.* Mexico City.

Bartra, Roger. 1982. *El reto de la izquierda.* Mexico City: Grijalbo.

Brailovsky, Vladimiro, Roland Clarke, and Natán Warman. 1989. *La política económica del desperdicio.* Mexico City: Universidad Nacional Autónoma de México.

Diarios de los debates de la Cámara de Diputados. 1965–1988. Mexico City: Congreso de la Unión.

Farías Mackey, María Emilia. 1990. "El PRI ante los resultados electorales del partido casi unico al partido mayoritario, 1946–1989." Pp. 217–254 in Abraham Talavera, ed., *El partido en el poder.* Mexico City: Instituto de Estudios Políticos, Económicos, y Sociales (IEPES).

Foweraker, Joe, and Ann L. Craig, eds. 1990. *Popular Movements and Political Change in Mexico.* Boulder and London: Lynne Rienner Publishers.

Garavilla Moreno, Jaime Miguel. 1991. "La legislación electoral en México, 1917–1991." *Exámen* 23:16–24.

Leal, Juan Felipe, Jacqueline Peschard, and Concepción Rivera. 1988. *Las elecciones federales de 1988 en México.* Mexico City: Universidad Nacional Autónoma de México.

Linz, Juan. 1978. *Crisis, Breakdown, and Reequilibration.* Baltimore, Md.: Johns Hopkins University Press.

Loaeza, Soledad, and Rafael Segovia, eds. 1987. *La vida política mexicana en la crisis.* Mexico City: El Colegio de México.

Luhmann, Niklas. 1991. *Sistemas sociales.* Mexico City: Alianza Editorial.

Meyer, Lorenzo. 1991. "Los límites del neoliberalismo." *Nexos,* 14(163):25–34.

Molinar Horcasitas, Juan. 1991. *El tiempo de la legitimidad.* Mexico City: Cal y Arena.

Moreira Alves, Maria Helena. 1984. *The State and the Opposition in Brazil.* Austin: University of Texas Press.

Nuncio, Abraham. 1988. *La sucesión presidencial en 1988.* Mexico City: Editorial Grijalbo.

O'Donnell, Guillermo, and Phillippe Schmitter. 1988. *Transiciones desde un gobierno autoritario: Conclusiones tentativas sobre las democracias inciertas.* Vol. 4. Buenos Aires: Paidós.

Paoli, Francisco José. 1984. "La infancia eterna." *El Buscón,* No. 9, March-April, pp. 53–69.

Salinas de Gortari, Carlos. 1989. *Primer informe de gobierno.* Mexico City: Gobierno de México.

Semo, Enrique. 1988. *Entre crisis te veas.* Mexico City: Editorial Nueva Imagen.

Semo, Ilán. 1989. "Cardenismo y neocardenismo." Mimeo. Colloquium: Mexico 1968–1988: Twenty Years After. San Diego, Calif.: Center for U.S.-Mexican Studies.

———. 1992. "Democracia de élites, democracia societal: El dilema de la pretransición." Pp. 191–221, in Ilán Semo, ed., *La transición interrumpida.* Mexico City: Universidad Iberoamericana.

Smith, Peter H. 1990. "Mexico since 1946." Pp. 83–157 in Leslie Bethell, ed., *The Cambridge History of Latin America,* Vol. 7 Cambridge and New York: Cambridge University Press.

Trejo Delabre, Raúl. 1991. *Los mil días de Carlos Salinas de Gortari.* Mexico City: El Nacional.

Valdés, Francisco. 1984. "Lo que la crisis se llevó." *El Buscón,* No. 14, November-December, pp. 81–98.

7

The Private Sector and Political Regime Change in Mexico

Francisco Valdés Ugalde

A key target of Mexico's economic reform has been the strengthening of the private sector as a fundamental actor in the economic arena. That sector has begun to exercise more political clout, establishing itself as a central force in the current reshaping of the Mexican body politic. More specifically, its political influence has transformed the character of state power and produced an array of notable consequences, including the move by the Institutional Revolutionary Party (PRI) to embrace institutionally the principles of neoliberalism and capitalist accumulation.

Despite the reshaping of various political structures (the presidency, the legislature, the ruling party, the party system), the future profile of the Mexican regime and its main political actors is still obscure. Mexico's transition has often been defined as a change in the balance of power between the state and society. In fact, not only is the general balance of power changing but so is the character of the regime itself: Since 1982 the state apparatus has been "modernized" with a view toward reducing its size and expenditures and increasing its efficiency. This program, the "reform of the state" implemented by the Salinas administration (1988–1994), is certain to drive a wedge between two elements that have been closely interrelated in postrevolutionary México: economic policy and social justice. Nothing expresses more clearly the government's determination to break with the heritage of the Mexican Revolution (Valdés, 1993:315–338). My purpose in this chapter is to describe and explain these developments and to suggest their implications with regard to the future course of Mexico's political transition and the reform of its regime. "Regime" is defined here as the set of institutionalized rules that regulate political representation and mediation and government decisionmaking (Therborn, 1978).

This chapter is divided into six sections. In the first I offer some theoretical considerations on politics and the private sector and propose some hypotheses for research. In the second I discuss the role of business organizations in the Mexican political arena. The two-decade conflict between the government and the private sector and the resulting changes in their relationship are examined in the third section. The fourth deals with the new dynamics of business's participation in the political process. In the fifth I endeavor to explain how this model has achieved a marked degree of success. The final section includes a summary of the new role of the private sector and an assessment of its probable consequences for the political transition in Mexico.

The Private Sector as Political Actor

Theoretical Approaches to the Private Sector

The analysis of business activity has often been restricted either to policy intervention or to structural constraints. In this chapter the business sector is considered as a political agent whose collective action must be understood in all its complexity. Taken into account are both economic structure and policy intervention as decisive aspects of such action, but also recognized are the organizational, cultural, and other strategies that are essential components of private-sector intervention. In conjunction with state reform, such intervention contributes substantially to the reshaping of civil society.

Analytical literature on this topic has primarily been informed by modernization and dependency theories. These are the theoretical expressions, respectively, of liberalism and Marxism as applied to the study of Latin American economies. Some major assumptions of both approaches as to the societal role of the private sector and its implications are questionable, as are the general ideas of society and the state that the theories employ.

Modernization theory assumes that the vitality of the private sector leads to a more efficient economy and to the gradual incorporation of "modern" social relations (Germani, 1971). With regard to Mexico, this school of thought has in its classical formulations emphasized the presence of an authoritarian regime that constrains private business by excluding it from the political decision-making process. According to extreme versions of this position, the private sector has been successfully confined to "doing business" with no significant involvement in the sphere of politics, except for two "natural" functions: interest representation and policy consulting through business associations. Proponents of this thesis advance two observations in its support: that certain state policies affecting business interests have at times been implemented in the face of private-sector opposition, and that there are significant differences between the patterns of personnel recruitment in the two sectors (Kaufman-Purcell, 1975).

By way of contrast, the dependency approach regards imperialism, national states, and local capitalists as links in a single chain. In this perspective, Third World states are continually faced with the dilemma of seeking the autonomy needed to achieve development, but in practice their only effective choice is to cultivate either foreign or domestic private interests. The latter are seen by dependency theorists as chronically incapable of furnishing the energy and vision normally ascribed to the classical European bourgeoisie. In the case of Mexico, this type of inquiry focuses on the policies pursued by the state in its efforts to gain such autonomy. The general conclusion is that structural constraints impose crippling limitations on efforts by the state to increase its autonomy vis-à-vis private interests, whether foreign or domestic. Almost no attention is given to the specificity of private political behavior, whose character is generally taken for granted (Cardoso and Faletto, 1979 [1971]; Jaguaribe et al., 1970).[1] In this regard, dependency theory proceeds from a verifiable fact—that Latin American elites are oligarchical in nature—from which it simply infers the characteristically exclusive and authoritarian behavior of this social category (Halperin-Donghi, 1969:11–73, 437–538).

In short, both approaches make reductionist simplifications. The first reduces empirical research to questions of public policy, aimed either at limiting or at fostering private economic interests, and the second focuses narrowly upon the economic alliance between the state and private business. The detailed particularity of the participation and interaction of business (and its allies) in the political arena is left out of the analysis, notwithstanding its manifest relevance and complexity.

Despite the decline of both paradigms, mainly because of their incapacity to account for recent historical developments, no theoretical alternative has yet emerged that can be applied to the study of Latin American society at a similar level of generality. Consequently, research continues to be guided by the basic principles of one or the other of these two seminal currents of thought. (Cardoso, 1986; Germani et al., 1985).

Proposed Hypotheses

In explaining the political participation of business, it is necessary to examine business's presence at all levels of society, including the economy, civil organizations, and the universe of public opinion as well as in the specifically or formally political sphere. A central aspect of an alternative approach is consideration of the "knowledgeability" of social actors (Giddens, 1984). According to this concept, what actors know or believe about their action and the context in which it takes place, including the behavior of other actors, is relevant in the explanation of such action. Such knowledge includes not only the common-sense consciousness of everyday life but also theories, which in turn influence the organization of the social institutions in which action takes place and objectives are carried out. If we are to account for the processes of transition currently under way in Latin American societies, we cannot ignore the efficacy of "subjectivity." In the Mexican case, we must attend not only to the reformation of political institutions but also to the actors' discourse regarding the necessity of such transformations. Among these actors, the private sector, in particular its economic and political leadership, has been remarkably consistent in elaborating, disseminating, and winning acceptance for a relatively novel series of proposals for the institutional reorganization of society.

Studies in historical sociology indicate that this role of the economic elite has always been central, at least in Western history in which private economic interests have played a key role in the development of social institutions (Braudel, 1982; Weber, 1942 [1923]). I suggest that the study of business in developed countries generally takes for granted the institutional setting of civil society and the private sector; both are assumed as given conditions, despite the fact that they are historically contingent. If such a simplification is admissible in investigating societies that have arrived at a condition of relative stability and institutional permanency, it is surely unsound when applied to societies undergoing processes of rapid and extensive change.

Most analyses of the relationship between the private sector and the state in Mexico share two assumptions: that the business elite and the upper echelons of the political bureaucracy are two *different* groups, formed and functioning according to different rationales; and that both groups were highly cohesive during the stages of accelerated industrialization (1940–1954) and stabilizing development (1954–1970).[2] The first idea implies that we are dealing with two social groups that are clearly differentiated in regard to the principles governing their formation and development. The second implies that despite their differences, they have established stable mechanisms to reproduce their unity (Valdés, 1988b). Neither argument is wholly true or false; both need to be qualified depending on the specific periods and aspects being considered.

As to the origin and present characteristics of the Mexican business elite, three observations may be adduced: First, the emergence of the contemporary business class occurred during the period of reconstruction and consolidation of the Mexican state led by military caudillos (1920–1940). The private sector had its roots in those elements of the old Porfirian oligarchy that survived the revolution as well as in the new entrepreneurial elements that emerged during its aftermath. In the ensuing period of industrialization, from 1940 onward, the political and economic elites managed to consolidate a historical compromise on the mutual ground of capitalist development. Their resulting alliance rests, somewhat paradoxically, upon the differences between them—that is, on those differences that promote the separate reproduction of political and economic elites.

Second, and still more paradoxically, it was during the periods of strong cohesion between the two groups (1922–1934 and 1940–1970) that conditions, projects, and strategies emerged that would later generate considerable degrees of conflict tending to undermine that cohesion. Their programmatic orientations began to diverge and at times became overtly contradictory, and the split opened a space for a private political will to function in opposition to the state. As a consequence, elite business policy became oriented toward the transformation of state structures at the level of the regime rather than being concerned only with the level of government.[3] This new course of action has brought the private sector into increasing conflict with various regime structures. The 1960s were the gestation period of this tendency, although it adopted the form of an independent program only during the administration of Luis Echeverría (1970–1976) and thereafter.

Third, business political activism has intensified with the changing orientation of state policies in the last two decades. The rise of democratic expression and the growth of political movements outside the PRI have challenged authoritarian rule. The four governments from 1970 to 1994 have reacted to the growing autonomy of civil society in very different forms, ranging from "populism" to liberalism. In this context, the private sector has developed its own independent political program and implemented strategies to reform the regime's structures of representation and mediation as well as its policymaking guidelines. One outcome of these strategies has been privatization policies.

In sum, the private sector and the political class have built a vigorous social bloc, whose consolidation must be ascribed to its own dynamic and not to that of either group. The form of this bloc has changed according to the characteristics of the relationship between the economy and the state. As Alan Knight has shown, the political elite emerging from the Mexican Revolution was less reform-oriented than has been assumed in previous historical research (to say nothing of official ideology). Public officials occupying the most important decisionmaking positions stemmed from the private sector's rank and file. On the whole, the transformative potential of legislative and policy reforms introduced by the Mexican Revolution remained subordinated to the alliance between the private sector and the political elite (Knight, 1986, vol. 2:517).

However, this observation does not apply to every policy implemented between 1920 and 1980. The political elite, to the extent that it was constrained by revolutionary ideology and legislation, maintained the principles of revolutionary legitimacy—the commitment to "social justice" with a strong class constituency among peasants and workers controlled by the official party—while at the same time managing to foster capitalist development.

During and after the 1980s, this power bloc changed in accord with the convergence between the private sector's demands and the altered relationship between the state and the economy in the wake of market-oriented reforms. In my view, these changes have been a result not only of the government's efforts to overcome the crisis of the Mexican economy in the 1980s but also of the private sector's determination to restructure key aspects of government policymaking.

At the core of business activism lies the need of the business community to monitor state policies institutionalized by the revolution, which bedevil the regime: They contain the fundamentally ambiguous commitment to promoting both capitalist development and social justice. Both tasks are enshrined in the 1917 Constitution and institutionally crystallized in traditions of social reformism and state economic regulation, but the capitalist modernization of the economy that occurred in the 1950s and 1960s and the heightened economic instability since 1965 have called their compatibility into question (Valdés 1988a). Since 1982 the dual constitutional mandate has gradually been abandoned, and neoliberal principles have been adopted in its place.

Business Organizations and Politics

The modern system of business organizations formed in postrevolutionary Mexico has been the institutional basis of private-sector politics. This system comprises several types of associations operating at the national, the regional, and the local levels. Groups with a sectoral or regional basis of affiliation include the confederations of industry and commerce, the bankers and insurance dealers associations, and the council of agriculture. More broadly based representation is provided by the employers trade union (COPARMEX), which affiliates "employers" rather than "industrialists," "merchants," or "entrepreneurs"; the Entrepreneurial Coordinating Council (CCE), which brings together the regional and sectoral organizations; and the Mexican Businessmen's Council (CMHN), an exclusive group representing the most influential capitalists in the country.

These organizations form an interlinked network that has evolved into an effective system for the representation of private interests. They show high levels of cohesion and coordination in the formation of policy and in channeling business interests (mostly economic but also political and ideological) through the state and civil society.

The business community is very heterogeneous, for it includes a wide variety of firm sizes, types of activity, and regional bases. There are three major financial and industrial regions in the country: the center, the west, and the north. The central region includes Mexico City and the contiguous state of Mexico. The west's main pole of economic and political activity is located in Guadalajara, and that of the north is in Monterrey. The economic crisis of the 1980s and the progress made by export-oriented investment in the Mexican-U.S. border have turned the northern region into an economic powerhouse by comparison with the rest of the country. Nonetheless, despite the fact that this region has and will continue for some time to have a decisive role in economic development, at present the main industrial and financial groups remain distributed throughout the three regions.

Not surprisingly, the largest, most influential industrial, agricultural, financial, and commercial enterprises tend to be dominant in their representative associations (Tirado, 1986). The same tendency can be observed in nonsectoral associations like COPARMEX and the CCE. Small business associations do not have significant influence in national chambers and councils and tend to be moderate and supportive of governmental policies, as they depend to a greater extent on government protection or government-related business or both.

The relationship between regional and organizational interests is clearly slanted in favor of the central and northern groups. The main associations (CMHN, CCE, COPARMEX, CONCAMIN, CONCANACO, and AMCB) are always controlled by representatives of companies located in those geographic areas. Even though an analysis of these associations would show high degrees of complexity, insiders commonly accept that the Mexico City and Monterrey groups are the most influential in controlling them. They are the principal loci of power and control over business associations.

The participation of business associations in politics is not a new phenomenon in Mexican history. It has been a keynote in their formation and evolution since 1917 when the confederations of industry and commerce, CONCAMIN and CONCANACO, were created to inaugurate a period of economic reconstruction. The employers union, COPARMEX, was founded to oppose the Federal Labor Law promoted by the government in 1929. Later, during the Lázaro Cárdenas administration, the associations strongly opposed the land reform and the policies that established a government-controlled education system and authorized the formation of labor unions. In 1940 they opposed the candidacy of General Francisco J. Múgica as Cárdenas's successor in the presidency. As a result of their political action, several top business representatives were in charge of key economic ministries in the administrations of Presidents Manuel Avila Camacho (1940–1946) and Miguel Alemán (1946–1952). In the 1960s various business organizations were involved in the formation of anti-Communist groups on the extreme right. They created the CMHN in 1962, which has been the most powerful business organization ever since. The CCE, founded in 1975, stands out among entrepreneurial organizations in seeking to unify capitalists as a class rather than as a corporate group, whereas the CMHN is reserved for the crème de la crème—the upper ranks of the bourgeoisie.

Conflict and Transition

During the three decades between 1940 and 1970, the format of business representation prescribed that the private sector should not intervene as such in political activities involving opposition to the one-party system.[4] This rule was normally accepted by the private sector and was violated only by some of its more radical ideologues and during periods of unusual conflict. However, business had the right to participate closely in the formulation of policy (including veto power) and in the selection—which at times amounted to self-selection—of government officials.

This format was created under the conditions of postrevolutionary state formation, when there was a differentiation of the political class's identity from that of the entrepreneurial sector. The former inherited the mantle of the revolution, claiming title to govern by right of military victory and by the 1917 Constitution; the latter embodied the modern capitalist sector and shaped development in a putative alliance with the Mexican people but with its sphere of action restricted to the economy. The new rulers' explicit repudiation of the old Porfirian symbiosis of economic and political power was to be inscribed in the constitution of their official party, first founded in 1929 as the National Revolutionary Party (PNR) and subsequently reorganized as the Party of the Mexican Revolution (PRM) in 1938 and as the Revolutionary Institutional Party (PRI) in 1945. The party's rules deliberately *excluded* the business elite from membership, whereas workers, peasants, and the middle classes (the "popular sector") were officially affiliated to the party after 1938—thereby being assimilated into the "revolutionary family."

By 1959, however, the beginning of the end of this arm's-length relationship between the country's economic and political elites was already in sight. By then the pace of postwar industrialization had slowed, but simultaneously the private sector had become a major economic force thanks to the "Mexican miracle." It was no longer weak and diffuse vis-à-vis a powerful, centralized state but had gathered strength from its bases in finance, industry, commerce, and agriculture and had likewise gained a higher level of organization and greater influence in state policymaking.

In the period of "stabilizing development" (1954–1970), it was tacitly understood that state intervention in the economy should be progressively replaced by private business (Labastida, 1972). As a result the state began to reduce its role in the industrialization process. At this point the relationship between the two actors entered a new phase, bringing to the forefront elements that had previously been inconspicuous.

From the 1960s onward, the evolution of the business organizations system was clearly led by the CMHN, formed in 1962 by a few powerful members. This organization owed its inception to a lack of business confidence in the López Mateos administration (1958–1964), whose left-of-center ideology reflected the influence in Mexico of the Cuban revolution. During the 1960s the CMHN forged a new consensus among big business and between the state and the private sector as a whole. The council's power and prestige grew rapidly, and its members were faced with few obstacles in coordinating their projects with other business organizations or with the state.

In 1970, when President Luis Echeverría announced a political opening combined with a package of populist economic reforms, the private sector began to challenge the traditional boundaries limiting its participation in the political system. Forcing the state to abandon its reforms clearly presupposed, among other things, unified and concerted opposition from the private sector (abetted by its national and international supporters). Under the stimulus of new and more audacious goals, business was able to mobilize and reshape its organizational network. The year 1973 marked the starting point of its public contestation of Echeverría's policies. COPARMEX took the lead, replacing moderate or progovernment representatives with hard-liners. At this juncture, a long-term feature of private representative organizations was clearly manifested: Since their inception, private organizations have been recognized as a political mechanism that distributes power rather widely and yet, notwithstanding such diffusion, delivers it ultimately into the hands of the big-business elites in Mexico City and Monterrey.[5] In the conflict with the government, organizations at all levels developed many different forms of pressure, which in time became more and more coordinated from above without losing initiative at the sectoral, regional, and local levels or unity on a national scale.

At first the dispute was thought to be temporary, caused by populist policies aimed at a readjustment of social inequalities—in effect, a new social contract. In the face of Echeverría's populism, however, the private sector's structure of representation appeared to be dangerously weak, potentially inadequate to ensure the successful defense of its interests. The response was the creation of the Entrepreneurial Coordinating Council (CCE) in 1975.

The CCE was not just one more organization but a hierarchical instrument articulating a forced convergence between the CMHN's program and that of the rest of the private sector. An initial objective was to redistribute functions among organizations. Those dedicated to *sectoral* interests would no longer expend their limited energies in efforts to promote *classwide* interests. The latter were reserved for class organizations, thus strengthening their capacity to act politically in a greater number of social and political processes.[6] The CCE was created to accomplish wider objectives in this arena, to coordinate the activities of business associations with regard to all kinds of policies and issues. Its aim was to present an aggressive, united front, intent upon shifting political life in Mexico away from populism in a more liberal, business-oriented direction and capable of intervening systematically across the entire spectrum of public affairs.

The new association was thus dedicated to promoting the expansion of private influence in the public sphere of society. Its project, as was soon evident, was to parlay the private sector's economic supremacy into supremacy within the state, purging the latter of populist or nonconservative officials in decisionmaking circles and reinforcing the linkages with the conservative (mostly financial) bureaucracy. At the same time, the CCE emphasized the need to start a neoliberal downsizing of the state's intervention in the economy and a concomitant loosening of its political control, summed up in the code words "privatization" and "modernization." The former translates into a massive reallocation of economic resources in favor of the largest firms and consortiums; the latter connotes a weakening or dismantling of the ties between government and labor as well as the eclipse of the traditional (i.e., nonmodern) sectors of the bureaucracy.

By the 1990s, capital's new forms of political participation had become a permanent feature of Mexican politics, even though reforms seen as contrary to business interests were definitively abandoned after 1976, when the López Portillo administration made the recovery of private-sector confidence the major aim of its economic policies. These policies, however, met with indifferent success and eventuated in the most serious bone of contention between business and government in recent times—the nationalization of banks in 1982.

Thus, the period from 1970 to 1988 can be seen as one of intense private-sector involvement in politics, with the objective of laying out alternative forms of participation in the regime of power by remolding the corporate structure of policy formation and decisionmaking. Underlying this activity were the two major crises that occurred in the relationship between business elites and government in recent times—the 1973–1976 business activism and the 1982 banking upheaval. It is important to point out that *distrust* of government, originally a response to economic crisis and an attitude limited to the most conservative groups, ultimately hardened into a sectorwide political program. Distrust came to underpin the most diverse claims, including the demand for a reform of state representation and mediation, and capital flight simultaneously became the favored strategy to evade the effects of economic crisis.

Program, Factions, and Strategies

Conceived along with the CCE in 1975, the private sector's political program has been amended and augmented in the light of subsequent events. A review of the major proclamations issued by business organizations during the last twenty years[7] reveals the following list of demands: (1) a market-oriented economy; (2) increased attention to the private sector's position, as opposed to that of other sectors, in government decisionmaking; (3) reduced bargaining power for trade unions; (4) an invigoration of civil society; (5) official recognition of the legitimacy of business participation in politics, education, public opinion, and so forth. The first demand involves the privatization of government-owned enterprises and the restriction of state intervention to regulatory functions. There are two aspects to the second demand: the reduction and specification of the president's power over economic decisionmaking and the establishment of *rational* institutional forms of *bilateral* decisionmaking. The third demand has been manifested in the attacks on collective contracts and negotiations (particularly in state enterprises, where labor has obtained the highest levels of income and social benefits) and on the formulation of proposals to modify Article 123 of the Constitution regulating labor, in accordance to the new status quo. A more robust civil society, the fourth demand, is conceived as one in which the individual, private initiative, entrepreneurship, modernity, citizenship, and the like are the regnant ideals, replacing statism, corporatism, and revolutionary nationalism in the public sphere. The final demand, which is self-explanatory, envisions a new and imposing profile for the private sector and its supporters in society.

The triumph of such a program represents a major reformation of the state in today's Mexico—a rupture with the "social justice" tradition of the Mexican Revolution. That tradition may be characterized as a reformist practice related to the aforementioned political ambiguity of the Mexican state. Its legal foundations are the so-called social rights protected by the Constitution—more specifically, by Article 3, which provides that education is to be state-supported and nonreligious; by Article 27, which defines land and natural resources as the property of the "nation" and specifies that private property can be limited according to the "public interest"; by Article 123, which permits the state to intervene in industrial relations on behalf of labor; and by Article 130, which legislates the separation of church and state.

The historical origins of these constitutional precepts are varied. The provisions concerning education date from the revolutionary period of 1910–1917; those dealing with land and natural resources harken back to the Bourbon reforms of the late colonial era; the prohibition of clerical involvement in politics is rooted in the nineteenth-century liberal reform, which expropriated the agrarian properties of the Catholic Church. In order to restore stability in the aftermath of the revolution, the president was granted "permanent exceptional powers" to enforce the Constitution, thus attaining a dominant position vis-à-vis the legislature and the judiciary in Mexico's authoritarian political system. Because constitutional law has thus been enforced in a discretionary manner, the private-sector program has concentrated on changing it.

The development of the private-sector agenda can best be observed in the forms of political activism adopted by business organizations. These may be grouped into two principal factions according to their attitudes toward politics in general: one moderate or technocratic, the other radical or populist (see Table 7.1) (Luna et al., 1987:13–43; Jacobo et al., 1989:6–9).[8]

The moderates are located in the sectoral and regional organizations involved in frontline defense of specific economic interests through negotiations with the government. Industrialists and financiers normally adopt guarded positions with respect to political issues, preferring to pursue their objectives by way of direct and discrete negotiations with the government. By contrast, the employers union (COPARMEX) and the Confederation of Commerce generally assume aggressively right-wing postures on a wide variety of issues, ranging from wage scales and economic policies to elections, education, culture, and religion. In accord with its mediating role, the CCE oscillates between the

TABLE 7.1
National Business Organizations and Their Position Toward the Political Regime

Moderate/Technocratic Faction			Radical/Populist Faction	
Unconditional Support		Moderate Criticism		Strong Criticism
I	II	III	IV	V
CNPP	CANACINTRA	CANACO-MEX	CONCAMIN	COPARMEX
CNPC		CNG	CCE	CONCANACO
		AMIS	CAMCO	
		CMHN	CNA	
		AMCB		

AMCB: Asociación Mexicana de Casas de Bolsa (Mexican Association of Stock Market Brokers).[a]

AMIS: Asociación Mexicana de Instituciones de Seguros (Mexican Association of Insurance Institutions).[a]

CAMCO: Cámara Americana de Comercio (American Chamber of Commerce).[b]

CANACINTRA: Cámara Nacional de la Industria de Transformación (National Chamber of the Transformation Industry).[a]

CANACO-MEX: Cámara Nacional de Comercio de la Ciudad de México (National Chamber of Commerce of Mexico City).[a]

CCE: Consejo Coordinador Empresarial (Entrepreneurial Coordinating Council, affiliates all national organizations).[b]

CMHN: Consejo Mexicano de Hombres de Negocios (Mexican Businessmen's Council, formed by 37 key heads of investment groups).[b]

CNA: Consejo Nacional Agropecuario (National Agricultural Council).[b]

CNG: Confederación Nacional Ganadera (National Livestock Confederation).[b]

CNPC: Confederación Nacional de Cámaras del Pequeño Comercio (National Confederation of Chambers of Small Commerce).[a]

CNPP: Confederación Nacional de la Pequeña Propiedad (National Confederation of Small Property Owners).[b]

CONCAMIN: Confederación Nacional de Cámaras Industriales (National Confederation of Chambers of Industry).[a]

CONCANACO: Confederación Nacional de Cámaras de Comercio (National Confederation of Chambers of Commerce).[a]

COPARMEX: Confederación Patronal de la República Mexicana (Employers' Confederation of the Mexican Republic).[b]

[a] Legally recognized as a mandatory affiliation and state policy consulting organization.
[b] Voluntary affiliation organization.

positions of the two factions, endeavoring to coordinate them in the general interest of the entrepreneurial class.[9]

Despite their differences, both business factions share a common view of the public sector. Both have criticized the political system, the excessive concentration of power in the presidency, and state intervention in the economy. Both maintain that they lack adequate representation in the political structure and claim that this lack is responsible for the current crisis of political representation. They propose to resolve the crisis by building up their own forms of political participation, both collective and individual, and by curtailing the institutional power of other social sectors. Three main strategies in establishing such new forms have been pursued to date: a corporate strategy, a partisan strategy, and a social or civic strategy. Respectively, these strategies involve enhancing business's position in economic policymaking, assuming a significant role in electoral processes, and attempting to influence other social groups ideologically in the arena of public opinion.

There are fairly clear lines of differentiation among the organizations, factions, and strategies. Organizations representing better established and highly concentrated interests (mainly industrialists and the CCE) promote technocratic rather than right-wing populist views; they prefer to stress the corporate instead of the partisan or civic strategies, which are left to second-rank and more ideologically oriented organizations. Nonetheless, these divergent agendas are better seen as reflecting a sophisticated division of labor rather than any serious division within the private sector, for factions and strategies are coordinated, notwithstanding that they apparently tend in somewhat different directions.

A further observation about the civic strategy it that it is one of the most difficult strategies to analyze because it is generally diffused in values, messages, mass-media campaigns, and the like. Its overriding aim is to convince citizens that by virtue of simply *being* citizens, they belong by definition to the so-called private initiative. This usage constitutes an innovation in public discourse, since "citizenship" has not been a prominent category in Mexico's political culture until very recent times, when (primarily middle-class) urbanites involved in the grassroots movements and the opposition parties began to construct new forms of identity in opposition to the Mexican variant of authoritarianism, the corporatist-presidentialist and state-party system.

Further insight into the civic strategy may be gained by applying Michel Foucault's concept of "pastoral power" (Rouse, 1988; Foucault, 1983). Foucault used this notion to account for the ideological coherence between the organization of a dominant ideology and the obedience paid by individuals to the social and political order. The concept of pastoral power departs from the classical definition of ideology in modern times, in that the latter has focused on ideology's role in ordering the public space as opposed to its effects within the intimate sphere of individual subjectivity. The original locus of pastoral power, in Foucault's view, was institutionalized Christianity: the central role of the pastor and pastoral ritual in the Catholic Church. But despite the decline of ecclesiastical authority after the seventeenth century, the function of the pastoral has endured as an "individualizing" power. Political rule in the modern world, according to Foucault, is founded not only in the control of the "public," conceived as distinct and separate from the "private," but in the very constitution of authority within the individual. This involved the process of secularization: The religious hope of salvation was transmuted, through the mediation of pastoral power, into secular assurance of the individual's biological life—health, welfare, social security. Instead of the church and the priest, multiple institutions take over this function—the family, medicine, psychiatry, education, entrepreneurs, the mass media.

Since independence, Mexico has experienced two major epochs in the organization of pastoral power. During the first, such power was still exercised by the Catholic Church. After the liberal reform of the midnineteenth century, the church's pastoral role was taken over by the state. This transition was consolidated after the revolution, when cultural rule was secularized through public education and health and the PRI's corporatist system. Very recently, however, a third epoch appears to have been inaugurated, as the ideological institutions and mechanisms used by the state were rendered increasingly obsolete and private communications firms and organizations became hegemonic in the cultural sphere. The advent of this last period signaled the final crisis and rupture of the pact between the state and the masses that had characterized the regime from the days of Lázaro Cárdenas's government until 1982.

Through this new "apparatus of private hegemony," the symbolic integration of Mexican society is being shifted from the pastoral power of the state toward the more modern, individualistic, and exclusionary pastoral power of the private sector. Multiple social and political associations, clubs, mass media, show businesses, and other institutions compose this apparatus. Despite pretensions of modernity and individualism, such pastoral power presides over a flock that is by no means constituted solely of businesspeople. On the contrary, it includes many other groups, but its ideological coloration is clearly probusiness.

The political dynamic of the private sector is thus no longer limited to the economic sphere and the mere *representation* of interests. It now involves a growing concern for and participation in the dynamics of society as a whole, including the economy, social and political organizations, public opinion, and the state.

The Model's Success

In December 1982, President Miguel de la Madrid sent to Congress a proposal for constitutional reforms that included a clear-cut division between the economic functions of the state and those reserved to private enterprise. An innovative measure, imposing unprecedented limitations on the power of the presidency, was the provision that Congress and not the president would be entitled to enact laws and decrees enabling the government to intervene in the economy; these would be in addition to the authority provided in the Constitution. In 1983 the government decided to indemnify bankers expropriated in 1982 by the previous administration and to return banking enterprises to their former owners. That same year the private sector was declared in various national plans to be the main agent of economic development. In 1987, after the stock exchange crash, the government called upon labor, peasant, and business organizations to sign an Economic Solidarity Pact (PSE) in which the key to achieving economic stability was acknowledged to be the confidence of big business and the adoption of economic policies designed to win that confidence.

The period 1982–1987 had brought almost incessant private-sector activism and opposition to the government, but with the acceptance of the PSE in December 1987, in which business agreed to participate, oppositional activities began to diminish visibly. Business elites had found in this pact the mechanism they had been seeking for many years. Its relative success in reducing inflation and restoring private-sector optimism by 1991 as well as its renewal by the Salinas administration demonstrated that it was the embryo of a new relationship between economic and political elites—clearly a sine qua non for a successful neoliberal reform of the state in Mexico.

Salinas's program was indeed nothing less than a reform of the state. It can be summarized in a few words: to disencumber the state of the burden of an obsolete and mismanaged system of publicly owned enterprises by selling them off to the private sector and, simultaneously, to organize a national program to "eradicate extreme poverty." Privatization proceeded faster in the Salinas *sexenio* (six-year presidential term) than in any previous one. With the exception of petroleum, railroads, and electricity, there is scarcely a state enterprise that has not already been sold or at least put up for sale. The most important sector to be privatized in 1991 and 1992 was banking. The corollary of the Salinas plan, established shortly after the new government was installed in power, was the National Solidarity Program (PRONASOL), intended to reduce the most glaring inequalities in Mexico's new economic order via a scheme of poverty alleviation. On balance, however, the concomitant propaganda campaign that attended the implementation of this program served to legitimate Salinas's privatization measures and other economic reforms, and this proved more important than its real effect in stemming extreme poverty.

Rhetoric aside, the Salinas administration's economic policies appeared to signal the definitive abandonment on the part of the postrevolutionary Mexican state of its constitutional commitment to intervene in economic relations to counteract the effects of social inequality. Regardless of one's verdict as to the extent to which the state ever complied with this obligation and of one's opinion about the appropriateness of Salinas's reforms, they clearly represent a historic change in the relationship among the state, civil society, and the economy.

Privatization of public enterprises, a falling nominal interest rate, and a stable exchange rate were the three major reasons for business confidence in the

Salinas administration. Renegotiation of the foreign debt and rising tax revenues provided the essential underpinning of these policies. The beginning of a new alliance between the most concentrated and competitive economic enterprises and the technocratic group in government was also achieved during the Salinas years (Baker, 1991). It would be no exaggeration to say that this alliance was based on a carefully thought-out strategy to bring public policy into line with private-sector demands, to effect a global reform of the relationship between the state and society, and hence to redesign Mexico's insertion into the emerging neoliberal global order. All this, of course, was presumably accomplished in perfect accord with the spirit of the Mexican Revolution and the 1917 Constitution—at least according to Salinas's frequent addresses to the nation and other major speeches.

To be sure, fundamental structural changes in the state and in the economy cannot be explained purely as a result of private-sector political action but must be seen as both condition and consequence of a new alliance within the ruling power bloc. Yet the business community has plainly been a central player in the institution of these changes. The private sector expanded its political influence in order to induce the reforms and policies constituting the new relationship between itself and the state. But revamping the regime and its policies also presupposed the emergence of a new ruling elite within the political bureaucracy.

Conclusion

The probusiness shift in the policy process introduced by the Salinas administration finally resulted in closing the gap between government and private sector. Business activism has decisively replaced the traditionally passive posture of business in the political arena. The economic and social changes Mexico has undergone since the close of the 1960s provided an environment in which the business community has reshaped its objectives, methods, and style of participation. Notwithstanding the coincidence of interests with the Salinas government, the private sector had no intention of relaxing its close monitoring of state policies, its continuing efforts to reshape its relations with other social groups, or its determination to forestall a possible resurgence of left-wing populism among the ruling elites. In this regard, the private sector strongly supported the constitutional reforms introduced by the Salinas administration, whose aim was to institutionalize the historic changes in the relationship between the state and the economy, thus thwarting in advance any backsliding on the part of future governments. These constitutional and legal changes were calculated to guarantee the private sector's position as the main economic and social actor.

How will these changes in the role of the private sector affect Mexico's political future? Mexico is evidently in a political transition, but it is a process of reformation occurring within an authoritarian system. The central institution characterizing authoritarianism is presidentialism, the effective concentration of power in the executive branch of government, which in turn rests on a single-party system exercising firm control over elections and subordinate sectors and, ultimately, on a societywide, authoritarian political culture. The reformation involves, on the one hand, the technocratization of all significant government agencies and, on the other, a modernization of corporate organizations. The current modernization discloses what augurs to become a permanent feature of policy and decisionmaking in Mexico: the consolidation of a privileged circuit of private and public officials insulated from the influence and pressures of social organizations and opposition political parties. There is, of course, a modicum of pluralism in the Congress and in municipal and state governments, but this has little effect upon decisionmaking at the national level.

Once the privatization process is completed, policy efforts are likely to be directed against whatever residual bargaining power remains in the hands of subordinate actors as a result of the populism of the past. After the reform of the agrarian law in 1992, a major reform of labor regulations was anticipated in order to eliminate obstacles to the international competitiveness of Mexican industry. Legal initiatives to this effect were already being discussed in the early part of Ernesto Zedillo's administration (1994–2000).

Neoliberal economic reform is essentially completed, but the future of political reform remains clouded. In spite of the electoral reforms of 1994, the PRI remains firmly ensconced in power at the national level, and the electoral playing field is still tilted in its favor. The effects of this are clear: Whereas the private sector has strengthened its position both economically and politically, the rest of society remains in the grip of the ruling party but with less bargaining power than in the past. The structures in which such power used to be exerted are in a process of rapid decay and are not being replaced by new institutions, either within the provenance of the state or that of civil society.

Thus, in a strict sense, the Mexican transition is not yet moving in the direction of a democratic political system but has thus far confined itself to adapting the old authoritarianism to new circumstances. Representatives of big business, whether of national or transnational origin, are being admitted to key positions in the decisionmaking process in order, reputedly, to improve the viability of the Mexican economy in the face of international competition. The "liberal" aspect of this transition lies in accepting that privatization and free trade policies must prevail over social policies. Its "corporatist" aspect is reflected in the fact that business participation in the policymaking process is structured sectorally and organized hierarchically—rather than operating through political parties, for instance. The *legal rationality* assumed by liberalism is being selectively implemented so as to instill confidence in foreign and national business, but the essentially authoritarian character of the regime persists and is unlikely to change unless the political-economic model undergoes a major crisis. Such a scenario, of course, is far from inconceivable.

In the present circumstances, the presidency must steer a narrow course. It is still the force in command of the process of economic and state reform, but its power is secure only to the extent that it maintains its legitimacy while minimizing that of the opposition. The Congress is now more pluralist than Mexicans would have imagined prior to the 1988 elections, but it is still dominated by the PRI, which has recovered much of its previous position by resorting to unfair electoral rules and practices in 1991 and 1994. But these trends are not written in stone, and should they be altered and reversed, we may witness a scenario of renewed social conflict—even a political crisis whose resolution might entail social reform and democracy.

In a long-term perspective, the multiparty system has been gaining strength, and elections are coming increasingly to resemble contests rather than coronations. The coalition assembled by Cuautémoc Cárdenas attained 31 percent of the votes in 1988; in consequence the PRD became the target of a systematic campaign of destruction orchestrated from the apex of state power. At the other end of the spectrum, the conservative National Action Party (PAN) is engaged in consolidating its role as a cogovernment party and at the same time trying to differentiate its conception of democracy from that of the PRD. This line of march was opened by the coincidence between the PAN's economic proposals and Salinas's policies. Rank-and-file members of the PAN have criticized the national leadership for adopting a course of action that threatens to reduce the PAN to a "second official party"—effectively playing Tweedledum to the PRI's Tweedledee—in a "democratic" political system without a third actor. In such a scheme the private sector could be represented alternately by one or the other of two interchangeable parties, without facing any serious electoral threat from the Left.

The 1994 federal electoral results, when compared with those of 1988, revealed an altered balance of power. The PRD's share of votes was reduced to over 17 percent; the PAN's rose to more than 27 percent. The combined opposition vote, including minor parties, reached almost 50 percent. These figures indicate a redrawing of the electoral map that will surely be confirmed in future elections, obliging the political structure to make room for a more pluralistic system of representation. In combination with a generalized political-economic crisis, such a development might well provide a unique opportunity for democratic transition.

On the side of the private sector, it is clear that the idea of alternating power between the PRI and PAN is gaining acceptance. But the possibility of a three-party political democracy, such as recent electoral results appear to suggest, is scarcely a prospect that business groups can be expected to greet with sympathy or even with equanimity.

The future, as always, remains elusive. Ten years of crisis, political conflict, and declining living standards have affected people's political orientation. The 1988 and 1994 electoral results represent a challenge to the newly formed governing coalition, whose rule has thus far benefited only itself—the private sector and the technocrats in power. Such a challenge betokens the presence of a popular will, however tentative and diffused, opting for a social contract different from the one offered by today's ruling elites. There is, however, no evidence at all of a change of heart on the part of Mexico's neoliberal modernizers with respect to those two essential features of modernity that they have studiously neglected to implement: equality and democracy.

It is as yet impossible to foresee the extent to or manner in which social discontent will be expressed, although it seems inevitable that the dismantling of the social institutions of the postrevolutionary Mexican state must eventuate in a period of social conflict in which the central demands will be either the restoration of those institutions or the construction of new ones capable of processing social discontent. The EZLN (Zapatista National Liberation Army) rebellion in Chiapas should be understood in this context.

Transitional processes are by definition highly indeterminate. Given the conditions considered in this chapter, it is unlikely that in the short run a situation that combines social equality and political democracy will be found. Mexico's history to date would suggest renewed forms of authoritarianism and social polarization as the more probable outcome. Any deviation from these secular trends can only result from the capacity of other actors—hitherto incorporated into the corporatist system in a subordinate role or else excluded from the political arena altogether—to oblige the dominant groups to take their interests seriously.

Notes

1. An explicit recognition of this fact can be found in Cardoso, 1986:139.

2. See, for instance, Camp (1989), Kauffman-Purcell (1975), Smith (1979), Vernon (1963), and Hansen (1974).

3. As applied to Mexico, "regime" refers to the structure of institutions compoing the state within a given, relatively long-term period, whereas "government" means the direct exercise of administrative authority during a six-year presidential term.

4. Business participation in the PRI during this period was evident at the top level of government. In the medium and lower layers of the political system, the tendency was in the opposite direction: Politicians were eager to participate in business. Naturally, government and the state party have always been a source of individual fortunes, which could then be invested in the private sector.

5. The Monterrey industrialist Luis G. Sada was, in the 1920s and 1930s, perhaps the most important theorist of this "model," according to which private-sector representation is legally organized along sectoral and regional economic lines but at the same time remains firmly controlled by the owners and managers of big companies, both national and foreign.

6. The formation of the CCE was conceived and implemented by the CMHN, which has always controlled it (Tirado, 1986).

7. Three documents are important to consider here: the *Declaración de Principios* (Declaration of Principles), the *Declaración sobre Problemas Nacionales* (Declaration on National Problems), and *Anteproyecto de un Programa para Crear una Imagen Adecuada y Fidedigna del Sector Empresarial en México* (Preliminary Plan for a Program to Create an Adequate and Faithful Image of the Entrepreneurial Sector in Mexico).

8. The use of the word "radical" indicates that this faction demands changes in the political regime that would modify its present structure.

9. Jacobo et al. (1989) have identified a third faction, the protectionist, made up of entrepreneurs that tried to counteract trade liberalization policies and their effects, including the North American Free Trade Agreement negotiations. This group, however, has not attained a presence comparable to that of the other two, at least with regard to the issues addressed herein.

Bibliography

Baker, Stephen. 1991. "The Friends of Carlos Salinas." *Business Week*, 22 July, pp. 40–42.

Braudel, Fernand. 1982. *The Wheels of Commerce.* Volume 1 of *Civilization and Capitalism, 15th–18th Century.* New York: Harper & Row.

Camp, Roderic Ai. 1989. *Entrepreneurs and Politics in Twentieth-Century Mexico.* New York and Oxford: Oxford University Press.

Cardoso, Fernando H. 1986. "Entrepreneurs and the Transition Process: The Brazilian Case." Pp. 137–153 in Guillermo O'Donnell, Philippe C. Schmitter, and Lawrence Whitehead, eds. *Transitions from Authoritarian Rule: Prospects for Democracy.* Baltimore and London: Johns Hopkins University Press.

Cardoso, Fernando Henrique, and Enzo Faletto. 1979 [1971]. *Dependency and Development in Latin America.* Berkeley and Los Angeles: University of California Press.

Foucault, Michel. 1983. "The Subject and Power." In Hubert L. Dreyfus and Paul Rabinow, eds., *Michel Foucault: Beyond Structuralism and Hermeneutics.* 2d edition. Chicago: University of Chicago Press.

Germani, Gino. 1971. *Sociología de la modernización.* Buenos Aires: Editorial Paidós.

Germani, Gino, Norberto Bobbio, S.N. Eisenstadt, Theda Sekocpol, et al. 1985. *Los límites de la democracia.* 2 volumes. Buenos Aires: Consejo Latinoamericano de Ciencias Sociales.

Giddens, Anthony. 1984. *The Constitution of Society.* Berkeley and Los Angeles: University of California Press.

———. 1985. *The Nation-State and Violence.* Berkeley and Los Angeles: University of California Press.

Halperin-Donghi, Tulio. 1969. *Historia contemporánea de América Latina.* Madrid: Alianza Editorial.

Hansen, Roger D. 1974. *The Politics of Mexican Development.* Baltimore and London: Johns Hopkins University Press.

Jacobo, Edmundo, Matilde Luna, and Ricardo Tirado. 1989. "Empresarios, pacto político y coyuntura actual en México." *Estudios Políticos* (Mexico City), Nueva Epoca, 8(1):4–15.

Jaguaribe, Helio, Aldo Ferrer, Miguel Wionzcek, and Theotonio dos Santos. 1970. *La dependencia político-económica de América Latina.* Mexico City: Siglo XXI Editores.

Kaufman-Purcell, Susan. 1975. *The Mexican Profit-Sharing Decision: Politics in an Authoritarian Regime.* Philadelphia: Institute for the Study of Human Issues.

Knight, Alan. 1986. *The Mexican Revolution.* 2 volumes. Cambridge: Cambridge University Press.

Labastida, Julio. 1972. "Los grupos dominantes frente a las alternativas de cambio." Pp. 97–164 in Jorge Marinez Ríos, Jorge Basurto, Jose Calixto Rangel C., et al. *El perfil de México en 1980,* Vol. 3. Mexico: Siglo XXI Editores.

Luna, Matilde, Ricardo Tirado, and Francisco Valdés. 1987. "Businessmen and Politics in Mexico, 1982–1986." Pp. 13–43 in Sylvia Maxfield and Ricardo Anzaldua, eds., *Government and Private Sector in Contemporary Mexico,* Monograph series, 20. San Diego: Center for U.S.-Mexican Studies, University of California, San Diego.

Rouse, Roger. 1988. "Foucault and the Mechanisms of Power in Mexico." Unpublished manuscript.

Smith, Peter. 1979. *Labyrinths of Power: Political Recruitment in Twentieth-Century Mexico.* Princeton: Princeton University Press.

Therborn, Göran. 1978. *What Does the Ruling Class Do When It Rules?* London: New Left Books.

Tirado, Ricardo. 1986. "Semblanza de las organizaciones patronales en México." In Julio Labastida, coord., *Grupos económicos y organizaciones empresariales en México.* Mexico City: Alianza Editorial Mexicana and Universidad Nacional Autónoma de México.

Valdés, Francisco. 1988a. "Empresarios, estabilidad y democracia en México: 1880–1982." In Octavio Rodríguez Araujo, ed., *México: Estabilidad y luchas por la democracia, 1900–1982.* Mexico City: Centro de Investigaciones y Docencia Económicas and Ediciones El Caballito.

———. 1988b. "Los empresarios, la política y el estado." *Cuadernos Políticos* (Mexico City), no. 53:47–70.

———. 1993. "Concepto y estrategia de la 'reforma del Estado.'" *Revista Mexicana de Sociología* (Mexico City), 55(2):315–338.

Vernon, Raymond. 1963. *The Dilemma of Mexico's Development: The Roles of the Private and Public Sector.* Cambridge: Harvard University Press.

Weber, Max. 1942 [1923]. *Historia económica general.* Mexico City: Fondo de Cultura Económica.

8

Economic Restructuring, State-Labor Relations, and the Transformation of Mexican Corporatism

Judith Teichman

Since Mexico's economic crisis of 1982, profound changes have occurred in the Mexican economy. A combination of deteriorating international economic circumstances and public policy initiatives has altered the nature of the Mexican economy from one almost entirely dependent upon the exportation of petroleum to one increasingly geared toward the exportation of manufactured products.[1] An economic restructuring program was initiated by President Miguel de la Madrid in 1983 and given further impetus by former President Carlos Salinas de Gortari (1988–1994). Coincident with changes in the economy, a transition has been occurring in the Mexican political system, as opposition to the government's economic model has become increasingly polarized and mobilized. Elements of a disaffected business class have lent support to the opposition National Action Party (PAN), and the opposition Left has coalesced around its own electoral front. The results of the 1988 federal election in which the official Institutional Revolutionary Party (PRI) presidential candidate received the lowest proportion of the popular vote ever (50.7 percent), even in the face of what is widely believed to have been extensive electoral fraud, marked an acceleration of the decline in PRI predominance that began with the economic stagnation and political turmoil of the late 1960s. With the 1994 federal election, however, the PRI has been surprisingly successful in stemming the downward spiral of its electoral fortunes: It won 48.8 percent of the popular vote (from valid votes cast), without large-scale electoral fraud, leaving its strongest opponent in the 1988 elections, a leftist coalition led by Cuauhtemoc Cárdenas, with only 16.6 percent of the popular vote. This electoral resurgence of the PRI occurred despite a peasant rebellion in Chiapas, division within the PRI over the selection of a new presidential candidate following the assassination of Luis Donaldo Colosio, and economic recession.

In view of the electoral challenge facing the PRI in recent years, there has been considerable scholarly interest in the Mexican electoral process (Gentleman, 1986; Alvarado Mendoza, 1987; Leal et al., 1988; Gómez Tagle, 1992). Only very recently, however, has attention been given to the transformation of Mexico's traditional mechanisms of societal state incorporation (Cornelius et al., 1994). This latter process is an equally important aspect of the political transition the Mexican political system is experiencing and is integral to the question of electoral support.[2] In this chapter I examine Mexico's economic restructuring program and argue that it has had an important role in accelerating the transformation of Mexico's corporatist-clientelist political arrangements—arrangements that have ensured the political dominance of the official PRI party. Although a form of neocorporatism is likely to replace the old corporatist structures in at least some sectors, this new form of corporatism is considerably weaker in its ability to control societal pressures than its older variant.

Mexico's Postrevolutionary Political System

Corporatism and patron clientelism are well recognized as fundamental operating principles of Mexico's postrevolutionary authoritarian regime.[3] In this chapter I argue that the clientelist-corporatist aspect of Mexico's political system has been seriously undermined by the economic restructuring policies implemented since 1983. Although operating at all levels of the social and political systems, corporatism and patron clientelism have been particularly important in mitigating dissent from the popular classes.[4] Mexico has been characterized by state corporatism (Schmitter, 1974) in which popular organizations purporting to represent workers and peasants are incorporated into the party-state apparatus in such a way as to minimize if not eliminate the potential for popular dissent. In Mexico, patron clientelism has operated to reinforce state corporatism. A "tie between two parties of unequal wealth and influence" that "depends upon the exchange of goods and services" (Powell, 1970:412–413), patron clientelism has been most extensively documented in the rural sector but exists at all levels and in all spheres of the political system. It normally involves the exchange of material rewards (from the more powerful patron to the weaker client) for political support from the client.

Corporatism has its roots in Mexico's postrevolutionary history. Formal incorporation of popular organizations within the official party occurred during the presidency of Lázaro Cárdenas (1934–1940). In 1938, the regional groupings within the party were dropped and replaced by sectoral representation from labor, peasants, the "popular sector," and the military (military representation later disappeared). Cárdenas sponsored the Confederation of

Mexican Workers (CTM) and the National Peasant Confederation (CNC) and incorporated them into the official party as sectoral representatives. Within the CTM, the most important union has been the Petroleum Workers Union (STRPRM)—indeed, the STRPRM was arguably the most powerful trade union in Mexico until recently. The popular sector, known as the National Confederation of Popular Organizations (CNOP), was constituted by organizations representing a number of important middle-class interests, along with elements of the urban poor. The most powerful organizations within the CNOP have been the Federation of Public Employees (FSTSE), representing federal civil servants, the National Union of Educational Workers (SNTE), and the National Confederation of Small Farmers (CNPP) (Bailey, 1988:94–95).[5]

In the years following the Cárdenas presidency, the party became a mechanism of popular control. Labor militancy was dampened as later administrations used the party to co-opt real and potential dissidents. Particularly during World War II, control over labor unions was tightened, as radical leaders were replaced by more acquiescent ones. Through a system of patronage, labor-government relations became characterized by *charrismo*, which is domination by union leaders who use their positions of power to amass great personal wealth and power at the expense of their rank and file.[6] Control of the party through the choice of candidates and their sectoral distribution came to be exercised from the top downward—by the president, governors, and sectoral leaders.

The archetype of this model of political control is found in the petroleum sector, where, until recently, union leaders who were allowed to amass sizable fortunes maintained the petroleum union as a fervent PRI supporter (Novelo O., 1989; Cruz Bencomo, 1989; *Proceso*, 3 December 1984:12; *Proceso*, 31 January 1983:15–16). Strong ties of clientelism have bound rank and file to leaders, and these ties have enabled union leaders to mobilize petroleum workers in support of the PRI. The material rewards dispensed by union leaders as a consequence of collective labor agreements have included the assignment of new or vacated jobs to rank-and-file workers, worker mobility within the enterprise (regional or departmental), the dispensing of loans, and the granting of vacations, housing, and scholarships. Consequently, union rank and file, in particular temporary workers because of their desire for full-time employment, made every effort to maintain good relations with union leaders. In general, workers would give money or political support or both to acquire these benefits.

There is no doubt that such benefits were manipulated by the union leadership in specifically political ways. According to union statutes, permanent jobs were to be distributed 50 percent to temporary workers on the basis of, first, the union militancy of workers and, second, seniority. The other half of vacated permanent positions were to go to the families of temporary workers (sons, brothers) under the same criteria. Union militancy was defined in terms of participation in the union and in the political activities it organizes. The quality of union militancy was assessed at the discretion of the union leadership and meant, in effect, loyalty and obedience.

The Petroleum Workers Union was able to amass great wealth that enabled it to provide housing, hospitals, and schools selectively in petroleum communities. One important source of funds came from a clause in the collective agreement that provided for the payment to the union of 2 percent of the value of all works contracted out by Pemex (Petróleos Mexicanos, Mexico's wholly government-owned petroleum corporation). Regional union leaders were kept in line through the distribution of such funds to those who cooperated and the withholding of funds from those who did not.

The system of material awards also bound the top union leadership to the highest levels of political power. These union leaders were aided in expanding their economic power in return for the delivery of loyal political support from their rank and file. A number of agreements between Pemex and the union during the 1970s and 1980s stimulated the proliferation of a large number of contracting companies, whose board of directors inevitably included the top members of the union bureaucracy. In 1977 Pemex conceded to the union the right to subcontract 40 percent of the drilling contracts. In 1980 this right was extended to the transportation of hydrocarbon, and in 1983 this figure was raised to 50 percent. In 1980 the union and Pemex signed an extra-contractual agreement under which Pemex would tolerate the granting of contracts without tender. The union's contracts committee acted as a subcontracting agent to provide work for these new companies, thereby facilitating the entry of the labor leadership into the bourgeoisie.

The Petroleum Workers Union's close ties with Mexico's top political leadership up until 1988 is well known: The union's most powerful leader until his arrest in 1989, Joaquín Herdández Galicia ("La Quina"), had been very close to both Presidents Luis Echeverría (1970–1976) and López Portillo (1976–1982). Until the 1988 national election, a memorandum was regularly sent to the union membership directing the rank and file to vote for and to show militancy in the PRI.

Although the Petroleum Workers Union was by far the wealthiest of Mexico's trade unions, the mechanisms at work here operated elsewhere (see, for example, Aguilar, 1987). The relationship between the government and the nation's official trade unions has been integral to its capacity to ensure social peace and co-opt political dissent from the most combative labor organizations within Mexican society. The economic restructuring program implemented after 1983, however, has radically altered the corporatist and patron-clientelist relationships. The following section thus turns to an examination of that program and an analysis of its impact upon labor-state relations.

Economic Restructuring in Mexico

The objectives and nature of Mexico's economic restructuring program are spelled out in the government's 1983 National Development Plan, which called for a reorientation and modernization of the productive apparatus both to fulfill domestic needs better and to break into export markets. Key to the plan was trade liberalization. It was believed that imposing greater international competition would force domestic firms to become more efficient (and export-competitive) and that inflation would be reduced by compelling domestic firms to lower their prices. The plan called for the establishment of an integrated and competitive industrial sector through a process that became known as "industrial reconversion." Technological advancement was a goal, but the major thrust in the drive for international competitiveness focused upon the modernization of labor relations. The National Development Plan, for example, called for "the modernization of the labor process" and "the rationalization of employment" (Poder Ejecutivo Federal, 1983:175).

Industrial reconversion was to be optional for the private sector but mandatory for public-sector firms. The state was to be trimmed and made more productive. Parastatal industrial policy was to be revised along the following criteria: (1) "Strategic" areas (as defined by the Constitution) were to be consolidated and strengthened, and (2) "priority" areas (the designation of which is at the discretion of the state) were also to be strengthened, with state ownership eliminated from those areas in which it was deemed not to be justified (Poder Ejecutivo Federal, 1983:133). In addition to the elimination of corruption and patronage within those firms remaining in state hands, tariffs and prices for public goods and services would be increased and subsidies would be rationalized (Poder Ejecutivo Federal, 1983:177).

Despite what appeared to be a firm commitment to structural change, however, the government proceeded slowly with its program. During 1983 and 1984, import controls and subsidies remained in effect. And although the state divested itself of over 200 public enterprises (through their liquidation, sale, transfer, or fusion), these enterprises were either paper companies or were in areas considered neither strategic nor priority. Moreover, as a result of the drastic cutback in government expenditure required by Mexico's 1983 agreement with the International Moentary Fund (IMF), capital investment in modernization of the state industries was delayed if not prevented entirely. The 1983 IMF agreement called for a reduction of public-sector deficit as a percentage of GDP to 8.5 percent in 1983 (from 17 percent in 1982), to 5.5 percent in 1984, and to 3.5 percent in 1985 (Teichman, 1988:141; Teichmann, 1996). The stiff austerity program also severely restricted investment in the modernization of industrial plant by the private sector. Public and private investment declined by 27.9 percent in 1983, grew at the rates of 5.5 percent and 6.4 percent in 1984 and 1985, and declined again in 1987 and 1988 (Bendensky and Godínez, 1988:66).

On the other hand, policy reform in the area of fiscal control, particularly with regard to measures to reduce corruption, proceeded more quickly. The office of Comptroller General of the Nation was established to monitor the expenditure of government departments, agencies, and parastatals, and corruption charges were laid against a number of government officials of the previous administration (1976–1982). In 1984 the Ley de Obras (Law of Public Works) was passed stipulating that all works contracted out by the public sector, including the parastatals, had to go to public tender.

External economic events were soon to precipitate a reinvigorated commitment to restructuring. In 1985 deteriorating petroleum prices, rising interest rates, and U.S. barriers against Mexican manufactured goods resulted in a sharp deterioration of Mexico's balance of payments. With the 1985 earthquake, Mexico was faced with a renewed economic crisis that forced the government to make budget cuts in addition to those made earlier in February and June. An estimated 51,000 government employees were laid off in fifteen ministries and fourteen departments, and the government was forced to suspend investment projects in steel and petroleum in 1985 (*Proceso*, 12 August 1985:34).

In the face of rising social and political unrest, Mexico's political leaders took a strong stand against further austerity in their negotiations with the IMF. Although promising growth by 1987 (widely believed to be a departure from traditional IMF policy), Mexico in its 1986 agreement with the IMF pledged a renewed commitment to economic restructuring, and measures to increase trade liberalization were accelerated. External pressures played an important role in the renewed emphasis on industrial reconversion: A key component of a World Bank loan for sectoral programs in late 1986 was the allocation of funds for rationalization and industrial reconversion. Indeed, it has been suggested that the World Bank stipulated that funds for this purpose were to be channeled exclusively to the private sector (*La Jornada*, 2 June 1988:30). Moreover, the 1986 agreement with the IMF committed Mexico to the divestiture of some 300 state entities (*Wall Street Journal*, 23 August 1986:25).

In 1986 tax incentives and technical support were made available to those enterprises deemed to have a strong participation in international commerce through the Program for the Promotion of Integral Exports (PROPIEX). After 1985 import permits were replaced by tariffs, and tariffs were reduced. Hence, the new economic program announced by the government in 1986, Program for Stimulation and Growth (Programa de Aliento y Crecimiento, PAC), called for a renewal of economic growth along with an intensification of industrial reconversion through the introduction of new technology, the closing of obsolete production processes, and increases in productivity.

But PAC's call for an acceleration in the divestiture of nonstrategic and nonpriority parastatals was also a response to domestic pressures, both from the Mexican private sector and from within the state. The government-commissioned Hiriart Report, published in 1986, recommended that the state divest itself of "unnecessary" public enterprises in the steel industry and that the industry concentrate on making fundamental changes in its labor relations (*Proceso*, 10 February 1986:9). The divestiture of state enterprises then began to move into a number of areas previously considered to be priority and strategic: air transportation, minerals, and petroleum. In 1986 Mexicana de Aviación (a state-owned airline company) was put up for sale, Fundidora de Monterrey (steel) was shut down, and thirty-six basic petrochemical products were reclassified as nonbasic so as to open them to private (including foreign) investment. In addition, there occurred a sharp reduction in transfer payments from the federal government to parastatals after 1986 (Teichman, 1989b:33; Teichman, 1996).

External economic events in 1987 and 1988 caused policymakers to deepen the process of economic restructuring further. Decline in the price and demand for hydrocarbons, a burgeoning public deficit (resulting in large part from increases in interest rates), and inflation of over 150 percent in 1987 continued to plague the economy. The agreement signed among the state, business, labor, and peasants in December 1987, known as the Pact of Economic Solidarity, in addition to price and wage controls, called for a deepening of the restructuring process: Tariffs on imports were to be further reduced, more state enterprises were to be sold, the prices of the goods and services of parastatals were to be increased, and many more subsidies were to be reduced or eliminated. As one of the agreements of the pact, seventeen sugar refineries, three shipyards, and an undetermined number of mining enterprises were to be sold.

After 1986 the state strove for international competitiveness by selling public enterprises to the private sector, a route that it was believed would inject the resources required (and that the public sector lacked) for modernization. At the same time, the government announced its intention to "intensify structural change in those public enterprises which continue to be strategic or priority" and to maintain austerity in government spending (Nafinsa, 1989:62). Aeroméxico was liquidated in 1988, and social institutions were also pared down. The National Company for Popular Subsistence Provision (CONASUPO), a state marketing board that sought to supply basic foodstuffs to the poor, was to be restructured with the closing of some 500 stores and the reorganization of other retail outlets. In 1989 six of its companies were sold. Cananea, a government-owned company producing silver and gold, which also possessed one of the ten largest copper mines in the world, was also sold in 1990.

While carrying out the privatizations anticipated in the last years of the de la Madrid administration, the Salinas administration announced a number of new privatization initiatives. In 1990 the government sold its shares in the telephone company, Telmex; in 1992 it sold the state steel companies, Siderurgica Lázaro Cárdenas–Las Truchas (Sicarsta) and Altos Hornos (a steel mill); and the banks, nationalized by the Lopez Portillo administration in 1982, were reprivatized in 1990 and 1991. By 1993 some 200 parastatals remained from the more than 1,150 that had existed in 1983. At the same time, the Salinas administration opened up areas such as petroleum and electricity, which had been exclusively reserved for the state, to private (including foreign) capital. Through the reclassification of basic petrochemicals to secondary (a policy introduced by President de la Madrid), all but a few petrochemical products were opened up to private capital. Remaining restrictions on foreign investment were removed with the 1993 Foreign Investment Law. Furthermore, the administration of Ernesto Zedillo (1994–2000) expanded the realm of petrochemicals open for private investment in 1995. And with the North American Free Trade Agreegment (NAFTA), Mexico agreed to open its finance sector to foreign competition and changed legislation to allow foreign financial institutions to establish fully owned subsidiaries by 1997.

Transforming State-Labor Relations

The package of policies that came to constitute Mexico's economic restructuring program called for both modernization of the industrial plant (industrial reconversion) and reduction of the public deficit. This package consisted of the following specific measures. First was a reduction of expenditures within the public sector and the parastatals by contracting out those functions that the private sector could carry out more economically. The second was the divestiture of parastatals in order to achieve both savings and investment for modernization. Purchasers of public enterprises were required to agree to invest in plant modernization in subsequent years. It was believed that the government could then focus its investment on select programs of modernization. Third was the elimination of the worst aspects of union patronage to achieve financial savings and, later, to make government companies more attractive for sale to the private sector. Finally, worker involvement in matters considered to be "administrative," such as promotions and movement through the ranks, was to be eliminated. Coupled with the alteration of collective agreements to achieve greater worker mobility between functions and departments, these measures were believed to be essential to increased productivity. All of these aspects of the government's program created confrontation with labor. The first two measures produced large numbers of layoffs, and the last two seriously eroded union gains and restricted the distribution of patronage.

The economic project of increased competitiveness through industrial reconversion produced ever increasing confrontation with Mexico's powerful labor unions and ultimately a forceful government assault against labor unions and collective contracts. Deteriorating economic circumstances appear to have forced the state to abandon a strategy of industrial reconversion with state investment in a substantial core of state enterprises. In the absence of sufficient capital to modernize and to achieve international competitiveness while maintaining ownership, the state increasingly opted for the divestiture of state enterprises in order to secure the modernization of firms. Industrial reconversion in itself was likely to generate conflicts with labor unions; it involved changes in collective agreements that labor was likely to oppose. The growing commitment of the government to sell parastatals, in the absence of sufficient capital to achieve their modernization, further hardened the state's stance toward labor.

Although at the outset the private sector had exercised one of the most important pressures for privatization, by 1988 it was demonstrating decreasing interest in purchasing the firms that the government had put up for sale (*La Jornada*, 21 April 1988:18). The private sector made it very clear that one of the most negative aspects in its consideration of the purchase of parastatals was the nature of their collective agreements. In the words of the president of the Employers Confederation of the Mexican Republic (COPARMEX), Jorge Ocejo Moreno, because union gains increase costs to a company, any assessment of assets and liabilities of a parastatal up for sale "must include an assessment of the collective contract of the respective union" (*La Jornada*, 21 April 1988:21).

It is not surprising, therefore, that the state embarked upon a tough labor policy that included not only stiff resistance to labor's wage demands but also frequent refusal of the right to strike (declaring a strike illegal or nonexistent). Although President de la Madrid took an increasingly hard line toward labor, President Salinas's position was even tougher. Strikes by the nuclear workers in 1983, the telephone workers in 1984, workers at Dina-Renault in 1985, electrical workers in 1987, and workers at Sicartsa in 1989 were declared nonexistent. Unions that resisted modernization plans, invariably involving a large number of layoffs and the elimination of a substantial number of clauses from collective agreements, could be confronted with their company being declared bankrupt and the collective agreement dissolved, as occurred with the cases of Fundidora Monterrey in 1986, Cananea and Aeroméxico in 1988, and Concarril and Sicartsa in 1991. In other cases, such as that of Masa (a bus manufacturing enterprise that was part of the Dina group), enterprises were closed and their collective agreements liquidated because of difficulties in selling the company. In the Masa and Cananea cases, the enterprises were later sold to private interests without the encumbrance of labor resistance. The cases of Sicartsa and Cananea also appear to be ones in which policymakers felt it necessary to introduce "flexibility" into labor-management relations before putting these companies on the market. Tough restructuring measures were imposed prior to the announcement that these firms would be put up for sale. The state also used the *requisa*, its right to intervene in a labor dispute (as in Teléfonos de México in 1984), annulling labor rights and the collective agreement and forcing the workers back to work.

As the state became bolder in its confrontation with labor under the Salinas presidency, it removed uncooperative labor leadership. Perhaps the state's most aggressive act in this regard was the removal and arrest of the top leadership of the Petroleum Workers Union soon after Carlos Salinas took office. His administration then imposed a cooperative leadership and dismantled the union's well-established patronage network. Zedillo's administration has taken an even tougher stance against unions, to judge by the violence that has plagued its crackdown on the Ruta 100 Union. With about 25,000 workers, Ruta 100 was the provider of bus service in Mexico City until May 1995, when the government decided to declare its bankruptcy and dismissed its workers. The combative response by the union caused at least three deaths and the incarceration of several union leaders (Golden, 1995).

These tactics had two effects, both of which undermined Mexico's corporatist-clientelist labor-state relationship. One effect was to erode the longtime solid support the official labor movement had rendered the PRI. Although the CTM has continued to support the PRI and, formally, the incumbent president, it remained consistently and increasingly critical of government economic policy after 1983. Protests sent to the cabinet from 1984 onward accused Mexico's political leaders of demanding sacrifices from only the workers and their families. By 1986 there was a concerted campaign initiated by the worker sector of the PRI to reform the party in such a way that its leadership and policy would "reflect rank-and-file demands." But the CTM remained weak in the face of the state's onslaught against union interests: In 1983 it was unable to achieve unanimity on the issue of a general strike within the CT (Congreso del Trabajo [Labor Congress], the peak labor organization containing independent unions as well as the CTM's corporatist rivals, the Regional Confederation of Mexican Workers [CROM] and the Revolutionary Confederation of Workers and Peasants [CROC]), and it remained vulnerable to the state's veiled threats that it could be replaced by the CROC as the official state-sponsored labor organization. In 1984 Secretary of Labor Arsenio Farrell began to refer to the CROC as the new "vanguard of official unionism" (*Proceso*, 30 April 1984:10).

By 1989 the CTM was threatening to withdraw from the Minimum Salary Commission if the government continued to ignore its views (*El Día*, 23 December 1989:6). In 1990 the CTM called for a 20 percent wage increase, a demand actively opposed by its rivals, the CROC and the CROM. The divisions within the labor movement deepened as CTM leader Fidel Velasquez withdrew the CTM from active participation within the CT (*La Jornada*, 9 February 1991:23). Salinas in his labor policy continued to play on these divisions, declaring in 1991 that the CTM was no longer the major worker organization (*Proceso*, 1 April 1991:28).

The official labor movement was weakened by internal divisions generated by the government's antilabor policies, and union leadership loyalty to the PRI was eroded by the dismantling of patronage. The dismantling of the lucrative privileges granted the Petroleum Workers Union bureaucracy generated intense opposition to the government from the union leadership. When the union's failed attempts to get Ramón Beteta, the director general appointed by de la Madrid to cut Pemex's expenditures, removed on corruption charges, PRI petroleum deputies broke openly with their party over the issue of endorsing the findings of the Attorney General's Office (Procuraduría General de la República, PGR), which cleared Beteta of any wrongdoing (*La Jornada*, 2 November

1988:9). By the end of 1983 the union was suggesting that it might leave the PRI (*Proceso*, 24 June 1985:8). By 1988 the alienation between the union and Mexico's political leadership was deepening: It has been suggested that La Quina secretly helped the Cárdenas electoral campaign in 1988, which accounts for the loss of PRI support in the petroleum zones in the country (*Proceso*, 25 July 1988:27). Hence, in the 1988 election, the presidential vote went overwhelmingly in favor of Cárdenas in the petroleum regions, and although the incumbent PRI petroleum deputies were all reelected for Congress, all had links with dissident groups within and outside the PRI (Loyola Díaz, 1990:290). Links between the petroleum workers and the opposition continued throughout the Salinas years with close ties between former La Quina supporters and the opposition PRD (Partido de la Revolución Democrática) (*Proceso*, 11 December 1989:8–9). In the 1994 elections, the PRI lost to the opposition PRD in five petroleum districts in Veracruz, a region severely affected by the restructuring of Pemex (*Reforma*, 24 August 1994:2A).

The second and probably more serious impact of the government's assault on previously powerful labor unions and their collective agreements was the erosion of rank-and-file support both for official unions and the PRI in view of the almost complete failure of the old labor leadership to protect its patronage system, jobs, benefits, or salaries. The strongest and most immediate rejection of PRI rule came from the steel sector with the closure of Fundidora Monterrey. A PRI mining deputy declared that he would resign if the enterprise were not reopened, and the leader of the Miners Union of Fundidora declared that "the number one enemy of the workers is the President of the Republic" (*Proceso*, 13 July 1986:38; 9 June 1986:22). Some 40,000 opponents to the closing reportedly burned their PRI membership credentials during a demonstration in Monterrey, the capital city of Nuevo León (*Proceso*, 2 June 1986:22).

Other groups of dissident workers, particularly in state enterprises affected by the government's modernization program, were also reported to have given support to Cárdenas during the 1988 election. Telephone and airline workers organized committees in support of Cárdenas (*La Jornada*, 31 July 1988:7; 19 August 1988:17). Rank-and-file support for the usually quiescent public employees union (FSTSE) began to erode with the formation of a dissident organization (Intersecretarial Front for the Defense of Employment, FIDE), which accused union leadership of failing to react to government layoffs (*Proceso*, 5 August 1985:10). Shouts against the *charro* leadership were interspersed with cries of "Viva Cárdenas" at FSTSE meetings (*La Jornada*, 21 July 1988:1).

Again dissension increased under Salinas's tough antilabor policies. In 1989 a bitter sixty-day strike in the government steel plant Sicartsa occurred as a consequence of management's proposal to cut some 2,183 workers, to remove union interference in contracting out, and to remove union participation in the allocation of temporary and permanent jobs. The government's tough handling of the strike is said to have caused the local population to move openly in

support of the opposition PRD, which resulted in the election of a local PRD
deputy and later a municipal president (*Proceso*, 12 March 1990:20). In 1990
the workers of Sicartsa repudiated their national leadership after it signed an
agreement to renegotiate the clause in their collective agreement that had
granted the workers a forty-hour week, foreseeing that renegotiation would ultimately force the union to give up that hard-won gain. In Altos Hornos, another government-owned steel plant, union acceptance of 3,958 layoffs resulted
in rank-and-file repudiation of both its leadership and the agreement. Yet in
subsequent negotiations, the union was forced to agree to 4,458 dismissals (*El
Cotidiano*, May–June 1989:60).

With the divestiture of state enterprises, the state removed itself perma-
nently from direct ties to many labor unions. Even for those labor unions that
have remained intact and those workers who have maintained their jobs, the
fundamental alterations that have occurred in the collective agreements make
the continued operation of Mexico's co-optative corporatist-clientelist system
problematic. By and large, the traditional mechanisms union leaders have used
to ensure their domination of the rank and file have been seriously eroded.
New collective agreements imposed by the state (in petroleum, mining, air-
lines, for example) have removed union control over technical innovations,
worker mobility, promotions, and movements through the ranks. In the 1989
collective agreement between Pemex and its union, following the removal of its
recalcitrant leaders, ninety-four clauses were modified and fifteen eliminated.
Profound administrative reorganization meant large-scale layoffs, the union's
access to Pemex's 2 percent contribution to its social fund for works contracted
out was restricted, union control over the mobility of workers was eliminated,
and the company gained unrestricted ability to hire nonunion personnel (*La
Jornada*, 5 August 1990:1). The 1991 collective agreement eroded the power of
the union even further, eliminating its participation in the allocation of jobs
and promotions and reducing the importance of seniority in deciding promotions. With the union weakened, Pemex's labor force was reduced between
1989 and 1992 by over 60,000 (*Proceso*, 13 April 1992:16). Mounting unrest
among the rank and file of the Petroleum Workers Union resulted in the government forcing the resignation of its compliant *charro* leadership in 1993 (*Los
Angeles Times*, 22 June 1993:12). The 1992 reorganization of Pemex into a
holding company for four subsidiaries had the twin purpose of making possible infusions of private (including foreign) capital and weakening labor even
further. Each subsidiary now signs a separate agreement with its workers,
thereby diminishing the importance of the national union leadership (*La Jornada*, 5 June 1993:41).

Economic restructuring, therefore, was achieved within a context of direct
confrontation with the organized core of Mexican corporatism. Only the telephone union was able to negotiate a modicum of participation in modernization. Although the union and its leader, Hector Hernández Juárez, had

maintained a position of "critical support" for the PRI, the union in fact took a nonconfrontational stance in the face of the government's modernization plans (unlike the hard-line opposition from other more progovernment unions of parastatals, such as the Petroleum Workers Union). There are likely two reasons for the telephone workers' inclination to negotiate. One was that the administration's thrust for modernization of the collective contract of the telephone company closely followed the liquidation of Aeroméxico and the government's tough handling of the Sicartsa strike—both events likely convinced the union leadership that a hard line in defense of union gains would end in defeat. Second, the nature of the requirements of modernization in the telephone industry that would ultimately necessitate the expansion of employment (though requiring its reduction in certain areas) made negotiating space available. But even here, as with other labor unions allied with the state, the sectoral incorporation of organized workers within the state-party apparatus has been severely tested and is in a process of transformation.

The CTM has been weakened considerably by the rise of more combative labor fronts both from within its ranks and from outside. In early 1990 a new federation of labor unions, named the Federation of Unions of Enterprises of Goods and Services (FESEBIS), was formed by the unions of state-owned and previously state-owned enterprises, which had recently struggled against the negative implications of government restructuring programs. Federation organizers were the unions of aviation workers, telephone workers, and electrical workers. Taking the view that both the CTM and the CT had failed to defend workers' interests adequately, the federation sought to defend collective agreements, employment, and the right to strike and to stop the privatization of public enterprises (*La Jornada*, 3 January 1990:3; 27 March 1990:16). Although remaining within the CT, the new federation called for its reorganization. The formation of FESEBIS was strongly opposed by the CTM.

Labor conflicts in the private sector (particularly in Ford Cuautitlán and Cervecería Modelo) have given rise to the Front for the Defense of Legality and Union Rights (FDLDS)—an organization given impetus by the Workers Revolutionary Confederation (COR), a CTM rival among official unionism. In September 1990 workers of twenty-nine unions began preliminary discussions for the establishment of a workers party, the major objective being the fight for labor rights. Supporters of this initiative included those unions, both in the public and private sectors, with recent labor conflicts over the requisites of restructuring: the workers of Ford, Chrysler, and Sicartsa; critical currents within the petroleum, bank workers, and teachers unions; and various unions representing university workers (*La Jornada*, 3 September 1990:8).

A new labor party did not emerge for the 1994 elections, and the labor movement has remained seriously fragmented, but it is also clear that PRI corporatist political control is in retreat. Leaders of the telephone workers and teachers unions and FESEBIS all repudiated the notion of collective support for the PRI, saying they would take no measures to ensure rank-and-file PRI support apart from their own personal declarations of loyalty (*La Jornada*, 14 August 1994:7). The leaders of the FSTSF and the Social Security Workers Union both emphasized in public pronouncements that their support for the PRI in no way restricted the political choices of rank-and-file members (*La Jornada*, 14 August 1994:1, 13).

Conclusion: The Future of Mexican Corporatism

In this chapter I have sought to demonstrate that Mexico's program of economic restructuring has severely undermined the corporatist-clientelist relations largely responsible for the predominance of the PRI. Although these relations began to break down with the economic and political crises of the late 1960s, the economic restructuring program instituted between 1983 and 1995 accelerated this process. The combination of economic austerity and a strategy geared toward increasing manufactured exports through industrial reconversion resulted in a serious erosion of the state's corporatist-clientelist ties with the labor unions forming the core of Mexico's traditional political structure: the workers of the parastatals, particularly petroleum, mining, and transportation, and the hitherto dependent and loyal public service unions. Moreover, although the CTM and its affiliates continued to operate in support of the PRI during the 1994 election campaign, the CTM's political weight both within the PRI and within the labor movement was now considerably diminished. The CTM lost only one candidate in the 1994 election, but its allocation of deputy candidates has been reduced by 25 percent since 1988 (*La Jornada*, 25 August 1994:11).

The requirement for severe cutbacks in government expenditures, the necessity of raising labor productivity and cutting costs, and later the requirement to make state enterprises attractive for acquisition by private capital were strong incentives for a concerted onslaught against labor unions and their collective agreements. The failure of union leaders to defend the interests of their rank and file, the eradication of much of the patronage network from the control of union leadership, and indeed the elimination of the state from many economic activities, have all served to deteriorate the ties that have hitherto bound the rank and file of powerful elements of organized labor to the state.

Mexican corporatism, of course, has faced severe challenges in the past. In 1958, for example, the rail workers' strike and in 1968 the student movement both represented serious threats to Mexico's authoritarian regime. But in each case, the regime was able to institute a combination of repression and adjustments in its economic model in order to ensure the continuity of its particular form of corporatist-clientelist authoritarianism. The "stabilizing development" program ensured economic growth with price stability from the late 1950s until the late 1960s, and the petroleum export strategy reinitiated economic growth between the mid-1970s and 1981. The import-substitution model was maintained, economic growth was renewed, and resources for the expansion of the state apparatus were secured for selective satisfaction of working-class demands and for patronage. With the 1982 crisis, however, the administration was no longer able to find a palliative for the structural defects (debt, chronic commercial deficit, and public deficit) of its old import-substitution economic model. It was forced to alter that model fundamentally from one based on import substitution, involving heavy protection for domestic industry with the strong participation of the state in infrastructure and basic inputs, to a new model geared toward export promotion in manufactured goods that entailed trade liberalization and withdrawal of the state from the economy. The former model was compatible with the corporatist incorporation of sectors of official unionism; the latter is far less so.

The Mexican regime, however, is unlikely to abandon corporatist control entirely, particularly of the labor movement. But corporatist control of labor organizations will probably be less effective than in the past (because of the diminished patronage leverage of labor leaders), and it will increasingly exist alongside different forms of labor-state relations. Because the regime's economic model requires that labor gains and strife be kept to a minimum, the regime can be expected to continue some of the practices of the old corporatist model—for example, to impose its own choices for labor leadership in many of the large, older trade unions, particularly those in sectors producing essential inputs and providing essential services. This has already occurred in the Petroleum Workers Union, where after removing La Quina and his cohorts in 1989, the government imposed a more cooperative, though no less corrupt union leadership in the person of Sebastián Guzmán Cabrera and later removed him when he could not control rank-and-file unrest. But because the new state-imposed *charro* leaderships have fewer means by which to control their rank and file, neocorporatism is a less secure form of political control.

In the unions of the *maquiladoras* (assembly plants) and the new high-technology export industries, on the other hand, neocorporatism is less necessary. The unions are weak and subordinate, and the government has no need to change collective contracts because such plants were established with flexible labor contracts from the outset. Moreover, as the workers tend to be younger and more mobile and to lack previous labor experience, they are less likely to engage in collective action (de la Garza, 1989:81). The state may be able to establish a new form of alliance with labor unions in two kinds of settings: the new *maquiladoras* and the few cases in which the state is able to negotiate an alliance with combative labor unions when there is sufficient maneuverability to allow labor a limited role in the modernization process. The latter will perhaps be based on selective patronage but without the corporatist structures of the old alliance.

The alteration of state-labor relations described here has important implications for the nature of the PRI and for its continued rule. It is likely that sectoral representation within the PRI will continue to decline in importance. The administration of Carlos Salinas made a concerted, though not entirely successful effort to reduce the importance of the traditional PRI sectors, particularly labor. Stagnant or declining economic growth rates over the next five to ten years raise the specter of worker radicalization and labor militancy in the form of mobilization against *charro* leadership and demands for union democratization. The failure of the new economic model would severely undermine the legitimacy of the regime. In such a scenario, worker organizations could move toward support of the opposition PRD while the PRI continues its march toward the neoliberalism of the Right. If such should occur, the state would be forced either to exercise increasing repression against the opposition or to speed up the process of political liberalization. Should it choose repression, a further erosion of legitimacy would no doubt occur, whereas political liberalization could well mean electoral losses, particularly if labor moves en masse to an opposition party or forms its own party. As the old corporatist-clientelist form of political control further declines, conflicts in a situation of continued economic stagnation or decline would become increasingly unmediated by state-party institutions. Such a chronic political instability and labor unrest would further erode the possibilities for economic growth.

But this outcome is unlikely because of at least two factors. One is the severe divisions within the Mexican labor movement, which render improbable a united labor front against the government's neoliberal program. In the past, the government has demonstrated adeptness at exploiting divisions within the labor movement. No doubt a judicious support of independent unions and CTM rivals (within the context of neocorporatism) might well be sufficient to keep labor off balance for some time and to ensure the continuity of neocorporatism in potentially combative sectors of the labor movement. As I have argued, the regime has demonstrated a propensity to maintain a form of corporatism but without the big worker confederations of the past. Second, the lack of democratic union participation and violence that characterized the old *charro* union structure is responsible for an attitude of passivity, political apathy, and fear of conflict on the part of many workers (Pérez Linares, 1984:186). These factors undermine the possibility of independent political mobilization and render workers susceptible to continued political manipulation. Although numerous sectors within the labor movement remain combative, the labor movement in general clings to the old populist, import-substitution economic formula of protection of industry and heavy state intervention in the economy. If labor is to overcome its weakness as a political force, it must be able to offer a viable alternative vision to both an unviable return to the past and the government's neoliberal program.

Notes

1. Petroleum as a percentage of all exports dropped from 74.8 percent in 1983 to 43.0 percent by 1987; manufactured goods as a proportion of total exports rose from 17.1 percent in 1983 to 49.3 percent by 1987. Petroleum export growth stagnated or declined between 1983 and 1986, with the exception of 1985, whereas manufactured exports averaged a growth rate of over 30 percent per year (Teichman, 1989a:34).

2. Whether there is such a direct connection must await the results of ongoing electoral studies. As I suggest later in this chapter, however, there is some preliminary evidence to suggest such a link.

3. Other factors, interrelated with those I shall focus on here, include revolutionary mythology, preemptive reform, and violent repression as a last resort. See Coleman and Davis, 1983; Hellman, 1988; and Stevens, 1974.

4. A classic work dealing with the operation of patronage in the Mexican political system is Brandenburg, 1964. See also Handelman, 1979. Brandenburg also deals with the evolution of Mexican corporatism, as do most standard works dealing with Mexican political history. Good discussions of the particular nature of Mexican corporatism are found in Reyna and Weinert, 1977.

5. CNOP changed its name in 1993 to FNOC, National Front of Organizations and Citizens.

6. The term *charro* (literally cowboy) has its origins in the nickname given to an early leader of the Mexican railway workers, Luis Gómez Zepeda, who was removed from office because of embezzlement of union funds.

Bibliography

Aguilar, Javier, coord. 1987. *Los sindicatos nacionales, minero metalúrgico.* Mexico City: G.V. Editores, S.A.

Alvarado Mendoza, Arturo. 1987. *Electoral Patterns and Perspectives in Mexico.* San Diego: Center for U.S.-Mexican Studies, University of California.

Bailey, John. 1988. *Governing Mexico: The Statecraft of Crisis Management.* London: Macmillan.

Bendensky, León, and Victor Godínez. 1988. "The Mexican Foreign Debt: A Case of Conflictual Cooperation." Pp. 51–69 in Riordan Roett, ed., *Mexico and the United States.* Boulder: Westview Press.

Brandenburg, Frank. 1964. *The Making of Modern Mexico.* Englewood Cliffs, N.J.: Prentice-Hall.

Coleman, Kenneth M., and Charles L. Davis. 1983. "Preemptive Reform and the Mexican Working Class." *Latin American Research Review,* 18(1):3–32.

Cornelius, Wayne A., Ann L. Craig, and Jonathan Fox. 1994. *Transforming State-Society Relations in Mexico: The National Solidarity Strategy.* U.S.-Mexico Contemporary Perspectives Series, 6. San Diego: Center for U.S.-Mexican Studies, University of California, San Diego.

Cruz Bencomo, Miguel Angel. 1989. "El quinismo, una historia del charrismo petrolero." *El Cotidiano,* no. 28:24–28.

de la Garza, Enrique. 1989. "La crisis del sindicalismo en México." Pp. 75–90 in Graciela Bensusan and Carlos García, coords., *Estado y sindicalismo, crisis de una relación.* Mexico City: Universidad Autónoma Metropolitana.

Gentleman, Judith, ed. 1986. *Mexican Politics in Transition.* Boulder: Westview Press.

Golden, Tim. 1995. "Mexico Judge in Union Case Is Shot Dead." *New York Times,* 21 June.

Gómes Tagle, Silvia. 1992. "Mexico 1991: Democratic Perspectives and the Middle Term Elections." Paper presented at the XVII International Congress of the Latin American Studies Association. September 24–27, Los Angeles, Calif.

Handelman, Howard. 1979. "Unionization, Ideology and Political Participation Within the Mexican Working Class." Pp. 154–168 in Mitchell A. Seligson and John A. Booth, eds. *Political Participation in Latin America: Politics and the Poor,* Vol. 2. New York: Homes and Meier.

Hellman, Judith Adler. 1988. *Mexico in Crisis.* 2d ed. New York: Holmes and Meier.

Leal, Juan Felipe, Jacqueline Peschard, and Concepción Rivera, eds. 1988. *Las elecciones federales de 1988 en México.* Mexico City: Universidad Nacional Autónoma de México.

Loyola Díaz, Rafael. 1990. "La liquidación del feudo petrolero en la política moderna, México 1988." *Mexican Studies/Estudios Mexcanos,* 6(3):263–297.

Nafinsa. 1988. "Criterios generales de política económica para 1987." *El mercado de valores,* no. 2:4–14.

Novelo O., Vitorio. 1989. "Las fuentes de poder de la dirigencia sindical en Pemex." *El Cotidiano,* no. 28:13–23.

Pérez Linares, Rosalía. 1984. "El charrismo sindical en la década de los setenta: El sindicato petrolero." Pp. 169–188 in Ana María Prieto Hernández et al., eds., *Historia y crónicas de la clase obrera en México.* Mexico City: Escuela Nacional de Antropología e Historia e Instituto Nacional de anthropología e Historia.

Poder Ejecutivo Federal. 1983. *Plan Nacional de Desarrollo, 1983–1988.* Mexico City.

Powell, John Duncan. 1970. "Peasant Society and Clientelistic Politics." *American Political Science Review* 64(2):411–425.

Reyna, José Luis, and Richard S. Wienert, eds. 1977. *Authoritarianism in Mexico.* Philadelphia: Institute for the Study of Human Issues.

Schmitter, Philippe G. 1974. "Still the Century of Corporatism." Pp. 85–131 in Fredrick B. Pike and Thomas Stritch, eds., *The New Corporatism.* Notre Dame, Ind.: University of Notre Dame.

Secretaría de Contraloría de la Federación. 1988. *Restructuración del sector paraestatal.* Mexico City.

Stevens, Evelyn. 1974. *Protest and Response in Mexico.* Cambridge, Mass.: M.I.T. Press.

Teichman, Judith. 1988. *Policymaking in Mexico: From Boom to Crisis.* Boston: Allan Unwin.

———. 1989a. "The Mexican State and the Political Implications of Economic Restructuring." Paper presented at the annual conference of the Canadian Association for Studies in International Development, Quebec City, Laval University, June.

———. 1989. "The State and Economic Restructuring: Restructuring the Parastatal Sector." Paper presented at the annual meeting of the Canadian Association for Latin American and Caribbean Studies, Ottawa, Carlton University, October.

———. 1996. *Privatization and Political Transition in Mexico.* Pittsburgh: University of Pittsburgh Press.

9

Democracy for Whom? Women's Grassroots Political Activism in the 1990s, Mexico City and Chiapas

Lynn Stephen

Two major issues have broadly defined Mexican politics at the end of the twentieth century—democracy and economic restructuring. The structural adjustment that Mexico began to undergo even before the 1982 currency crises and that has continued into the 1990s has profoundly influenced the lives of all Mexicans. The most concrete manifestation of policies aimed at promoting foreign investment, production for export, and overall economic growth has been continued and accelerated social and economic inequality. For those at the bottom, particularly women and children, the difficult consequences felt by all have been even harsher. As material resources, social services, and income for family maintenance dwindled, women began to alter their consumption patterns and the amount and type of paid and unpaid labor they engaged in. Studies conducted on the impact of economic crisis on urban women concluded that increasing numbers of women and children were entering the informal and formal wage labor forces, self-provisioning of goods and services formerly purchased was increasing, forced family cooperation was on the rise, and women continued to carry heavy domestic workloads (Arizpe, 1977; Arizpe et al., 1989; Benería and Roldán, 1987; Benería, 1992; del Castillo, 1993; González de la Rocha, 1989, 1991, 1994; Gutmann, 1994a, 1994b; Sánchez Gómez, 1989; Stephen, 1992, forthcoming).

These trends can be viewed as strategies for privatizing the economic crisis. At the same time, however, some women began to participate in what have often been called urban survival movements focused on procuring land, housing, basic resources, and infrastructure. In the countryside as well, indigenous and peasant women began participating in local and regional movements and advancing agendas focused on economic survival. During the past twenty years, Mexico has seen the emergence or continued existence of significant social movements making demands on an array of issues: human rights, rural and urban living conditions, land reclamation, the "disappeared," labor rights, abortion and reproductive rights, democratization of political systems, and more. Women were and are a major presence in these movements. The participation of women in these movements and their increased importance in Mexican politics are a critical factor in cultural demands for increased democratization in all spheres of life, including formal political systems.

Although 98 percent of the Mexican political elite is male (Rodríguez, 1995:22), women have played significant political roles through their presence in social movements as well as in political parties. In this chapter I examine how women's grassroots organizing in Mexico City and Chiapas has contributed to the possibility of a more democratic political culture in Mexico. The term "democracy" is used here to denote widespread citizen participation. It is not confined to electoral democracies in which the primary exercise of citizenship is voting. As Mary Dietz noted, politics as participation and citizenship, as the active engagement of peers in the public realm, assumes a notion of democracy that is neither the negative liberty of noninterference nor the legitimization of every individual interest nor the transformation of private into public interests. "The conception is perhaps best called the democratic one, and it takes politics to be the collective and participatory engagement of citizens in the determination of the affairs of their community" (Dietz, 1992:75).

The case studies presented in this chapter also challenge the primary theoretical dichotomy used by many social scientists to classify women's organizing. Many analysts of women's grassroots movements divide them into either (1) feminist or strategically oriented movements that challenge women's gender oppression or (2) feminine or practical movements that focus on helping women to fulfill their "traditional" gender roles (Kaplan 1982 ; Logan, 1990).

Maxine Molyneux applied the strategic-practical differentiation in analyzing women's political participation in revolutionary and postrevolutionary Nicaragua under the Sandinistas. In her analysis, Molyneux refused to make a unitary judgment about the success of the Sandinistas in serving the needs of women. Rather she divided the types of interests women have into practical interests that further women's ability to fulfill traditional gender roles associated with the gendered division of labor versus strategic interests that challenge gender inequalities. She concluded that on the practical front the Sandinistas did not do too badly in terms of improving the position of poorer women, at least until the Contra war. In terms of strategic interests, she found that the progress made was " modest, but significant," citing legal reforms holding men responsible for the financial welfare of their families, political discussion about the division of domestic labor, and land reform that encouraged women's participation (Molyneux 1985:248–249).

In analyzing women's collective action in early twentieth-century Barcelona, Temma Kaplan (1982) elaborated a theory of "female consciousness." Kaplan stated that when women who have internalized their designated roles as domestic providers and caretakers are unable to carry out their duties, they will be moved to take action in order to fulfill their social roles as females. This may even include taking on the state when it impedes their normal activities (Stephen, forthcoming).

Other recent analyses of women's political participation in Latin America question the utility of the strategic versus practical gender interest dichotomy and by implication the categorization of social, economic, personal, and political relations as either public or private. In an article on popular women's organizations in Ecuador, Amy Conger Lind suggested that although women's organizing projects may focus around procuring basic needs, "basic needs are not tied solely to survival, but rather to constructions of identity and relations of power" (1992:137). Organizing around any kind of needs automatically involves challenging traditional gender roles. The mere act of organizing and its implications—such as occupying public spaces, being absent from the home, and confronting officials, police, and sometimes the military—challenge feminine stereotypes in many Latin American countries.

Others such as Jennifer Schirmer (1993) and Lynn Stephen (forthcoming) have pointed out that women may hold interests that are simultaneously strategic and practical and that interests change over time. The fact that not all members of an organization think identically or necessarily share the same identity is also important in understanding variation within one organization. The notion of categorizing all of the demands of one organization according to one typology, in this case feminine or feminist, tends to homogenize important differences among women and to simplify the contextual construction of gender that occurs in relation to other hierarchies, including class, race, ethnicity, location, and age.

Some Mexican women are challenging this dichotomy through their integration of spheres and issues that have been deemed separate by social scientists. Common themes in women's grassroots organizing bridge the division between "strategic" and "practical" gender concerns. These include democratization of organizations and of the home, the right to basic survival and health, respect for women's physical integrity and control over their bodies and reproduction, and political representation. However, the meaning of these themes can vary not only by movement but also in accordance with the diversity reflected within one organization. Here I use separate examples to illustrate the convergence of these issues in three different sectors: women organizing for urban survival among the poor (the Women's Council of the National Coordinating Committee of the Urban Popular Movement, CONAMUP; women in revolutionary organizations (women combatants of the Zapatista National Liberation Army, EZLN); and women from NGOs (nongovernmental organizations) and peasant and indigenous organizations participating in a larger movement for democracy (Chiapas State Women's Assembly of the National Democratic Convention).

I have chosen these three case studies to reflect different geographic locations, different ethnic identities, and different political strategies and thus to illustrate the important convergence of issues that women are organizing around in Mexico. If women in a range of political organizations are overlapping significantly in their agendas in terms of calls for democracy, economic justice, respect for women's rights in the home, and control over their own bodies, then this is an important signal about shared dimensions of gender oppression in contemporary Mexico.

Urban Survival:
The Women's Regional Council of CONAMUP

The year 1980 stands out in the history of Mexico's urban movements because it marks the seminal event of approximately twenty-one organizations and 700 delegates attending the first national congress of urban movements in Monterrey (Moctezuma, 1983:7).[1] The congress allowed activists and participants in movements from different parts of the country to debate and compare strategies, ideologies, and specific programs. The first congress concluded with a pact of solidarity and a promise to hold a second congress in 1981 (Moctezuma 1983:7; Bennett 1992). At that congress in Durango the CONAMUP was formally created with 2,000 participants from sixty organizations representing fourteen states. The constituency at the founding congress covered a range of class subgroups, including the urban poor, renters, working-class and some middle-class homeowners, people looking for housing, workers from the informal sector, small-scale vendors and merchants, and more (Ramírez Saiz, 1986:175).

The demands of the CONAMUP focused not only on improving the living conditions of its members but also on democratizing Mexican society and easing repression against those organizing for change. During the 1980s the CONAMUP emerged as one of Mexico's most powerful urban social movement organizations, but a majority of its members remained invisible. Overwhelmingly the backbone of the urban popular movement, women within the CONAMUP (particularly those who were in contact with feminist organizations focused on the integration of class and gender-based concerns) began to question their lack of representation in CONAMUP's leadership, decisionmaking processes, and agenda for political struggle. The lack of internal democracy within the CONAMUP was a major mobilizing force for women to organize their own space within the organization.

Women within the CONAMUP came from varied class fractions and had varying experience within political organizing, but most shared in a common struggle to make ends meet with no or decreasing resources and felt that their particular struggles such as urban living conditions, domestic violence, and their health were not being addressed. The impetus for forming a women's organization within the CONAMUP came out of discussions focused on the theme of democracy. A few women who had previous organizing experience as well as some men, particularly those from one political faction within the CONAMUP, began to push for the formation of an autonomous women's organization. In 1983 a national women's meeting of the CONAMUP was held at the headquarters for the Committee for Popular Defense in the city of Durango. Several hundred women attended.

After the first national meeting, the Women's Regional Council of the CONAMUP was formed from women who participated in thirty urban organizations in the Valley of Mexico. This regional group has remained the most successful instance of women organizing within the CONAMUP and has had an important presence in Mexico City.

The most striking aspect of the organizing project of the Women's Regional Council of the CONAMUP is the combination of issues activists have focused on since its inception. Workshops and campaigns bring together domestic violence, women's sexuality, and women's political participation with poverty and urban survival. This range of issues, more than anything, is responsible for the successful integration of women from a variety of backgrounds into one organization. The issues also reflect the different dimensions of women's lives relating to gender, class, age, and ethnicity. While the larger CONAMUP remained focused on the material conditions of living, often filtered through rhetoric focused on class and class position, the Women's Regional Council developed a more wide-ranging discourse that incorporated different aspects of women's identities.

After the second national women's meeting of the CONAMUP in 1985, members of the Women's Regional Council organized several campaigns. From August 1985 until February 1986, they organized their first campaign to oppose violence against women. The activities focused on consciousness-raising about domestic violence and education through films, flyers, and discussions in and around Mexico City (Brugada and Ortega, 1987:101). In 1987 after the fourth meeting of Latin American and Caribbean feminists in Taxco, Mexico, the Women's Regional Council joined women across Latin America in observing an International Day Against Violence Against Women. The date chosen, 25 November, was selected in commemoration of six Dominican peasant women who were killed after resisting sexual violation by military troops (Miller, 1990:245).

In 1986 the Women's Regional Council organized a second campaign against inflation. A major focus of this struggle was to persuade the Ministry of Trade and Industrial Promotion (SECOFI) to let them control the distribution and sale of gas used for cooking in thirty neighborhoods. They got SECOFI to donate gas tanks and to give them a distribution contract. This program continued into the 1990s. That same year the Women's Regional Council also began to organize to keep the price of subsidized corn and tortillas down as well as to control distribution of subsidized milk from the government-run LICONSA (CONASUPO, Industrialized Milk, Inc.).

By the end of the 1980s, the economic situation of Mexico's urban poor and working classes had worsened significantly. The creation of PRONASOL (Solidarity Program) by the government was a turning point for organizations like the Women's Regional Council. Many grassroots organizations were ultimately squeezed out of existence for economic reasons, and many women in the CONAMUP believe that their participation in government Solidarity programs was critical not only to their continued existence but also to forcing the government to make such programs function as they should. Well aware of the possibility of being co-opted by government programs, women in the CONAMUP have always approached their participation critically. Their position is based on holding the government accountable for its responsibilities to women, children, and families. In many instances they have organized large marches, sit-ins, hunger strikes, and other actions to pressure government officials. By the 1990s, when they appeared at the offices of Solidarity officials, it was well known that they would not back down and would be happy to stay until their demands had been met.

In 1988 the Women's Regional Council moved into a building occupied by a feminist organization called "The Moon Crescent" (Cuarto Creciente). Moon Crescent members solicited the support of the CONAMUP to avoid being evicted from the house they had taken over in the center of Mexico City. They donated all of their materials to council members who valiantly tried to defend the space. Once they were evicted from the original location, the women decided to petition the city for a space. They maintained a strong presence in the city and kept constant pressure on the mayor to give in to their demands. A sit-in organized by the Women's Regional Council was the first one faced by Mayor Manuel Camacho Solís, who capitulated to the pressure and gave the women a credit from the city to be used as a twelve-year mortgage in order to acquire a permanent space. They used the credit to purchase a large house in the center of Mexico City, which is now a women's center with a wide range of activities (Mogrovejo Aquise, 1990:42–43).

The experience of winning the struggle for their space as well as prior confrontations over access to control of gas distribution, tortilla programs, and milk emboldened the women in their efforts. Once they moved into their new space, the Women's Regional Council organized a school for women, a collective kitchen that serves breakfast to schoolchildren and lunch to the elderly, a health clinic, and a wide range of workshops focusing on women's health and sexuality, battering, and strategies for generating household income. Economic production workshops emphasize clothing production, small crafts, food processing, and tarot card reading. The Women's Regional Council distributes over 16,000 government-subsidized breakfasts to children each day and uses the center for weekly meetings with representatives from the neighborhood committees that make up the council. In 1994 the council also began organizing monthly cultural outings.

Women within the Women's Regional Council have not been ideologically united by any means. The council's relationship with local self-identified feminist organizations has been difficult, and although some members embrace feminism, other emphatically reject it. A few women within the leadership of the CONAMUP began and continued with a vision of feminism; others never adopted the terms. The few women who identified as feminists were interested in combining class and gender struggles into a "popular feminism." This brand of feminism takes the concrete daily struggles of poor urban women as its starting point. Most CONAMUP women who called themselves feminists were clearly aligned with other feminist organizations such as the Integral Revolutionary Project (CRI, Colectivo Revolucionario Integral) that emerged from a working-class identity and focused on labor issues. Feminist organizations such as the Collective of Human Development in Latin America (CIDHAL) that worked with the Women's Regional Council were interested in having it take on a more explicit feminist identity. This entailed difficult considerations about what this identity would mean, how it would be framed, who would embrace it, and when and for what purpose that would occur.

Some leaders in 1989 declared the organization to be feminist and talked about "popular feminism," which integrates class and gender concerns as an appropriate label for the work of the organization, but other women were more reluctant to claim that label. Some key activists who worked with the Women's Regional Council continue to embrace the term and integrate the concept into their work; others are more skeptical and indicate they never really understood the term. They prefer to talk about "organizing" and to focus on the concrete issues women struggle around. However, even those women who do not actively embrace the term respond to the issues raised by popular feminism. One activist interviewed by this author identified the work of the Women's Regional Council simply as follows: "Our primary goal is to improve the lives of women, to help them get the basic things they need in life and prevent them from suffering from violence."

The task of initiating and maintaining organizations such as the Women's Regional Council is no small feat. The women in the council have faced a long path of struggle not only at home but also with one another and with men in the larger CONAMUP (see Stephen, forthcoming; Mogrovejo Aquise, 1990). Although all do not necessarily share the same perspective about what their participation in the council means, most women who are active in the organization have the following in common. They (1) leave their homes several times a week to participate in local and regional meetings, marches, and health and nutrition programs; (2) have participated in workshops and events that discuss domestic violence, women's health, and reproduction; (3) have had to renegotiate the household division of labor in their absence in terms of child care, cooking, and cleaning; and (4) have participated in wider political meetings and events in mixed organizations and in discussions about women's lack of political representation within the CONAMUP and elsewhere.

These shared experiences have resulted in a group of women who have a common set of questions regarding the various dimensions of inequality found within the class, gender, ethnic, and generational relationships they participate in. They seem unified in agreeing strategically how to combat economic marginalization, domestic violence, and a lack of democracy within the CONAMUP and in society at large. Their entrance into a bargaining relationship with the state to obtain resources they feel they have a right to takes them out of a passive relationship with the formal political sphere. Their insistence that they have the right to an autonomous organizational space within the larger CONAMUP and their complaints about their lack of representation in the organization are tied to an emerging discourse about internal democratization. Like the themes reflected in the Zapatista's Revolutionary Law of Women (discussed in the next section), their work also defies dichotomies that label the contents of movement demands as feminist or not. The examples of women in the EZLN and the Chiapas Women's Convention bring out these themes even more clearly.

The EZLN and the Revolutionary Law of Women

When the EZLN burst onto the international scene on 1 January 1994, a few observers noted that there were significant numbers of women among their ranks and that the temporary takeover of San Cristóbal had been directed by a woman whose nom de guerre was Major Ana María. Not until sixteen days after the now famous "Declaration from the Lacandon Jungle" was released did the newspaper *El Financiero* make mention of the the the "Women's Revolutionary Law" that was distributed simultaneously with the Lacandon declaration (Castellanos, 1994:4). It states:

> *First*, women have the right to participate in the revolutionary struggle in the place and at the level that their capacity and will dictate without any discrimination based on race, creed, color, or political affiliation.
>
> *Second*, women have the right to work and to receive a just salary.
>
> *Third*, women have the right to decide on the number of children they have and take care of.
>
> *Fourth*, women have the right to participate in community affairs and hold leadership positions if they are freely and democratically elected.
>
> *Fifth*, women have the right to primary care in terms of their health and nutrition.

Sixth, women have the right to education.

Seventh, women have the right to choose who they are with and should not be obligated to marry by force.

Eighth, no woman should be beaten or physically mistreated by either family members or strangers. Rape and attempted rape should be severely punished.

Ninth, women can hold leadership positions in the organization and hold military rank in the revolutionary armed forces.

Tenth, women have all the rights and obligations set out by the revolutionary laws and regulations (*Doble Jornada,* 1994:8).

The wide-ranging set of issues discussed in the law points to the importance of the EZLN as a political organization and suggests an underlying conception of democracy that includes the right of women to have full political participation and control over all decisions that affect their lives, whether in sexual matters, child raising, work, politics, or participation in a revolutionary organization. The issues highlighted in the Revolutionary Law of Women did not emerge spontaneously in the wake of armed struggle but came out of a sustained organizing context in which women slowly articulated the need for attention to their life experience as well as that of male campesinos.

The Cañadas region of Chiapas, which is the stronghold of the EZLN, is one of the most diverse areas of the state. The region is populated largely by migrants from other parts of Chiapas and elsewhere in Mexico who were encouraged to resettle in the Mexican frontier as part of colonization programs. Groups in the area include Choles from Palenque, highland Tzotziles pushed out of San Juan Chamula by traditional caciques aligned with the PRI, Tzeltal and Tojolobal Indians who were plantation workers or lost their land to local elites in the northern and eastern highlands, and landless mestizo farmers from a variety of states (Harvey, 1994:27; Ross, 1994:256; Rus, 1994). This ethnic diversity was further complicated by grassroots organizing efforts promoted by the church of liberation theology under the direction of Bishop Samuel Ruíz and independent peasant organizations and ejido unions promoted by Maoist activists of varying political lines (Harvey, 1993; 1994).

In 1976 three regional ejido unions were formed: Ejido Union "United in Our Strength" (Quiptic Ta Lecubtecel, UEQTL) in Ocosingo; Ejido Union "Land and Liberty" (Tierra y Libertad, UETL) in Las Margaritas; and Ejido Union "Peasant Struggle" (Lucha Campesina, UELC) in Las Margaritas (Harvey, 1994:29). Organizers from the Maoist-oriented Proletarian Line were active as advisers in each of these ejido unions. In the late 1970s a statewide effort to improve the terms of coffee marketing resulted in the unification of the three ejido unions as well as other smaller producer groups to form the Union of Ejido Unions and Solidarity Peasant Organizations of Chiapas (UU, often known as Unión de Uniones) (Harvey, 1994:30; 1993). UU focused primarily on peasant appropriation of the production process.

Many other sources of independent peasant organizing emerged in the 1970s and 1980s. The National Coordinator "Plan de Ayala" (Coordinadora Nacional "Plan of Ayala," CNPA), which takes its name from Zapata's 1911 plan to redistribute land, was founded in 1979 with ten regional peasant organizations. Their principal demands included "the legal recognition of long-standing indigenous land rights; the distribution of land exceeding the legal limits for private property; community control over and defense of natural resources; agricultural production, marketing, and consumption subsidies; rural unionization; and the preservation of popular culture" (Paré, 1990:85). CNPA participants included indigenous peoples with communal land or no land, minifundia peasants, peasants who were soliciting land, and some groups of small producers and agricultural wage workers.[2]

During the 1980s the CNPA began to experience debates about whether it should organize an autonomous women's presence within its ranks. The first effort toward this end came in 1981, but the national organization decided that an autonomous women's presence would be an invitation for internal division. A second attempt in 1984 during a CNPA congress resulted in the creation of a women's commission charged with organizing a national meeting of peasant women in 1986. Women in the CNPA were mobilized around organizing to create jobs, obtain social services, lower the cost of basic goods, and address health and educational issues.

The official report from the 1984 CNPA meeting reflected considerable dissatisfaction within the women's commission about the role of women in the organization. It stated that women had little participation in official negotiations with the state, received little political training, and had not participated in choosing authorities or reached positions of authority themselves within the CNPA. The commission enumerated particular problems related to women and asked for financial support, child care, and other resources that would help them to participate more fully in the CNPA. The official report also encouraged the inclusion of women's specific demands as part of those adopted by the organization, requested that women be given ejidal plots regardless of their marital status, and urged that the CNPA include at least one woman in its directorate (Documentos del Movimiento Campesino, 1984:123–126). Such efforts no doubt filtered down to other organizations, including those of the church, that formed part of the political terrain the Zapatistas encountered in the 1980s.

Subcomandante Marcos of the EZLN acknowledged that when he and a few other organizers first arrived in the Lacandon jungle, they had traditional leftist ideas about how to run a guerrilla organization. They viewed themselves as organic intellectuals in the revolutionary vanguard who would educate others. One of their biggest mistakes was to question the existence of God and the authority of Bishop Samuel Ruíz. They had chosen an area with over twenty years of varied organizing experience from different strains of Maoism as well as from the church. They had to adjust their organizational style to the political culture that had already been established by the church and a variety of peasant and indigenous organizations. This organizing style emphasized consensus and inclusion of everyone in the process, including women and children. As described by Guillermoprieto:

> The Maya communities' notion that no one person should be above any other, the Church's goal of empowering all members of a community and the secular organizer's belief in political mobilization—all translated into a working, if cumbersome democracy. Women were brought into discussions, children were given a voice. So successful were these efforts that decisions took hours, or weeks, or months of debate (1995:38).

According to the Zapatistas, the Women's Revolutionary Law went through a long process of discussion and consensus decisionmaking before it was adopted. In an interview during the peace accord dialogues with the government in San Cristóbal de las Casas in February 1994, EZLN Major Ana Maria commented on the birth of the Revolutionary Law of Women:

> They had given us the right to participate in meetings and to study, but there were no laws specifically relating to women. We protested this fact and that is how the Women's Law was born. We all decided that we wanted to write this law and we presented it in meetings in all of the communities. Men and women voted for it. There weren't problems. In the process of doing this we solicited the opinions of all the women in the communities. The women who are insurgents helped to write the law (Pérez and Castellano, 1994:12).

Women combatants interviewed by me in 1994 indicated that there were widespread discussion and exchange about the women's law within the EZLN.[3] Captain Mirabel stated:

> The laws are about women's rights to participate in organizations in accordance with their skills. No one is obligated to participate. The law also talks about how women should be paid a just wage. Sometimes women are paid less than men. This isn't fair if they do the same kind of work. . . . If a compañera is raped, then this rapist has to be punished. The compañeras from the small villages were the ones who insisted that this point be included. These are laws for women here. Not everyone has to adopt them. Other kinds of women can make other kinds of laws. Like women who are students. They can make their own laws. These are ours.

Men interviewed also spoke of the importance of respecting women according to the rank they had and as individuals. Major Eliseo explained, "We have to obey women who are our commanders, even if we don't want to. Of course that is hard for some men, but they have to learn." Not all of the women felt that the laws were easily adopted by men. Lieutenant Ana responded to a question about how well men obeyed the women's law with, "Well, they are supposed to obey, but it takes some men a long time to learn to obey women. I had a hard time with some of them."

For women who are combatants in the EZLN, making a commitment to the armed struggle entails many changes in lifestyle. Lieutenant Norma talked about changes in her life upon entering the EZLN:

> I joined when I was twelve years old. My whole family is part of the EZLN. I started working in social projects, in farming, and in health. Probably the most striking part of participating is the education you get. Especially for women. We were taught about our bodies, about reproduction, and about different diseases. As a young woman where I grew up we never learned about these things. We even heard about condoms. That is not something you hear about in most villages.

According to EZLN combatants, women are integrated into many different levels of the EZLN and into local councils. As detailed by EZLN members, those called insurgents live in military-style camps and go into communities to carry out political education and social welfare projects such as those mentioned by Norma. The militants, or "milicianos," continue to live in their communities, receive military training, and participate in coordinated local militias. Coordination among local militias appears to have been the first step in building a larger army to fend off the attacks of the White Guards (Guardias Blancas) of local landowners. Each community sympathetic to the EZLN organizes its own Clandestine Revolutionary Indigenous Council (CCRI) that incorporates local militants. The local CCRI then organizes local committees and elects officers in local assemblies who are responsible for communal safe houses, education, and health. These officers meet regionally to coordinate plans. Local CCRIs also elect representatives to four regional CCRIs, which in turn choose delegates to sit on the CCRI–General Command, well known for the communiqués it issues (Ross, 1994:287).

EZLN representatives have consistently stated that women are about 30 percent of the insurgents and are also representatives on local and regional CCRIs. The CCRI–General Command has two women among its eleven members. If local governance operates as it is described by the Zapatistas, this is a significant change in communities where women do not participate actively in local politics and community assemblies. According to Captain Mirabel:

> It has been very difficult to integrate indigenous women into the movement. It is very different than a group of students. They need a lot of support. What we are trying to establish is that women don't have to just work in the kitchen. Women are also capable of leading society and not just leaving this up to the men. They also have the capacity to govern. What happens is women aren't trained to do this. In the EZLN we have this opportunity. In all of the towns that we control there are women with local positions of responsibility and authority. Slowly things are changing. We have to start in each community and with young people. Most of the women in the EZLN are between seventeen and twenty years old.

Although it is difficult to assess the extent to which such changes have widely permeated society in the Lacandon, the example of the female Zapatista combatants, the dissemination of the Revolutionary Law of Women, and the dedication of local women to the EZLN provided an important political open-ing and a forum for discussion, and these trends have moved well beyond the communities under EZLN control. The vision of democracy projected by women in the EZLN demands democratization not only of formal political sys-tems and political organizations but also of the daily-life arena of marriage, family life, and work. In the state of Chiapas, many of the issues underlying the Revolutionary Law of Women have been taken up in a statewide coalition.

The Chiapas Women's Convention

The Chiapas Women's Convention was first formed in July 1994 in preparation for the historic first meeting of the National Democratic Convention in Aguas-calientes, Chiapas, called by the EZLN. The call for the convention came in mid-June after the Zapatistas rejected the government's thirty-four-point peace plan. The plan was widely discussed in base communities in the Zapatista area of support and rejected by a majority because it did not adequately address questions of political democracy that came to form the centerpiece of the con-vention platform. The convention focused on a range of themes, including (1) the peaceful transition to democracy; (2) constructing a new nation and ways to implement the eleven points of the EZLNs Lacandon declaration distributed that January (work, land, housing, food, health, education, independence, liberty, democracy, justice, and peace); (3) the structure and direction of a transition government; and (4) establishing a constitutional congress and rewriting the Mexican constitution (Stephen, 1995). Each state in Mexico held a statewide convention before the national meeting and elected delegates.

In order to ensure that women's issues were not diluted in the convention, women from twenty-five nongovernmental organizations and peasant and in-digenous groups came together to articulate the needs of women in the state of Chiapas. The women's program demanded an end to violence against women, including rape, used as a way of intimidating the civilian population by large landowners, their White Guards, and the army; demilitarization of the state of Chiapas; respect for human rights; economic justice; an end to discrimination against women; democratic processes and practices that include women in all levels of politics and representation; economic programs and training that allow women to take care of their families; equal rights under the law; the right for women to marry whom they please; equal rights with fathers and children; the right to decide how many children to have; the right to inherit property; and punishment for men who disrespect, rape, or mistreat women and who do not meet their obligations to their families.

The women elected five delegates to the National Democratic Convention who attended subsequent meetings of it. The Women's Convention continued to meet on its own and to provide a statewide network for women who work within mixed organizations (the majority of peasant and indigenous organizations) and in explicitly women's organizations. The Chiapas Women's Convention has also developed linkages with feminists in Mexico City and organized workshops on health, violence, and economic survival (Convención Estatal de Mujeres Chiapanecas, 1994). This is the first independent statewide women's network in Mexico and also the first large-scale organization of indigenous women.

The Women's Convention met again in October and November 1994 and in January 1995. At the third national meeting of the National Democratic Convention in Queretero in February 1995, the example of the Chiapas Women's Convention was followed at the national level. Before the meeting of the National Democratic Convention, hundreds of women from all over Mexico from "diverse ideologies, personal histories, ethnic groups, sexual preferences, religions and different political tendencies" met in the first National Women's Convention (Convención Nacional de Mujeres, 1995:1). Their manifesto called for a transitional government that would reject

> all forms of discrimination and oppression. A government that results from the coming together of free will, where women have the right to propose, decide and to represent themselves. The government of transition will not be democratic if it does not include the knowledge, ability, and sentiments of women. This government should be a space for the reformation of politics which considers generic democracy in all of the fields of public and private life (Convención Nacional de Mujeres, 1995:1).

The resolutions of many of the working sessions reflected concerns raised in the Revolutionary Law of Women and by the Chiapas Women's Convention. They included issues of women's control over reproduction, violence against women, rape, representation at all levels of government and in formal terms in the Constitution, and equal working conditions and pay.

The National Women's Convention (CNM) is one of the few sections of the National Democratic Convention (CND), along with the National Indigenous Convention (CNI), to take the disparate politics, alliances, and ideologies that have continually threatened to divide the CND and forge them into a unified platform that is being discussed locally and regionally. The National Women's Convention does not represent a majority of Mexican women, but its presence and the content of its manifesto have opened up critical space in the national discourse on women's rights, democracy, and what is meant by political participation.

Comparative Conclusions: Democracy, Neoliberalism, and the Integration of Public and Private Spheres

The discourse on democracy inspired by the Zapatista women and their revolutionary laws is featured front and center in the manifestos and documents of the Chiapas Women's Convention and the National Women's Convention. Democratization is proposed as a critical ingredient in improving the lives of women at all levels. In the demands of the Women's Regional Council of the CONAMUP, democracy takes more of a back seat to issues of economic survival, domestic violence, and women's representation within the CONAMUP. The agenda of the CONAMUP questions the legacy of structural adjustment and its implications for poor urban women, but the Chiapas Women's Convention and the CNM clearly state that without democratization at federal, state, and local levels and through legal reform of the Constitution, the poverty and economic inequality associated with structural adjustment cannot be effectively dealt with.

The coupling of demands for democratization with a call for economic justice poses a clear challenge to the neoliberal model implemented in Mexico over the past two decades. The Salinas government maintained that economic liberalism could go hand in hand with a transition to democracy, but history and the lived experience of many Mexicans have suggested otherwise. Continued questioning of the political system by both women and men and demands for a transition government by the Chiapas Women's Convention and the CNM indicate a sector of society that feels no progress has been made in achieving participatory democracy under a neoliberal economic model.

A renewed economic crisis set off by a major devaluation of the peso in December 1994 that resulted in double-digit inflation, interest rates of over 90 percent annually, and increasing unemployment has confirmed the suspicions of many men and women that economic liberalism not only is an economic failure but also creates a profoundly nondemocratic political culture. Mexican men and women watched as government officials negotiated with the United States and representatives from international banking and finance to salvage their economy. The result was a "rescue plan" that no one voted on, discussed, or was consulted about. People such as women active in the CONAMUP and the Chiapas Women's Convention expressed their opinions by taking to the streets and protesting tax hikes and increases in the costs of basic goods. Their belief in their right to participate in economic decisionmaking that affects their lives brought them out quickly and in force to challenge new austerity measures that are supposed to improve the economy but offer no relief for those who have nothing left to "adjust."

Women in Mexico City and in Chiapas have also used the theme of democratization to legitimize their right to self-determination in both public and private spheres. By arguing for the democratization of all spheres of Mexican social life in terms of gender equity, they have refused to recognize the dichotomy between public and private life that for so long has relegated women to what is called "the home" and has been used to exclude them from participating in a wide range of institutions commonly seen as "male."

Beneath the dichotomy of "feminist-strategic" needs versus "feminine-practical" needs is an assumption of a universal division between the public world of politics that is viewed as male and the private domestic world that is seen as female. Feminist anthropologists, including some such as Michele Rosaldo who proposed the existence of a universal male public and female private dichotomy to explain the universal subordination of women, later recanted and noted that universal dichotomies, including that of the public and private, reinforce the tendency to naturalize gender and for theorists to declare that women's present lot derives from what in essence women are. If gender and gendered behavior are a social construction, then neither women nor men can be intrinsically bound to particular spheres or sets of behavior. These categories tend to reflect more about the social and cultural world of social theorists than of their subjects. Anthropologists have demonstrated repeatedly that the neat division between public and private is a historically bound construction relevant to industrial societies at particular points in time. The daily-life world of many sectors of Latin American society is not built around such a division (Stephen, 1992).

If women in Mexico City and Chiapas are demonstrating the irrelevancy of public-private dichotomies, it makes no sense for observers of their movements to continue this false division and repackage what they do as either "feminine" (demanding women's traditional rights linked to the private concerns of mothering, being a wife, and raising families) or "feminist" (challenging women's gender subordination and breaking into the public sphere). In fact, women are taking action in both directions. As seen in the case of activists in the Women's Regional Council of the CONAMUP, even women within the same organization do not agree on the label for what they do together. Women activists must be conceptualized as having many different facets to their identity that will influence their interpretation and experience of political, social, and cultural events. Individuals also change their perspective over time. Although individuals do act collectively based on a partially shared experience or perception, each participates in many sets of social relations, including gender, kinship, race, ethnicity, nationality, and vicinity (Mouffe, 1988). These social relations and positions modify the meaning of particular events, demands, and ideas for people within the same movement. This does not mean, however, that they cannot act in concert to confront structural relations of power.

Rather than try to pigeonhole the actions of women in Mexico City and Chiapas according to a fixed structural framework, it seems more fruitful to look at the contributions their movements are making toward larger social change in Mexico. In a country whose mainstream political culture is often characterized by authoritarianism, corporatism, and clientelism, the democratic demands and models emerging from women's grassroots organizing and from other sectors as well are critical ingredients in beginning a transition to participatory democracy in Mexico.[4] In addition, the collective survival strategies being attempted by some groups such as the Women's Regional Council provide important alternative models to the trend of privatizing economic crisis.

Notes

1. The following discussion of the CONAMUP is condensed and somewhat rewritten from Stephen (forthcoming).

2. The following discussion of the CNPA and efforts to organize women within it comes from Stephen (1992).

3. Combatants and supporters of the EZLN were interviewed by the author in August 1994 in and around Guadalupe Tepeyac. Captain Mirabel's statements are from an interview conducted by Eduardo Vera in October 1994. All translations here and elsewhere in this chapter are by the author.

4 . Not all of Mexico shares a dominant political culture. Works such as that of Rubin (1996) and Knight (1990) suggest that corporatism has not permeated Mexico to the degree that many people imply.

Bibliography

Arizpe, Lourdes. 1977. "Women in the Informal Sector: The Case of Mexico City." *Signs*, 3(1):24–37.

Arizpe, Lourdes, Fanny Salinas, and Margarita Velázquez. 1989. "Efectos de la crisis económica 1980–1985 sobre la condición de vida de las mujeres campesinas en Mexico." In *El ajuste invisible: Los efectos de la crisis económica en las mujeres pobres.* Bogota, Colombia: UNICEF.

Benería, Lourdes. 1992. "The Mexican Debt Crisis: Restructuring the Economy and the Household." Pp. 83–104 in Lourdes Benería and Shelly Feldman, eds., *Unequal Burden: Economic Crises, Persistent Poverty, and Women's Work.* Boulder: Westview Press.

Benería, Lourdes, and Martha Roldán. 1987. *The Crossroads of Class and Gender: Industrial Homework, Subcontracting, and Household Dynamics in Mexico City.* Chicago: University of Chicago Press.

Bennett, Vivienne. 1992. "The Evolution of Urban Popular Movements in Mexico Between 1968 and 1988." Pp. 240–259 in Arturo Escobar and Sonia E. Alvarez, eds., *The Making of Social Movements in Latin America: Identity, Strategy, and Democracy.* Boulder: Westview Press.

Brugada, Clara, and Zenaida Ortega. 1987. "Regional de mujeres del valle de México de la Coordinadora Nacional del Movimiento Urbano Popular (CONAMUP)." Pp. 97–102 in Alejandra Massolo y Martha Schteingart, eds., *Participación social, reconstrucción mujer: El sismo de 1985.* Mexico City: Reproducción de Documentos de El Colegio de Mexico.

Castellanos, Laura. 1994. "Las mujeres de Chiapas, protagonistas invisibles." *Doble Jornada*, 7 February:4.

Convención Estatal de Mujeres Chiapanecas. 1994. *Escribiendo nuestra historia.* San Cristobal de las Casas.

Convención Nacional de Mujeres. 1995. *Manfiesto: Solo habrá patria para las mujeres cuando juntas luchemos por ella.* Queretero. Mimeo.

del Castillo, Adelaida R. 1993. "Covert Cultural Norms and Sex/Gender Meaning: A Mexico City Case." *Urban Anthropology* 22(3–4):237–258.

Dietz, Mary. 1992. "Context Is All: Feminism and Theories of Citizenship." Pp. 63–85 in Chantal Mouffe, ed., *Dimensions of Radical Democracy*. London: Verso.

Doble Jornada. 1994. "La ley revolucionaria de mujeres." 7 February:8.

Documentos del Movimiento Campesino. 1984. "Acuerdos y resoluciones del II congreso nacional ordinario de la CNPA." *Textual*, 5(17):115–127.

Foweraker, Joe, and Ann Craig, eds. 1990. *Popular Movements and Political Change in Mexico*. Boulder: Lynne Rienner.

González de la Rocha, Mercedes. 1989. "Crisis, economía doméstica y trabajo femenino en Guadalajara." Pp. 159–176 in Oliveira, 1989.

———. 1991. "Family Well-Being, Food Consumption, and Survival Strategies During Mexico's Economic Crisis." Pp. 115–128 in Mercedes González de la Rocha and Augustín Escobar Latapí, eds., *Social Responses to Mexico's Economic Crisis of the 1980s*. San Diego: Center for U.S.-Mexican Studies, University of California, San Diego.

———. 1994. *The Resources of Poverty: Women and Survival in a Mexican City*. Oxford: Blackwell Publishers.

Guillermoprieto, Alma. 1995. "Marcos and Mexico." *The New York Review of Books*, 42(4):34–43.

Gutmann, Matthew. 1994a. "The Meanings of Macho: Changing Mexican Male Identities." *Masculinities*, 2(1):21–33.

———. 1994b. "The Meanings of Macho: Changing Male Identities in Mexico City." Ph.D. dissertation, University of California, Berkeley.

Harvey, Neil. 1993. "Concertación, violencia y la legalidad imaginaria: Conflictos sociales en Chiapas, 1989–1993." Unpublished manuscript. Author in Department of Government, University of New Mexico, Las Cruces.

———. 1994. "Rebellion in Chiapas: Rural Reforms, Campesino Radicalism, and the Limits to Salinismo." The Transformation of Rural Mexico, no. 5. La Jolla, Calif.: Ejido Research Project, Center for U.S.-Mexican Studies.

Kaplan, Temma. 1982. "Female Consciousness and Collective Action: The Case of Barcelona, 1910–1918." *Signs*, 7(3):545–560.

Knight, Alan. 1990. "Historical Continuities in Social Movements." In Foweraker and Craig, 1990.

Lind, Amy Conger. 1992. "Power, Gender, and Development: Popular Women's Organizations and the Politics of Needs in Ecuador." Pp. 134–149 in Arturo Escobar and Sonia E. Alvarez, eds., *The Making of Social Movements in Latin America: Identity, Strategy, and Democracy*. Boulder: Westview.

Logan, Kathleen. 1990. "Women's Participation in Urban Protest." Pp. 150–159 in Foweraker and Craig, 1990.

Miller, Francesca. 1990. *Latin American Women and the Search for Social Justice*. Hanover, N.H.: University Press of New England.

Moctezuma, Pedro. 1983. "Breve semblanza del movimiento urbano y popular y la CONAMUP." *Testimonios*, 1(1):5–17.

Mogrovejo Aquise, Norma. 1990. "Feminismo popular en México: Análisis del surgimiento, desarrollo y conflictos en la relación entre la Tendencia Feminista y la Regional de Mujeres de la CONAMUP." Master's thesis, Facultad Latinoamericana de Ciencias Sociales.

Molyneux, Maxine. 1985. "Mobilization Without Emancipation? Women's Interests, the State, and Revolution in Nicaragua." *Feminist Studies*, 11(2):227–254.

Mouffe, Chantal. 1988. "Hegemony and new political subjects: Toward a new concept of democracy." Pp. 89–104 in Carl Nelson, ed., *Marxism and the Interpretation of Culture.* Urbana: University of Illinois Press.

Oliveira, Orlandina de. 1989. *Trabajo, poder y sexualidad.* Mexico City: El Colegio de México.

Paré, Luisa. 1990. "The Challenge of Rural Democratization in Mexico." *Journal of Development Studies,* 26 (July):79–96.

Pérez, Matilde, and Castellano, Laura. 1994. "'No nos dejen solas': Mujeres del EZLN. Nuestra esperanza es que nos traten con respeto, justicia y democracia." *Doble Jornada,* 7 March:10–12.

Ramírez Saiz, Juan Manuel. 1986. *El movimiento urbano popular en México.* Mexico City: Siglo XXI Editores.

Rodríguez, Vicki. 1995. "Women in Contemporary Mexican Politics." Proceedings of Conference on Women in Contemporary Mexican Politics. The University of Texas, April 1995. Mexican Center.

Ross, John. 1994. *Rebellion from the Roots: Indian Uprising in Chiapas.* Monroe, Maine: Common Courage Press.

Rubin, Jeffrey. 1996. *Decentering the Regime: History, Culture, and Radical Politics in Juchitán, Mexico.* Durham, N.C.: Duke University Press.

Rus, Jan. 1994. "The 'Comunidad Revolucionaria Institucional': The Subversion of Native Government in Highland Chiapas, 1936–1968." Pp. 265–300 in Gilbert Joseph and Daniel Nugent, eds., *Everyday Forms of State Formation: Revolution and the Negotiation of Rule in Modern Mexico.* Durham, N.C.: Duke University Press.

Sánchez Gómez, Martha Judith. 1989. "Consideraciones teórico-metodológicas en el estudio del trabajo doméstico en México." Pp. 59–80 in Oliveira, 1989.

Schirmer, Jennifer. 1993. "The Seeking of Truth and the Gendering of Consciousness: The CO-MADRES of El Salvador and the CONAVIGUA Widows of Guatemala." Pp. 30–65 in Sarah A. Radcliffe and Sallie Westwood, eds., *'Viva': Women and Popular Protest in Latin America.* London: Routledge.

Stephen, Lynn. 1992. "Women in Mexico's Popular Movements: Survival Strategies Against Ecological and Economic Impoverishment." *Latin American Perspectives,* 19(1):73–96.

———. 1995. "The Zapatista Army of National Liberation and the National Democratic Convention." *Latin American Perspectives,* 22(4):88–100.

———. Forthcoming. *Power from Below: Women's Grassroots Organizing in Latin America.* Austin: University of Texas Press.

10

Rural Reforms
and the Zapatista Rebellion:
Chiapas, 1988–1995

Neil Harvey

The January 1994 rebellion of the Zapatista National Liberation Army (EZLN) shook the foundations of the Mexican political system. In the name of the country's indigenous peoples, the EZLN declared war on the federal army and the government, called for the removal of the president, and demanded the holding of free and fair elections. Over 3,000 rebels took control of seven towns in the central highlands and eastern Chiapas and issued a call for all Mexicans to support their struggle for "jobs, land, housing, food, health, education, independence, liberty, democracy, justice and peace." Many analysts debated the causes of the uprising and its implications for the country. There was consensus that poverty, racism, and social inequalities had created the conditions for such a rebellion. Others went further, arguing that the Mexican government's neoliberal economic model was to blame and that it was therefore necessary to reorient the type of development strategy followed since the debt crisis of 1982. The government responded by maintaining that its economic reforms were part of the solution in Chiapas and not part of the problem.

Establishing causality between one factor and another is not easy, especially when there are so many local intervening variables as in the case of Chiapas. But it is also evident that the prospects of indigenous peoples are shaped by the changes the government has promoted, particularly when these directly affect their sources of income. For the majority of Chiapas state's 1 million Indians,

Research for this chapter was made possible by a grant from the Instituto de Investigaciones Sociales, UNAM. The chapter is drawn from a longer work on the Chiapas rebellion (Harvey, 1994) and is reprinted with permission of *Third World Quarterly*.

access to land and the cultivation of maize and coffee form the basis of their economy and their cultures. Thus, the restructuring of the coffee sector, the abandonment of maize producers in rain-fed areas, the signing of the North American Free Trade Agreement (NAFTA), and the modifications to Article 27 of the Mexican Constitution governing land tenure have a clear impact on the livelihood and expectations of the rural and indigenous population. The fact that the EZLN timed its uprising to coincide with the effective date of NAFTA demonstrated the link the guerrillas themselves had made between the government's economic model and its social impact. In one of the first EZLN declarations, Subcommander Marcos declared that NAFTA represented a "death certificate for the indigenous peoples of Mexico, who are dispensable for the government of Carlos Salinas de Gortari." The EZLN also called for the breakup of all latifundio holdings in Chiapas and the repeal of the reforms made to Article 27.

Regional factors shape the ways in which agrarian restructuring is felt, and the case of Chiapas has specific characteristics that cannot be generalized to the rest of the country. Nevertheless, Chiapas does share similarities with other predominantly rural states of the south and southeast where extreme poverty afflicts a large part of the indigenous population. The majority of the country's 2.5 million maize producers who will be unable to compete with cheaper U.S. imports are located in the states of Chiapas, Oaxaca, Guerrero, Puebla, and Veracruz. Unlike their northern counterparts, these farmers lack access to credit, irrigation, machinery, and marketing outlets. They have the clear perception that NAFTA threatens their livelihood without providing the means to convert to other crops or obtain alternative sources of income. The rebellion in Chiapas can be seen as an indication of the level of desperation being reached among the small farmers and as a warning that neoliberal restructuring in rural Mexico threatens not only campesino livelihoods but also political stability.

The uprising also occurred at a time when campesino movements in Mexico were beginning to respond to the new free trade environment. Since the 1970s, politically independent movements had fought first for land and then for the appropriation of the productive process. Both of these fronts of struggle had evolved within an institutional framework of extensive state intervention in rural development. This framework began to be transformed with the liberalization of trade in 1986 and the subsequent withdrawal of agricultural subsidies, the privatization of state enterprises, and the reforms to Article 27. In the early 1990s, the new challenge for campesino organizations became the defense of small producers in an increasingly liberalized market. The Chiapas rebellion revealed that the earlier struggles for land and autonomy were still alive, but it also demonstrated resistance to reforms that would force campesinos out of the market and off their land.

In this chapter I analyze the relationship between rural modernization in Chiapas and the Zapatista rebellion. To what extent did the reforms implemented by the Salinas administration accentuate existing inequalities in

Chiapas? Why was the government unable to defuse land conflicts through the policy of consensus building, known in Mexico as "concertación"? What might the rebellion imply for the future of campesino and indigenous movements in Mexico? In order to answer these questions, I have divided the chapter into six sections. In the first I contrast the decapitalized social sector in Chiapas with the modernizing private sector during the 1980s.[1] In the second I focus on the reforms in two particularly sensitive sectors, coffee and maize production. In the third I discuss the implications of the reforms to Article 27 in Chiapas and detail the context in which their announcement was received. I attempt in the fourth to illustrate some of the limits to the policy of consensus building during the governorship of Patrocinio González Garrido (1988–1994) by describing the selective approach to land conflict resolution and the manipulation of the National Solidarity Program (PRONASOL). The fifth section is a description of the role of the Catholic Church in the defense of human rights and the political conflicts that led up to the January 1994 uprising. In the conclusion I address the prospects for indigenous and campesino movements in Mexico in the light of the rebellion and the government's responses to the Zapatistas' demands.

Modernization and the Social Sector in Chiapas

In order to understand the impact of rural reforms in Chiapas, it is necessary to present some general characteristics of the social sector. The data in Table 10.1 are an indicator of the relatively poor level of development of ejidos and comunidades agrarias in Chiapas. Virtually all of the sector is dedicated to rain-fed areas. If each of the almost 200,000 ejidatarios and comuneros has five or six dependents, the population is over 1 million persons occupying a little over 3 million hectares of land, of which only 40.8 percent is classified as good for agricultural use. Maize is clearly the principal crop for most ejidos and comunidades agrarias, followed by coffee. However, the figures do not indicate the combination of crops within each ejido. Survey data for 1990 also revealed that 44.6 percent of ejidatarios possessed between 0.1 and 4.0 hectares, and 42.0 percent had plots between 4.1 and 10.0 hectares (SARH-CEPAL, 1992:3).

In terms of opportunities to convert to new cash crops, it should be noted that the sixteen soybean-producing ejidos were all located in the more developed Soconusco region. Ten percent of ejidos in Soconusco also had access to irrigation. As for the limited use of inputs, the category of "public services" tends to present a somewhat distorted picture of reality. This rubric includes electricity, drinking water, and paved and unpaved roads. The fact that three-quarters of the ejidos reported that they had unpaved roads (1,224) hardly constitutes access to public services. A more accurate indication is given by the low proportion that had paved roads (10 percent). Installation of electricity and drinking water was said to benefit 50 and 35 percent of ejidos, respectively (INEGI, 1991).

TABLE 10.1
The Social Sector in Chiapas in 1988

General characteristics		
Number of ejidos and comunidades agrarias	1,714	
Number of ejidatarios and comuneros	193,515	
Land surface in social sector	3,130,892 hectares	
Share of total land area in Chiapas	41.4 percent	
Land use in hectares and as percent of sector		
Agriculture	1,278,147 hectares	40.8 percent
Forestry	700,381 hectares	22.4 percent
Pasture	923,182 hectares	29.5 percent
Other uses	229,182 hectares	7.3 percent
Irrigation in hectares and as percent of sector		
Rain-fed area	1,225,831 hectares	95.9 percent
Irrigated area	52,316 hectares	4.1 percent
Principal crops by number of ejidos and communidades agrarias		
Maize	1,264	
Coffee	349	
Sugarcane	19	
Soybeans	16	
Beans	8	
Green vegetables	8	
Rice	3	
Inputs by number of ejidos and communidades agrarias and as percent of sector[a]		
Farm installations	495	28.9 percent
Tractors	318	18.6 percent
Agroindustry equipment	206	12.0 percent
Credit	951	55.5 percent
Public services	1,390	81.1 percent

[a] In the case of inputs, "percent of sector" refers to the percent of ejidos and comunidades agrarias with the corresponding input. For example, of the total 1,714 ejidos and comunidades agrarias 495, or 28.9 percent, have farm installations.

Source: "Encuesta nacional agropecuaria ejidal, 1988," published in INEGI, 1991, *Atlas ejidal del Estado de Chiapas, 1988.* Note that the number of ejidos and comunidades agrarias in Chiapas increased by 358 during the 1989–1992 period to 2,072 (PROCEDE, 1993:10).

According to the 1988 survey, 62.5 percent of the rural social sector in Mexico received credit in 1988. In Chiapas the figure was 55.5 percent. The regions with the lowest proportion of credit were Altos and Selva (30 and 38 percent, respectively). However, the validity of these figures is contradicted by other sources. More recent data show that at a national level, during the period 1985–1989 only 22.2 percent of ejidatarios and comuneros had access to credit each year, and this fell to 16.3 percent in 1990. In fact, between 1985 and 1990,

62 percent of producers in the social sector had no access whatsoever to agricultural credit (SARH-CEPAL, 1992:19). In Chiapas the number of producers
with credit for planting fell from an annual average of 20.4 percent in the period 1985–1989 to 12.7 in 1990, and only 5.7 percent of producers received
credit for machinery in the 1985–1990 period.

As productivity of basic grains declined, the growth of private-sector commercial agriculture boomed in Chiapas. The land area dedicated to new cash
crops of soybeans, peanuts, sorghum, and tobacco grew by 51.4, 64.5, 146.8,
and 194.9 percent, respectively. Production of these four crops grew by 150.8,
244.1, 144.8, and 261.2 percent in the same period. The more traditional export crops also continued to expand. Banana production increased by over 25
percent, and output of cacao and sugarcane doubled. For the 1982–1987 period
the volume of meat production also increased by over 400 percent, reflecting
the support that ranchers found in the state government (Thompson González
et al., 1988:225–230).

The modernization policies were continued by Governor Patrocinio González Garrido (1989–1993). In 1989 his government ordered the privatization
of two state-owned enterprises, the Chiapas Forestry Corporation (CORFO)
and the Pujiltic sugar mill.[2] The 1989–1994 government plan was also designed
to promote export agriculture through improvements to port facilities at Puerto
Madero and continued support for producers of sorghum, peanuts, soybeans,
and safflower. The most significant reforms of this period, however, concerned
the two main crops produced by campesinos in Chiapas: coffee and maize.

Reforms in the Coffee and Maize Sectors

After 1973 small coffee growers could sell part of their crop to a state agency,
the Mexican Coffee Institute (INMECAFE). With the economic crisis of the
1980s the position of INMECAFE declined. Its share of the market fell from
44 percent for 1982–1983 to just 9.6 percent for 1987–1988 (Hernández, 1991:
62). Like many of the state agencies in this period, it suffered from internal inefficiencies, corruption, and mismanagement. By 1988 the institute had an accumulated debt of approximately $90 million.

The response of the Salinas government in 1989 was to begin the process of
privatization. INMECAFE immediately withdrew from purchasing and marketing and reduced its provision of technical assistance. Although the reform
was originally designed to include the producer organizations in the transfer of
infrastructure, the plan lacked the necessary political will and much of the infrastructure lay idle or passed into private ownership.

In 1988 there were 194,000 coffee growers in Mexico cultivating over
560,000 hectares in twelve states. The skewed nature of production units in this
sector is well known. Of the growers, 71.3 percent have plots of less than two

hectares, 20.6 percent have between two and five hectares, and just 2 percent have over ten hectares (Hernández 1991:52).

Chiapas, Mexico's principal coffee-producing state, presents a similar pattern. There 73,742 growers occupy 228,264 hectares of land; 91 percent of producers have less than five hectares, and 116 private owners possess 12 percent of the area under coffee cultivation (Table 10.2). In the Selva region, of the almost 17,000 producers, 93 percent have plots of less than two hectares (Hernández, 1994).

At the same time that the state was withdrawing from coffee marketing, in June 1989 the International Coffee Organization failed to agree on production quotas, which caused the world price to fall by 50 percent. In the ensuing period the Mexican government did not support efforts by other Latin American countries to reestablish a quota system and increase the price paid to producers. Another consequence of Salinas's macroeconomic reforms that hurt coffee producers was the overvalued peso. Potential export earnings that might have offset lower world prices were lost as a result. Between December 1987 and December 1993 domestic inflation increased by 89.3 percent, and the exchange rate increased by under 50 percent. As a result, the cost of inputs rose faster than the principal source of income. In addition, in the absence of IMECAFE, marketing costs had to be absorbed by the producers themselves or alternatively through the reappearance of unregulated private intermediaries, known as "coyotes" (Hernández, 1994).

After the 1989 crisis it took over three years of negotiations and mobilizations by producer groups before the government agreed to an emergency support program. With less income and the simultaneous reduction of credit, thousands of growers were unable to invest in their crop. Both productivity and total output in the social sector fell by around 35 percent between 1989 and 1993. On average, small producers suffered a 70 percent drop in income in the same period (*La Jornada*, 23 January 1994:47). Most producers were

TABLE 10.2
Distribution of Coffee Producers by Plot Size, Chiapas and Mexico

Plot Size (hectares)	Chiapas	Mexico
up to 2	48,762	194,538
2–5	18,248	64,377
5–10	5,102	17,881
10–20	1,202	4,291
20–50	208	808
50–100	104	246
More than 100	116	178
Total	73,742	282,319

Source: Data from Instituto Mexicano del Café (IMECAFE), 1992, *Censo Cafetalero.* Mexico City: IMECAFE.

caught in a cycle of debt and poverty. Unable to repay loans because of the fall in prices and income, they became ineligible for new loans. The accumulation of debt in this sector reached approximately $270 million by the end of 1993. In these conditions thousands of small growers in Chiapas abandoned production in the 1989–1993 period.

As with coffee, Chiapas is Mexico's largest maize-producing state. Consequently, reforms in this sector, which began with the onset of the 1982 debt crisis, have been directly relevant to its indigenous population. Under the administration of Miguel de la Madrid (1982–1988), governmental subsidies to the agricultural sector decreased on average by 13 percent a year. Most of the country's 2.5 million maize producers faced higher input costs and declining access to credit. By 1987 the National Rural Credit Bank (BANRURAL) provided credit for only 37 percent of the area under maize cultivation and 43 percent in the case of beans. In contrast, it financed 52 percent of the land area dedicated to soybeans and 49 percent of sorghum cultivation (Robles, 1988). Peso devaluation made inputs more costly, but producers were partly protected by the guaranteed prices established by the government, which more or less increased in line with 1983–1986 inflation (Hewitt de Alcántara, 1992:10–12).

This situation began to deteriorate with the signing of the Economic Solidarity Pact (PSE) in December 1987. The pact was primarily designed to control inflation, which reached almost 200 percent in 1987. Its various renewals were aimed at controlling wages and prices as well as limiting further devaluation of the peso. Although inflation was brought down to under 20 percent by 1991, the agricultural sector suffered disproportionately. The real value of guaranteed maize prices fell behind the rate of increase in input costs. As a result, the proportion of maize producers operating at a loss jumped from 43 percent in 1987 to 65 percent in 1988 (Hewitt de Alcántara, 1992:13).

In Chiapas, the withdrawal of state support had a negative effect not only on output and productivity but also on the environment. In the Selva region many campesinos, unable to capitalize their production, continued to clear forested land for subsistence needs. Tropical soils are notoriously unsuited for sustainable agriculture once the biomass has been destroyed. The land may be good for just three or four cycles before it is turned into pasture for grazing and the process of deforestation begins anew. Thus, although the land area in Chiapas dedicated to maize increased by 20.6 percent between 1982 and 1987 (from 600,374 to 795,053 hectares), output of this crop in the same period fell by 19.6 percent (from 1.5 million to 1.25 million tons). The same trend was observed for beans (Thompson González et al., 1988:225–230).

The Salinas administration accelerated these trends with a series of institutional reforms that were also recommended by the World Bank. The bank conditioned the disbursement of new structural adjustment loans on a radical overhaul of the agricultural sector, calling for the privatization of state-owned enterprises and the gradual elimination of price supports and other input subsidies (McMichael and Myhre, 1991; Robles and Moguel, 1990; Gates, Chapter

3, this volume). The inclusion of maize and beans in the NAFTA negotiations represented the final break with policies to protect small producers. In Chiapas, as in Mexico as a whole, over 80 percent of ejidatarios grow maize. For over 70 percent of ejidos and comunidades agrarias in Chiapas, maize is the principal crop. As many authors have pointed out, Mexican producers cannot compete with the United States or Canada. Average maize yields in Mexico are 1.7 tons per hectare compared with 6.9 tons in the United States. Disparities in terms of technological development, subsidies, infrastructure, and climatological factors place Mexican producers at a great disadvantage (Calva, 1992).

As officials tried to determine how many maize producers would lose from free trade, the crucial issue became the fixing of new pricing mechanisms. Under NAFTA the Mexican government decided that guaranteed prices would have to be phased out and the international price gradually allowed to take its place. After several months of debate, Salinas announced PROCAMPO in October 1993, described by the SARH as "a new support program for the Mexican farm sector" (SARH, 1993).

Under PROCAMPO over 3.3 million producers of nine crops became eligible for direct payments to be made on a per hectare basis.[3] All those who had planted one of these crops during the period between December 1990 and December 1993 and who had been included in a national directory compiled by SARH during 1993 could request payment of 330 new pesos (US$103) for each hectare cultivated during the autumn-winter crop cycle of 1993–1994. The payments were due to be made at the time of harvest in March 1994. One of the distinguishing features of PROCAMPO is that it included 2.2 million farmers who produced solely for their own subsistence needs and had been isolated from any type of official credit.

Although welcoming the direct subsidy to the very poorest sector, critics of the program pointed out serious negative implications for small and medium farmers who depend on the sale of surplus maize for a significant part of their income. Because the replacement of Mexico's guaranteed price by the international price, scheduled for March 1995, would not be compensated for by the new direct payments, many farmers would have to convert to other crops (Bartra, 1993; Moguel, 1993). These implications applied to many producers in Chiapas. Contrary to popular opinion, the proportion of maize output in Chiapas sold on the market is much higher than that consumed by the family unit. According to the SARH-CEPAL survey, 67 percent of maize production in 1990 within the social sector of Chiapas was sold on the market, and 33 percent went to family consumption (SARH-CEPAL, 1992:92).

Implications of Ejido Reform in Chiapas

The reforms to Article 27 were announced in November 1991 and passed into law just three months later. Four of the main changes were the following: Ejido and communal land could be legally sold, bought, rented, or used as collateral for loans. Private companies could purchase in accordance with the legal limits for individual holdings. At a maximum, a company with at least twenty-five member-shareholders could acquire an area equivalent to twenty-five times the individual legal limit for the different categories of land. The reforms also allowed for new associations between capitalists and ejidatarios. Finally, in line with the intention of guaranteeing security for private property, the sections of Article 27 that allowed for campesinos to petition for land redistribution were deleted from the new law (Moguel, 1992).

In Chiapas the reforms were criticized by several organizations that had been struggling to gain ejido titles for many years. They also expressed fear that land ownership would be reconcentrated in the hands of a small elite. For example, under the new Agrarian Law of 1992 a company made up of twenty-five ranchers could also feasibly own an area equivalent to 12,500 hectares. The regional ranchers associations applauded the "valiant reforms to Article 27" that had guaranteed security of land tenure and would allow them to attract new investments. In one of their reports they revealed that foreign investors were interested in establishing modern farms for the fattening of cattle in Chiapas and developing the region's meat-processing industry (*El Financiero*, 10 June 1993:46).

The end of land reform also canceled the hope of many campesinos who still aspired to receiving land under the former legislation. At the same time, campesino organizations claimed that in Chiapas there existed several latifundio holdings that went beyond the legally permitted limits for private property. This argument was taken up by the EZLN, which demanded a full investigation of alleged latifundistas (*La Jornada*, 1 February 1994:5).

At a January 1992 workshop organized by the Diocese of San Cristóbal, representatives of different campesino and indigenous organizations concluded that the ejido reform was part of the government's general strategy in favor of private capital; that the spirit of the original law had been broken as the public interest was subordinated to individual interests; that the reconcentration of land in few hands was likely; and that the reform reflected the objectives of NAFTA. A more specific fear referred to the deepening of divisions within communities as village caciques (strongmen) moved to buy up land from poorer neighbors (Taller de San Cristóbal, 1992).

The direct effects of ejido reform were only gradually emerging by the end of 1993. According to officials of the National Agrarian Registry (RAN), only 100 of the state's 2,072 ejidos had requested the assistance of the government's certification program (interview, Registro Agrario Nacional, Mexico City, January 1994). The main problem with the reform concerned the lack of solution to a backlog of land petitions, known as the "rezago agrario." Although in 1992 the state government announced that it would purchase land in order to deal with the rezago, the program did not advance. Campesino leaders blamed the delays on bureaucratic inefficiency, the reluctance of private owners to sell, and collusion between functionaries and landowners. Although such delays are not unique to Chiapas, the need to speed up the process was clearly demonstrated by the rebellion.

In the Lacandon forest region the lack of definitive titles has been a major problem for many communities. The lack of legal definition not only increases the possibility of eviction by landowners or other campesino groups but also restricts access to credit. This obstacle hindered those ejidos that began to devote more land area to livestock in the 1980s (Leyva Solano and Ascencio Franco, 1993:274). The lack of secure titles further weakened the social organizations located in the area of rebellion.

One of these organizations, the ARIC (Asociación Rural de Interés Colectivo) Unión de Uniones, was particularly affected.[4] During 1992 its leaders proposed several measures to deal with the agrarian problem. In addition to its existing legal petitions, ARIC offered to buy land and asked for the redistribution of private estates that had been declared bankrupt. None of these proposals was taken up by the state government. For the president of ARIC, the reason was a familiar one: "The agrarian authorities are friends of the landowners. They carry out their studies and reject our petitions. In this past year we have gotten nowhere. The landowners are refusing to sell, and the [Secretaría de la Reforma] Agraria says the ranchers all have documents protecting themselves from expropriation. This is the case in Patihuitz, Avellanal, and La Estrella" (interview, January 1993). It is no coincidence that the EZLN has been able to recruit campesinos in precisely these subregions of the Lacandon forest.

It should also be noted that the Castellanos Domínguez government of 1982–1988 helped protect private landowners from possible expropriation by issuing more documents of inaffectability (certificados de inafectabilidad) than all the previous state governors combined. The main beneficiaries were the private ranchers who were issued 4,714 certificados, or 95 percent of the total number distributed in the state since 1934. By the end of this administration, at least 70 percent of private holdings was legally beyond the reach of agrarian reform (Reyes Ramos, 1992:119).

The Limits of Consensus Building in Chiapas

"The participation of campesinos as direct actors in their own reality is an essential condition for achieving rural modernization in Chiapas" (SRA, 1989). With these words the new official policy of consensus building was announced in Chiapas. Such a policy was a response to the unavoidable presence of independent organizations that had been built up since the 1970s. However, the policy of concertación lacked more permanent commitments, and by 1993 the concept was left as an unfulfilled promise. Although Governor González Garrido began by negotiating with a new set of campesino leaders, the space for achieving representation was restricted and became more so as time went by.

In 1989 the subdelegation of the Agrarian Reform Ministry (SRA) in Chiapas embarked on a plan to resolve eight of the most protracted land disputes in
the state. It sent out brigades of functionaries to the selected communities in
order to work with local people in devising solutions. One case was the indigenous community of Venustiano Carranza, which had seen a long and bitter
struggle for land with private cattle ranchers. As a result of this struggle, the
community had become divided into three political factions. One of these had
demanded the return of land that ranchers had taken over with the help of the
other factions. Supporters of the first group, known as the Casa del Pueblo,
were given over 2,000 of the 3,000 hectares they had been claiming.

Although the state government attempted to resolve some of the oldest conflicts, the new policy left out many other land petitioners. According to the
same subdelegation of the SRA, in 1989 there were 547 petitions awaiting solution in Chiapas representing over 22,000 campesinos. It was not surprising,
therefore, that new conflicts would continue to arise during the rest of the
administration.

At the same time, repression of campesino leaders did not abate. In Decem-
ber 1988 private gunmen at the service of a local landowner killed Sebastián
Pérez Núñez, a regional leader of the Independent Confederation of Agricultural Workers and Peasants (CIOAC). This was followed by the murder in
March 1989 of Arturo Albores Velasco, leader of the Emiliano Zapata Peasant
Organization (OCEZ). Repression became more frequent as the sexenio passed.
Several settlements in the municipality of Chiapa de Corzo were destroyed by
state police and landowners on two separate occasions in April 1990 and April
1991. Members of OCEZ claimed that the disputed lands were in fact covered
by a presidential resolution in their favor. In June 1990 six people were injured
when private gunmen shot at a crowd of over one hundred cane producers
who were demanding full payment for cane delivered to the Pujiltic sugar mill.
In July of the same year women from the highland settlement of San Felipe
Ecatepec staged a hunger strike in Mexico City's central square to demand a
hearing with the president. They protested the repression of their organization,
the National Council of Indigenous Peoples (CNPI), at the hands of the state
government. In October 1990 two members of OCEZ were injured when unknown assailants opened fire on a peaceful march from Venustiano Carranza to
Tuxtla Gutiérrez (Horizontes, 1990, 1991a, 1991b). In July 1991 a protest
march by 300 Indians from the Selva Lacandona was broken up by police in
Palenque using clubs and tear gas grenades. Seven leaders were arrested and
forced to sign confessions linking them to Central American guerrillas and drug
trafficking. They were protesting the illegal confiscation of timber by state police and the corruption of municipal authorities (Harvey, 1992). As will be discussed in the next section, agrarian conflicts evolved into political polarization
that pitted the state government against the principal defenders of indigenous

rights in Chiapas, the bishop and clergy of the Diocese of San Cristóbal de las Casas.

The limits of concertación were also illustrated by the reaction of Governor González Garrido to the federal government's antipoverty program, PRONASOL. In Chiapas, PRONASOL helped strengthen the National Indigenous Institute (INI), and it was through INI that some programs to support independent producer organizations were made possible. González Garrido did not like the fact that PRONASOL funds were controlled by functionaries who were accountable only to Salinas and who intervened in an attempt to centralize funds under Salinas's command. For example, in 1990 the regional director of the INI in Las Margaritas was forced to resign by Gonzalez Garrido after assisting independent organizations of small coffee producers to purchase a coffee-processing plant from INMECAFE. Then in March 1992 three top INI functionaries were arrested: the state director and the regional director and treasurer at the Ocosingo office. They were accused of corruption in the use of funds to support small-scale livestock activities. Local campesino leaders came out in their defense, arguing that their only crime was to have supported the projects of independent groups. Although they were later released, none could return to his previous post (*La Jornada,* 21 March 1992:13).

Although Chiapas ranks first in the number of local solidarity committees (8,824, or 8.26 percent of the national total), according to Moguel (1994) the figure is misleading because it includes any type of group that has received funds from the program. Most of these (7,474) participate in basic infrastructure and social welfare projects (Dignified Schools, Municipal Funds, and Children in Solidarity). These tend either to have a short time span between the disbursement of funds until the end of the project or, as in the case of Municipal Funds, to be tightly controlled by the local political bosses. One factor that contributed to divisions and unrest within indigenous communities was precisely the manipulation of Solidarity funds by municipal presidents loyal to the Institutional Revolutionary Party (PRI) and the state governor.

This manipulation was promoted by Governor González Garrido. For example, one of the programs designed to support subsistence farmers was the Credit on Demand scheme (Crédito a la Palabra).[5] This involved the disbursement of interest-free loans on an individual basis (principally to maize and bean producers) that when repaid were meant to be recycled in the form of new loans and investment in community welfare projects. Chiapas had the distinction of being the state with the highest recuperation rate. In 1992 88 percent of loans were repaid, and over 70 percent had been recuperated in 1993. However, the supposed benefits were not distributed equitably. Although loan recuperation was highest in the Altos and Selva regions, the share of the state's Solidarity credit these regions received fell between 1990 and 1993 from 23 to 16 percent and from 17 to 6 percent, respectively.

Part of the explanation for this paradox was the governor's political control of the program. In other parts of Mexico the repayment of Solidarity loans was used to generate new sources of financing for community projects. In Chiapas, by contrast, the governor created a state-level fund directly under his control. The disbursement of credit in this way favored political allies in the PRI and the National Peasant Confederation (CNC), strengthening the control exercised by municipal presidents and marginalizing independent organizations. A state-level Ministry of Community Participation, staffed by loyal PRI and CNC leaders, was set up in early 1992 in an effort to institutionalize these arrangements.

Solidarity as a whole was not such a threat to González Garrido as he had feared. Although Chiapas received more funds than any other state in the period 1989–1993, only 12 percent of these resources went to supporting agricultural production (Moguel, 1994). This is important to note given the effects of the rural reforms pointed out in the first section of this chapter. However, the program's limitations were compounded by the political manipulation at municipal and state levels. A clear indication of this was the way in which the Zapatista rebels directed much of their anger against municipal presidents. An immediate repercussion of the uprising was the resignation of the state delegate of the Ministry of Social Development (SEDESO) in January 1994. The new interim governor, Javier López Moreno, also announced his intention to meet with municipal authorities to investigate the misuse of Solidarity funds. During the first week of February 1994 several town halls were occupied by campesino groups calling for the dismissal of municipal presidents.[6]

Agrarian Conflicts, Human Rights, and the Church

The agrarian question in Chiapas was increasingly associated with the abuse of human rights and attempts to discredit the work of the Diocese of San Cristóbal de las Casas. The case that most illustrated this was the arrest in September 1991 of the parish priest of Simojovel, Joel Padrón, on charges of robbery, damages to property, and provocations. Campesinos belonging to the official CNC claimed that members of the CIOAC had evicted them from their land with the help of Joel Padrón. The state government attempted to condition the release of Padrón on a series of commitments from the bishop of San Cristóbal, Samuel Ruíz García, to order the eviction of alleged land invaders and declare his opposition to actions against private property. Ruíz was also requested to drop charges against police for the illegal detention of Joel Padrón and to order Padrón to leave Chiapas once released (Aguilar Zinser, 1991; Correa, 1993). Although these conditions were not accepted and charges against Padrón were eventually dropped, they were a clear indication of the governor's openness to the demands of ranchers and landowners. They also reaffirmed the central role of Samuel Ruíz, the Diocese of San Cristóbal, and the Centro de Derechos Humanos "Fray Bartolomé de las Casas" in defending indigenous rights.

Political pressure against the church increased in 1993. In March of that year two soldiers were killed in the Tzotzil community of San Isidro el Ocotal in Los Altos. Members of the community feared that the clandestine use of local timber would be discovered by the army, and the two soldiers were mistakenly identified as forestry agents.[7] The Centro de Derechos Humanos denounced the killings but also denounced the abuse of human rights carried out by soldiers in the arrest of thirteen suspects who were allegedly subjected to torture. Police returned to the community in April and May 1993 and carried out further illegal arrests and beatings. The original thirteen were eventually released without charges being brought against them (Minnesota Advocates for Human Rights, 1993:10–16). During the rest of 1993 political pressure against the Diocese of San Cristóbal increased, culminating in the efforts of the papal nuncio in Mexico to remove Samuel Ruiz from his position in Chiapas. The outbreak of the rebellion frustrated this move as Ruíz became a key mediator in negotiations between the EZLN and the government.

Until 1992 events in Chiapas had largely escaped national attention, but that began to change with a march of 400 Indians from Palenque to Mexico City in early 1992. The catalyst was another violent eviction by state police, this time of members of the Comité de Defensa de la Libertad Indígena (CDLI) who had gathered in Palenque on 28 December 1991. Their protest was to draw attention to the corruption of municipal presidents, the imposition of village authorities (agentes municipales), the failure of the government to carry out promised public works, the lack of solution to the rezago agrario, and their opposition to the reforms to Article 27. Over 100 were arrested and several people were beaten and tortured. The government used a 1989 reform to the state Penal Code in breaking up the demonstration. Articles 129 through 135 of this code classified participation in unarmed mass protests as threats to public order that were punishable by two to four years imprisonment.

The "Xi'Nich" march left Palenque on 7 March and arrived in the capital six weeks later.[8] In the meantime participants received national coverage in the independent press and solidarity from communities in Tabasco, Veracruz, Puebla, and the state of Mexico. The impact of the event on national consciousness was to display the repressive nature of the state government in Chiapas. It also coincided with a growing awareness regarding the conditions of indigenous peoples in the country (Cepeda Neri, 1992; Reyes Heroles, 1992; Bellinghausen, 1992). Although the marchers were able to gain promises of solutions from federal agencies, by the end of 1992 several of the demands had not been met. The state's Penal Code was not reformed; no police officers were ever brought to trial for alleged human rights abuses; and municipal presidents continued to impose agentes municipales. There were still thirty arrest orders out against CDLI members, and new public works had not begun.

In this context a new organization was formed in the Selva and Altos regions. In late 1989 the Alianza Campesina Independiente Emiliano Zapata

(ACIEZ) emerged in Altamirano, Ocosingo, San Cristóbal, Sabanilla, and Salto de Agua. In early 1992 it changed its name to ANCIEZ by adding "Nacional" to its title, claiming member organizations in six central and northern states. However, it was clearly strongest in Chiapas and had extended its base of support in just two years among Tzotzil, Tzeltal and Chol communities in the highland municipalities of El Bosque, Larrainzar, Chenalhó, Chanal, Huixtán, Oxchuc, Tila, and Tumbalá. The size of this movement was revealed by the march in San Cristóbal on 12 October 1992 to commemorate 500 years of indigenous resistance. Approximately half of the 10,000 Indians who participated were members of ANCIEZ. During the march the statue of Diego de Mazariegos, the Spanish conqueror and founder of Ciudad Real, was pulled down. Then in early 1993 ANCIEZ went underground, presumably to begin training for the armed rebellion. The clash with a federal army column in Ocosingo in May 1993 was the first clear sign of guerrilla activity, although the state government insisted that there were no guerrillas in Chiapas.

Conclusion

The social base of the EZLN was made up principally of Indians from municipalities in the Lacandon forest and central highlands of Chiapas who had felt the adverse effects of rural reforms and repression of their legal organizations. The crisis in the coffee sector, the withdrawal of price supports and other subsidies, and the reforms to Article 27 contributed to the radicalization of thousands of Indians who did not see solutions to the problems being achieved through the mechanisms of concertación. These mechanisms were selectively applied and manipulated politically by the state government. The sudden growth of ANCIEZ demonstrated its appeal in a political climate marked by increasing hostility to the Diocese of San Cristóbal and legal campesino organizations.

What does the Zapatista rebellion imply for rural development policy in Chiapas and Mexico more generally? On the one hand, some of the official statements made in the aftermath of the uprising indicate that little is set to change. The new interim governor of Chiapas told representatives of the ranchers associations that the reforms to Article 27 would not be amended. Private landowners in the area of conflict also declared that there were no latifundios in Chiapas and further land redistribution was not possible. For the state government the problem continued to be the lack of security of land tenure, not redistribution. At a national level, the minister of agrarian reform and the leader of the CNC also stated that the new Agrarian Law did not require modifications.

On the other hand, the federal government approved a new support program for small coffee growers and an emergency package to rescue the coffee harvest affected by the war. However, it still refused to back efforts of other producer countries to withhold surplus coffee from the international market in order to force higher prices. At the same time, the director of BANRURAL made it clear that the rebellion would not affect the bank's policy of ordering foreclosures on farms that fail to repay loans (*La Jornada*, 1 February 1994).

The federal government responded to the demands of the EZLN by trying to delink them from national policies, particularly its macroeconomic strategy. In this context, there will not be major changes in rural policy unless the other campesino and indigenous organizations articulate an alternative set of proposals and gain some form of political power within policymaking circles. In Chiapas a potential space for the emergence of new alternatives is the Council of Indigenous and Peasant Organizations (CEOIC), a network of 280 organizations formed at the end of January 1994. This council backed the demands of the EZLN for the repeal of the reforms to Article 27 and for an investigation into alleged latifundio holdings in the state. The CEOIC also called for reforms to Article 4 of the Constitution with the goal of creating a new section to stipulate the rights of indigenous peoples in Mexico. These would include the right to use natural resources in accordance with their social priorities and cultures, the right to consultation with all levels of government and private actors in decisionmaking processes affecting their lands and resources, and the right to elect their own authorities.

In 1992 the government reformed Article 4 by recognizing, for the first time, the multiethnic nature of the population. This measure was not enough to satisfy advocates of indigenous rights who demanded more specific and far-reaching changes. As a result of these different positions, the implementing legislation was not passed. Furthermore, in the context created by the Zapatista uprising, mobilization around the issue of indigenous autonomy increased, culminating in the declaration of five multiethnic autonomous regions in Chiapas in December 1994. Although the precise meaning and implications of autonomy remained somewhat unclear, CEOIC leaders were eager to point out that they did not equate it with secession or separation from the Mexican nation. Rather, the movement for autonomy should be seen as a struggle to redefine the relationships between indigenous peoples and the Mexican state in ways that permit those peoples to have more democratic control over their own economic, social, and cultural development. As of June 1995 no agreements on these demands had been reached. Indeed, any accord on indigenous peoples' autonomy can only result from the negotiations between the federal government and the EZLN.

Negotiations between representatives of the EZLN and the government's peace commissioner, Manuel Camacho Solís, were held in late February and early March 1994. The government responded to the Zapatistas' demands with a list of proposed reforms that included the breakup of latifundios in Chiapas for the purposes of redistribution. Significantly, the proposals did not meet the demand for the repeal of reforms to Article 27. The government instead offered to draw up a General Law for the Rights of Indigenous Communities. This law would guarantee that community lands could not be sold, rented, or used as collateral. It would also allow communities greater political autonomy. Other proposals included the formation of new municipalities in Ocosingo and Las Margaritas, repeal of the state Penal Code, antidiscrimination measures, and a program to ameliorate the effects of NAFTA for indigenous communities in Chiapas. These proposals were taken back to the EZLN bases for consultations and were rejected in June 1994. The Zapatistas argued that the proposals lacked guarantees of political reforms that could lead toward a real process of democratization. Camacho resigned as peace commissioner, and the government's new envoy was unable to restart direct talks.

The EZLN turned its attention to the support groups and networks of civil society that had been instrumental in halting the armed phase of the war. The Zapatistas proved very effective in convening a National Democratic Convention in August 1994 at Aguascalientes, an ejido in Zapatista territory. This initiative was designed to gain popular support for the EZLN's political strategy of bringing about a democratic transition through peaceful means. Stating that it would not impede the 21 August presidential elections, the EZLN nevertheless declared the unviability of the PRI government and the dominant party system and called for the formation of a transition government that would convene a constitutional assembly to draw up a new federal constitution.

The failure of the government to assure clean elections further antagonized the EZLN and many of its civilian supporters. The problems of fraud were particularly evident in the Chiapas governorship race, held on the same day as the national elections. The PRI candidate, Eduardo Robledo, was declared the winner and installed as governor in December, despite the threat of renewed armed conflict. The EZLN responded by occupying the county seats of thirty-eight municipalities in the central and northern highlands of Chiapas before retreating again in the face of federal troop movements. Negotiations between the two sides appeared to be resuming when the new interior minister met with EZLN leaders and Subcomandante Marcos in mid-January 1995. However, less than a month later President Zedillo announced that several EZLN cells operating in central Mexico had been discovered and that arrest orders had been issued against their leaders, including Marcos, whom government investigators claimed to have identified as Rafael Sebastian Guillen, a former university professor from Tampico. There followed a rapid deployment of federal troops, who retook villages in EZLN-controlled areas of Chiapas. A broad counterinsurgency plan accompanied the military operations, including the provision of much needed financial support to loyal campesino organizations and leaders. When talks finally resumed in April 1995, the EZLN was severely limited as a military force, although it continued to command considerable respect and legitimacy within Mexican society. The armed offensive against Zapatista bases was condemned in a series of mass demonstrations throughout the country, and brigades of sympathizers helped provide food and assistance to those displaced by the federal army.

In this context, attention necessarily shifted from the substantive issues that led to the rebellion, including rural poverty and development, to the immediate issues of physical survival. When talks resumed again in April, the only item on the agenda was the separation of the two armies and the establishment of guarantees for negotiators and the indigenous communities. In the face of the overwhelming military might of government troops, the EZLN looked again to allies and supporters in civil society to help build a national movement for democratic change that would strengthen its negotiating position. It remains to be seen if such a movement is able to consolidate itself and provide the platform to continue the struggle for progressive reforms.

With regard to the campesino and indigenous movements in Mexico, the Chiapas rebellion presented challenges in at least three areas. First, the assertion of indigenous rights introduced a relatively neglected dimension into discussion of new policies. Official as well as independent movements had tended to adopt the same productivist discourse as the state, calling for subsidies, price supports, inputs, and access to markets. The cultural meanings attached to notions of development continued to be those of the dominant sectors. The EZLN, in contrast, advocated a project of development in which indigenous knowledge and cultures were central rather than peripheral elements. In this respect, one of the Zapatistas' demands was to overcome excessive centralism in the Mexican political system through a new federal pact that allowed regions, municipalities, and indigenous communities to govern themselves with political, economic, and cultural autonomy. This struggle for local autonomy challenges the traditional form of campesino mobilization, namely the presentation of demands to agencies of the federal government and the executive. As the state withdraws from the rural sector, earlier strategies of petitioning and mobilization may be losing their effectiveness, and the option of local autonomy and decentralization of control over resources may present a more fruitful path for rural social movements in the future.[9] Further research would reveal to what extent the struggle for autonomy is replacing the more familiar patterns of mobilization and negotiation.

Second, whereas most campesino movements tended to avoid the electoral arena as they concentrated on productive projects and negotiations with state officials, the EZLN has demonstrated the type of linkages that can be formed between economic and political struggles at the local and regional levels. The lack of governmental accountability and the partisan use of public funds were seen in the way in which PRONASOL was managed in Chiapas. The immediate enemies for the Zapatistas were the region's municipal presidents. With a few notable exceptions, the campesino movement had neglected the control exercised through the PRI's local allies, preferring to try to bypass municipal power and establish direct linkages with federal agencies. Yet this strategy has been frustrated by the political intervention of municipal presidents and state governors. The removal of the INI officials in Las Margaritas and Ocosingo may not have been so inevitable if political power had been less monopolized. Only where social movements have contested municipal politics have they been able to use PRONASOL funds and other federal programs effectively to their own advantages.[10] Future research on campesino movements must take account of the importance of municipal politics.

Finally, the campesino movement can no longer concern itself with purely agricultural issues. Migration and temporary employment in capitalist agriculture have been increasing and are likely to continue in the free trade era. The composition of regional organizations is changing accordingly. Women, children, and indigenous people now make up the majority of temporary workers, in contrast to the traditional image of male mestizo adults. The issues that concern these workers are no longer restricted to conditions at the point of production but also involve access to decent housing and basic services in the provincial towns and cities where they settle. Not only are the demands new, but also the patterns of organization and identity are changing. Gender and ethnicity play a greater role in recruitment of new members and development of new strategies of resistance and mobilization. In Chiapas the lack of basic services was as important as agricultural issues in the mobilization of indigenous communities during the 1970s and 1980s. The pastoral work of the Catholic Church was designed to promote women's participation in cooperatives and health and literacy projects. The EZLN also made a clear strategic decision to recruit young indigenous women into its ranks. As a result, approximately one-third of the EZLN is made up of women. Other rural movements in Chiapas and Mexico should learn from this experience and overcome traditional organizational structures that tend to marginalize women.

The rapidity of change in rural Mexico has challenged the campesino movement to develop new strategies in defense of the social sector. The new era of deregulation and free trade is modifying the institutional framework that for a long time characterized state-campesino relations. The Zapatista uprising also represented the emergence of a new force in rural politics. In the future greater attention must be given to the cultural construction of development, the relationship of social struggles to the transformation of political power, and to the changing composition and identity of rural movements. The 1 January 1994 uprising was a watershed not only for the political system but also for the campesino and indigenous movement in Mexico.

Notes

1. The social sector is composed of individual small holdings of less than ten hectares and lands redistributed under Mexico's agrarian reform program, either as ejidos or

comunidades agrarias. The former refers to land given to petitioners from the breakup of private holdings or the colonization of unused land. The latter refers to the transfer of land back from private ownership to indigenous communities. The recipients are known as ejidatarios and comuneros. By 1992 there were almost 30,000 ejidos and comunidades agrarias in Mexico, representing just over half the land surface.

2. The mill was sold for approximately $14 million (42,000 million old pesos) to the Empresa Operadora Grijalva. The Pujiltic sale caused discontent among the cane growers who had been arguing for the transfer of the mill to their ownership.

3. These were maize, beans, sorghum, soybeans, rice, wheat, safflower, barley, and cotton.

4. The Asociación Rural de Interés Colectivo generally refers to an umbrella association for several smaller associations of ejidos. The ARIC Unión de Uniones was formed in March 1988 with six ejido associations (known as uniones de ejidos) located in the municipalities of Ocosingo, Altamirano, and Las Margaritas, representing over 12,000 Indian families.

5. Information contained in this section is drawn from Cano (1994). In Chiapas the program was renamed Crédito a la Solidaridad by González Garrido.

6. The announcement in August 1993 of a further $55 million for social projects in the border region of Chiapas obviously came too late to forestall the rebellion. Solidarity moneys were also allegedly used for such nonpriority works as the construction of hundreds of basketball courts, a sumptuous convention center in Tuxtla Gutiérrez, and the refurbishment of central parks and town halls (Hughes, 1994).

7. Despite a 1989 ban on exploitation of forestry resources in Chiapas, this activity has continued for lack of adequate alternative sources of income. Moreover, the ban has led to several conflicts with the police and army. The July 1991 protests in the Selva originated in application of the 1989 decree.

8. "Xi'Nich" is the Chol word for ants. One of the leaders of the march explained how the government had tried to stamp out the Palenque demonstration but had only succeeded in disturbing an ant's nest.

9. The question of autonomy in rural social movements is raised by several contributors to Moguel et al. (1992).

10. Two examples from Oaxaca are the Worker, Peasant, and Student Coalition of the Isthmus (COCEI) and the State Network of Coffee Producers of Oaxaca (CEPCO).

Bibliography

Aguilar Zinser, Adolfo. 1991. "Todo en Chiapas es Centroamérica." *El Financiero*, 21 October, p. 56.

Bartra, Armando. 1993. "¿Subsidios para qué? Los quiebres finisexenales de la política rural." *La Jornada del Campo*, supplement of *La Jornada*, 26 October, pp. 5–7.

Bellinghausen, Hermann. 1992. "Xi'Nich y la cultura de la victoria." *La Jornada*, 27 April, p. 26.

Calva, José Luis. 1992. *Probables efectos de un tratado de libre comercio en el campo*. Mexico City: Fontamara.

Cano, Arturo. 1994. "Lo más delgado del hilo: Pronasol en Chiapas." *Reforma*, 23 January, pp. 3–7.

Cepeda Neri, Alvaro. 1992. "Chiapas: La lucha por los derechos humanos." *La Jornada*, 21 April, p. 5.

Correa, Guillermo. 1993. "En cuatro años, Patrocinio estableció en Chiapas récord de violaciones a los derechos humanos." *Proceso*, no. 845, 11 January, pp. 6–10.

Harvey, Neil. 1990. "Peasant strategies and corporatism in Chiapas." Pp. 183–198 in Joe Foweraker and Ann Craig, eds., *Popular Movements and Political Change in Mexico*. Boulder: Lynne Rienner Publishers.

———. 1992. "Conservación a costa de la miseria." *Campo Uno*, supplement of *Unomásuno*, 1 and 8 June.

———. 1994. "Rebellion in Chiapas: Rural Reforms, Campesino Radicalism, and the Limits to Salinismo." Pp. 1–43 in *Transformation of Rural Mexico*, no. 5. La Jolla, Cali.: Center for U.S.-Mexican Studies, University of California, San Diego.

Hernández, Luis. 1991. "Nadando con los tiburones: La experiencia de la Coordinadora Nacional de Organizaciones Cafetaleras." *Cuadernos Agrarios*, 1 (January–April):52–75.

———. 1994. "El café y la guerra." *La Jornada*, 30 January, pp. 1, 48.

Hewitt de Alcántara, Cynthia. 1992. *Economic Restructuring and Rural Subsistence in Mexico: Maize and the Crisis of the 1980s*. Geneva: UNRISD Discussion Paper 31.

Horizontes. 1990. *Boletín del Centro de Derechos Humanos "Fray Bartolomé de Las Casas."* No. 2, San Cristóbal de Las Casas, Chiapas. November.

———. 1991a. *Boletín del Centro de Derechos Humanos "Fray Bartolomé de Las Casas."* No. 3, San Cristóbal de Las Casas, Chiapas. March.

———. 1991b. *Boletín del Centro de Derechos Humanos "Fray Bartolomé de Las Casas."* No. 4–5, San Cristóbal de Las Casas, Chiapas. September.

Hughes, Sally. 1994. "You Can't Eat Basketball Courts." *El Financiero International*, 24–30 January, 1994, p. 15.

INEGI (Instituto Nacional de Estadística, Geografía e Informática). 1991. *Atlas ejidal del Estado de Chiapas. Encuesta nacional agropecuaria ejidal, 1988*. Aguascalientes: INEGI.

Institute Mexicano del Café, 1992. *Censo cafetalero*. Mexico City: IMECAFE.

Leyva Solano, Xochitl, and Gabriel Ascencio Franco. 1993. "Apuntes para el estudio de la ganaderización en la Selva Lacandona." Pp. 262–284 in *Anuario de cultura e investigación 1992*. Tuxtla Gutiérrez, Chiapas: Instituto Chiapaneco de Cultura.

McMichael, Phil, and David Myhre. 1991. "Global Regulation vs. the Nation-State: Agro-Food Systems and the New Politics of Capital." *Capital and Class*, 43:83–105.

Minnesota Advocates for Human Rights. 1993. *Civilians at Risk: Military and Police Abuses in the Mexican Countryside*. New York: World Policy Institute. North America Project Special Report 6.

Moguel, Julio. 1992. "Reforma constitucional y luchas agrarias en el marco de la transción salinista." Pp. 261–275 in Moguel, et al., 1992.

———. 1993. "Procampo y la vía campesina de desarrollo." *La Jornada del Campo*, supplement of *La Jornada*, 26 October, pp. 8–9.

———. 1994 "Chiapas y el Pronasol." *La Jornada del Campo*, supplement of *La Jornada*, 25 January, pp. 7–8.

Moguel, Julio, Carlota Botey, and Luis Hernández, eds. 1992. *Autonomía y nuevos sujetos sociales en el desarrollo rural*. Mexico City: Siglo XXI Editores and Centro de Estudios Históricos del Agrarismo en México.

PROCEDE (Programa de Certificación de Derechos Ejidales y Titulación de Solares Urbanos). 1993. *Documento guía*. Mexico City: Procuraduría Agraria.

Reyes Heroles, Federico. 1992. "Esa vergüenza nacional." *La Jornada,* 22 April, p. 19.

Reyes Ramos, María Eugenia. 1992. *El reparto de tierras y la política agraria en Chiapas, 1914–1988.* Mexico City: Universidad Nacional Autónoma de México and Centro de Investigaciones Humanísticas de Mesoamérica y del Estado de Chiapas.

Robles, Rosario. 1988. "El campo y el pacto." *El Cotidiano,* 4(23):65–72.

Robles, Rosario, and Julio Moguel. 1990. "Agricultura y proyecto neoliberal." *El Cotidiano,* 7(34):3–12.

SARH (Secretaría de Agricultura y Recursos Hidráulicos). 1993. "PROCAMPO: A New Support Program for the Mexican Farm Sector." Mexico City: SARH, mimeo.

SARH-CEPAL (Secretaría de Agricultura y Recursos Hidráulicos and Comisión Económica para América Latina y el Caribe). 1992. *Primer informe nacional sobre tipología de productores del sector social.* Mexico City: Subsecretaría de Política Sectorial y Concertación.

SRA (Secretaría de la Reforma Agraria), Subdelegación de concertación agraria en zonas indígenas. 1989. "Acciones agrarias." Tuxtla Gutiérrez, Chiapas, mimeo.

Taller de San Cristóbal. 1992. "Reformas al artículo 27 constitucional." Unpublished workshop proceedings. San Cristóbal de las Casas, Chiapas.

Thompson González, Roberto, Ma. del Carmen García Aguilar, and Mario M. Castillo Huerta. 1988. *Crecimiento y desarrollo económico en Chiapas, 1982–1988.* Tuxtla Gutiérrez: Universidad Autónoma de Chiapas.

11

Crossing Borders: Labor Internationalism in the Era of NAFTA

Barry Carr

Mexico's march toward the internationalization of its economy and society was initiated by the country's accession to the General Agreement on Tariffs and Trade (GATT) in 1986 and greatly accelerated by the government of Carlos Salinas de Gortari and the signing of the North American Free Trade Agreement (NAFTA). But the exquisite timing of the 1994 Chiapas rebellion demonstrates that globalization is eliciting some unusual and largely unforeseen responses (Cleaver, 1994). More than a decade of frenzied neoliberalism—privatization, deregulation of the economy, the demolition of populist traditions, and attempts to roll back the "strong state"—was designed to encourage and placate domestic and, especially, foreign capital. However, the challenge of globalization has also promoted the development of a complex web of cross-border coalitions embracing labor organizations and activists, immigrant rights workers, and environmentalists. Grassroots activists have been given an unparalleled opportunity to raise major issues before the public, "crashing their way into the trade policy arena," as one scholar described the process that links trade, labor, human rights, and environmental issues in a way never seen before in the Americas (Mumme, 1993:215). Globalization has clearly changed the dynamics of debate, making politics less predictable (Thorup, 1991, 1992).

In this chapter I identify some of the key strands of transborder internationalism in which North American and Mexican workers and unions have been involved this century. Noted is the degree to which many of these forms of internationalism were contingent on factors that in the 1990s are weaker or nonexistent. In particular, I underline the dependence of earlier internationalisms and solidarities on the radical grand narratives (the many "isms"—anarchism, Marxism, and communism) that have been weakened by the collapse

209

of the Cold War and the waning of optimism about projects of global transformation. Also identified are several forms of transborder internationalism
that have emerged during the 1990s, partly in response to the challenge posed
by free trade, globalization, and their local manifestation in NAFTA.

The first section includes some cautions about the ambiguities present in the
term "labor internationalism." Next I identify some of the factors that promote
and constrain international labor solidarity and cooperation. Throughout the
chapter there are references to some significant examples of transborder networking and cooperation. The conclusion drawn is not an uncritical celebra-
tion of the reemergence of transborder labor internationalism but rather the
observation that it exhibits a striking asymmetry—a situation in which initiatives flow mainly in only one direction (from north to south) and in which
Mexico is frequently constructed as the "problem" rather than as a source of
ideas and experiences on which a nonpaternalistic, trinational labor practice
can be constructed.

Labor Internationalism: Cautions and a Definition

Labor internationalism has changed over time and taken a wide variety of
forms, including cooperation and exchange within centralized organizations
affiliated with one of the Cold War–era blocs; the activities of "official" organs
of workers in the same industries in different countries; and the sponsorship of
horizontal relations among rank-and-file workers of several countries with or
without the support of their union leaderships. The content of labor internationalisms has also varied along other lines, consisting of the sharing of economic data among workers in subsidiaries of the same transnational firm;
exchange of visits by rank-and-file unionists; the establishment of sister locals;
the forging of solidarity campaigns to support strikes and demand the release
of imprisoned unionists; struggles for the implementation of international
labor rights and standards; and the establishment of ties among labor activists
and human rights, women's, and indigenous peoples' organizations.

The topic here is labor, not socialist, internationalism. As the overview of the
early history of Mexican-U.S. labor internationalisms will demonstrate, the two
forms have frequently merged, one subsuming the other. Internationalisms
centered on relations among individuals and groups in different countries need
not be based on commonly recognized historical objectives and therefore not
on "a universalistic and ultimate vision of history," although this has been the
case with many internationalisms of the Left in the past (Mires, n.d., cited in
Waterman, 1991:11).

It is also important to distinguish among the different levels on which labor
internationalism unfolds and among the protagonists involved. Are the actors
involved in the internationalisms discussed in this chapter "abstract" classes,

grassroots workers, national organizers of unions and parties, or theoreticians (Waterman, 1991:19)? One could also make a distinction between labor internationalism and trade-union internationalism, although in this case as well the two are constantly conflated. Labor internationalism is a much broader phenomenon because it may incorporate "new" actors and issues (of the kinds associated with "social movements") as well as issues traditionally not directly related to the politics of the workplace.

It is also important to recognize that much of the activity that has been labeled "labor internationalism" stresses the kinds of "lobbying and legislative activity and . . . new international institutions and arrangements which do not involve ordinary working people and which they are unlikely to be able to control" (Waterman, 1991:47). The distinction here is between labor internationalist action that privileges political lobbying and that which targets individuals and groups involved in production and in the communities in which workers live. The choice is acknowledged by some participants in labor internationalist actions—hence these remarks (in a somewhat syndicalist tone) of Baldemar Velázquez, a leader of the Farm Labor Organizing Committee (FLOC) in Ohio that has developed close links with Mexico's Union of Agricultural Workers and Peasants (SNTOAC), a farm workers union affiliated with the Confederation of Mexican Workers (CTM):[1]

> Political lobbying uses up resources and personnel time in an area workers do not
> control and rarely win. FLOC considers it a dead-end response for labor in this
> country. Why waste time with it? Why not organize the industries and negotiate
> directly with the people who are going to make the difference? In general, legisla-
> tion may involve important philosophical concepts, but it isn't a reality that will
> make the difference in favor of working people in this country (Velázquez and
> Blackwell, 1993:23).

One must, therefore, rigorously query references to the "grassroots orientation" of labor internationalism. It is always possible that the new internationalist networks may be responding to the careerist needs of "specialists" in the communications and networking community rather than to the needs of grassroots workers. In an interesting experiment conducted in 1991 in Hong Kong, Derek Hall compared responses to a message he had posted about solidarity with a new autonomous Indonesian labor union with responses to news of a "rewarding academic job opportunity." There were plenty of responses to the latter and very few to the former (Waterman, 1992:72, fn. 28).

Finally, judgments ought to be made with caution. During a period of declining fortunes for organized labor, there are already signs of a tendency among writers and activists to indulge in the wishful thinking characteristic of many traditional revolutionary groupings faced with declining fortunes. Analysis should steer away from "constant emphasis on the hopeful signs, deemphasis on the setbacks, discussion in generalities only, clutching at each straw and a refusal to acknowledge the possibility of ultimate failure" (Hawarth and Ramsey, 1988:309).

Transborder Internationalisms: Historical Precedents

From Mutual Solidarity . . .

Certain workers have played a major role in carrying the seeds of internationalism in the Americas. In some cases, mobility was built into the nature of a particular work process. Sailors are a prime example. One thinks of the seamen who were members of radical maritime unions that, unlike much of the early American Federation of Labor (AFL), were open to nonwhites, women, and the foreign-born. For example, the Maritime Transport Workers Union (MTWU), affiliated with the Industrial Workers of the World (IWW), spread the Wobbly message and the principles of industrial unionism throughout the period of its existence—from 1913 to the mid-1920s. Spanish-speaking members of the IWW based in east-coast U.S. ports were active in carrying propaganda and forming MTWU branches in cities all over the Caribbean, Mexico, and Central and South America. A particularly vivid Mexican example was the Wobbly presence in the port city of Tampico and the petroleum camps of Veracruz and Tamaulipas states in northeastern Mexico (Bird et. al, 1985:177–178, Zogbaum, 1991). In the 1930s, this internationalist crusade was picked up by the Marine Workers Industrial Union (MWIU) (affiliated with the CPUSA's "Third Period" Trade Union Unity League) and later by the Congress of Industrial Organizations (CIO) (Richmond, 1972:202–214, Nelson, 1990: chap. 1). U.S. railroad worker brotherhoods also played a significant role in extending trade union organization beyond the borders of the United States before the outbreak of the Mexican Revolution, although the racism and ethnic exclusivism shown by American railroad workers employed in Mexico were almost as striking as their union proselytization (Parlee, 1984).

Another important zone in which links developed between workers in Mexico and the United States at an early stage was in the geographically contiguous border regions of the two countries—in particular, Sonora, Chihuahua, California, Arizona, New Mexico, and Texas. The background dynamic was the agricultural, mining, and industrial expansion of the United States westward and southwestward and the (in many ways linked) economic and demographic expansion of northern Mexico in the period before World War II. These economic developments provided the material base upon which a new bloc of "border proletarians" could develop.

There were many sites of transborder union cooperation, including the Arizona and Sonora copper mining zone where Mexican-U.S. worker links arose in the period when the Western Federation of Miners and the exiled Mexican Liberal Party (PLM) assisted Mexican miners at the U.S.-owned Cananea copper mines. These links, which were facilitated by the size of the Spanish-speaking workforce in such U.S. mine companies as Phelps Dodge, operated intermittently until the late 1940s when the Cold War destroyed the last carriers of this tradition, the leftist International Union of Mine, Mill, and Smelter Workers.

The smelting and refining plants of El Paso, Texas, were another important location. The organization of Mexican workers in the plants of American Smelting and Refining (some of whom lived in Ciudad Juárez and commuted to AS&R's El Paso plants) received support from union organizers south of the border. In 1939 and 1940, the mine-mill union negotiated the "loan" of several organizers who were active in the newly founded Mexican CTM branches in towns in Chihuahua state. In this way, the U.S. union "helped in creating a communications network that helped influence Mexicano workers not to scab at either the smelter or refinery" (García, 1990). In 1946, the union exploited the ties it had established with the Chihuahuan labor movement to forestall labor scabbing during a major strike against AS&R. Similar assistance was provided by Mexican unions to embattled workers in Douglas, Arizona (García, 1990:83–104).

There are a number of striking points about these cases. One is the fact that the more highly developed Mexican unions provided assistance to their North American counterparts. Also, the initiation and viability of cross-border cooperation were dependent on a degree of symmetry in the political and ideological composition of the Mexican and U.S. unions involved. Both the CTM and the mine-mill union at this point were leftist organizations in which the respective Communist parties—the Mexican Communist Party (PCM) and the Communist Party of the United States (CPUSA)—played an active role. Moreover, the wartime mood of antifascist "national unity" also facilitated cross-border cooperation. By the late 1940s, however, the purge of CTM leftists carried out during President Miguel Alemán's frenzy of development and the anti-Communist thrust within the CIO (which led to the expulsion or withdrawal of Left-led unions in 1949 and 1950) would dissolve this kind of cooperation (Rosswurm, 1992; Carr, 1992).

The movements of migratory workers between Mexico and the United States also provided opportunities for the circulation of ideas about emancipatory politics and labor organization in areas far removed from the immediate border region. In the 1920s, for example, Mexico's first national labor confederation, the CROM (Regional Confederation of Mexican Workers), provided resources for organizing Mexican agricultural workers in the south and southwest of the United States. Migrants returning to Mexico might also carry with them valuable political and organizing skills acquired while working with unions and leftist organizations. An excellent example would be Primo Tapia, who appropriated the skills he had acquired while working with IWW activists in the western United States and put them to use as an agrarian organizer in his home state (Michoacán) in the early 1920s (Friedrich, 1970). But ideas and organizational skills moved in the opposite direction as well. Many of the boldest and most experienced participants in the organization of agricultural workers in California's Imperial Valley in the first half of the 1930s were Mexican immigrants with a background acquired in the Magonista (PLM) and IWW movements (Weber, 1978:183–184). This south to north flow is worrisomely absent in recent transborder labor actions.

The earliest examples of labor internationalism were often sustained by commitments to radical, transformative, and emancipatory politics—the grand narrative internationalisms. The protagonists included the communist parties of Mexico and the United States and anarchist and anarcho-syndicalist bodies such as the PLM and IWW and, to a lesser degree, the Socialist Party of the United States. The cooperation and solidarities practiced by these organizations were anchored in two main bodies of commitment: to proletarian emancipation (in its self-managed or state socialist versions) and to solidarity with the nationalist, agrarianist, and antiimperialist banners of the Mexican Revolution. Mexico, far from representing a threat to the living standards and future well-being of working peoples in the Americas, appeared rather as a beacon of progress and a repository of ideas and strategies on which the social transformation of the larger American region might be modeled.

There are many examples of this cooperative radical internationalism. They include the collaboration between Mexico's Magonistas and the IWW in which the IWW (and even AFL unions in Los Angeles) helped finance publication of the Magonistas' newspaper *Regeneración* and participated in the abortive attempt to establish a revolutionary enclave in Baja California in 1911; the publicity and lobbying campaigns of the U.S. Socialist Party against the dictatorship of Porfirio Díaz and in favor of the government of Francisco Madero; and the contributions to the early Mexican socialist and feminist movement made by U.S. antiwar activists (the "slackers") who fled south of the Río Grande in 1917 and 1918 (Hernández Padilla, 1984:140–141, Christopulos, 1980).

Grand-narrative internationalism, much of it fueled by the communist parties and their allies, peaked during the Popular Front (1935–1939) which coincided with the sharp leftward move in the Mexican Revolution under President Lázaro Cárdenas and in the Rooseveltian New Deal. During this period, the newly established CTM national labor confederation worked closely with the CIO and embarked on a campaign to win U.S. labor and progressive support for the reformist project of the Cárdenas administration. The common interests of Mexican and U.S. labor could be easily identified as the need to fight domestic and foreign fascism and to promote cross-border solidarities. To promote this shared platform, the CTM, with help from the Cárdenas government, instituted summer schools for English-speakers at its Universidad Obrera and published a bulletin (*Mexican Labor News*) that circulated widely among U.S. radical and labor circles. Concrete support was provided by the CIO on a number of occasions. John L. Lewis threw his support behind the new Left-aligned Confederation of Latin American Workers (CTAL) in 1938, and after the nationalization of the U.S. and British-Dutch oil companies in the same year, Lewis tried to help the Mexican government find markets for its oil and defeat the boycott imposed by the expropriated companies. But international labor solidarity, as already noted in the case of the El Paso smelting workers, did not move in only one direction. Mexican workers in the CTM supported labor mobilizations within the United States. Thus, unions within the CTM assisted CIO locals in organizing Mexican workers on the West Coast and in the southwestern United States, and the Mexican confederation blocked the unloading of cargo in Mexican ports during a CIO maritime workers' strike in California (Levenstein, 1971:153–160, Peterson, 1993–1994:9).

. . . To Anti-Communism and Paternalism

The grand-narrative solidarities sampled here, heroic though they may have been, rested on some rather fragile bases. For a start, they were made possible by the existence of a temporary symmetry in the composition of the labor movements in the United States and Mexico, in particular the presence of a significant Left within labor's peak bodies. Second, the cooperation between Mexican and U.S. labor during the 1920s and especially the 1930s often received the endorsement of governments of the Mexican Revolution that saw the strengthening of transnational labor links as a way of neutralizing hostility to their reformist projects. But by the middle of the 1940s, Mexican government interest in transborder labor contacts had almost disappeared. When the Mexican state's interest in the international labor arena revived, it was marshaled in support of the Cold War labor diplomacy of the AFL-CIO and U.S. State Department. Moreover, in spite of the many internationalist actions initiated in Mexico, grand-narrative internationalism was frequently deformed by practices and discourses influenced by U.S. paternalism and interventionism. This was seen most clearly in the almost tutelary relationship established by the CPUSA toward the Mexican Communists (as witnessed by the frequent interventions in PCM business by envoys of the U.S. party) as well as by the broader drive to subordinate international worker relations to the logic of Comintern and Soviet interests.

A final source of labor internationalism in the pre–World War II period was the interest of the U.S. State Department and anti-Communist labor groups in shaping development of the Latin American labor movement in a class-collaborationist and anti-Communist direction (Spalding, 1992–1993; Scott, 1978; Andrews, 1991). Mexican government representatives, in particular

Mexican diplomatic consuls, also used their influence and prestige to undermine the impact of radical unionism on their countrymen who were resident in the United States.

From this brief account of pre-1945 transborder labor connections several patterns emerge. There was abundant evidence of paternalism and interventionism within U.S. labor initiatives toward Mexico, and initiatives like the Pan American Federation of Labor revealed the interest of the U.S. government and anti-Communist unions in using inter-American labor contacts to promote U.S. imperial objectives and curb "radicalism." But cooperation between Mexican and U.S. labor unions was also frequently driven by a mutual interest in using Mexican organizing expertise to unionize Mexican and Spanish-speaking workers in the United States. Internationalist action and discourse were often shaped by sentiments of admiration for and solidarity with the proworker and peasant achievements of Mexican revolutionary governments. Mexican reformism, therefore, was more likely to be represented as a model to be appreciated (although its radicalism might also be feared) than as a source of problems. Finally, although the language employed in Mexican-U.S. labor contact sometimes paid lip service to the need to prevent labor competition from reducing the living standards of North American workers, the desire to preserve U.S. wages and working conditions by "uplifting" Mexican standards played only a marginal role.

Questions can also be raised about how deeply these early forms of labor internationalism penetrated the consciousness of Mexican and U.S. workers. Moreover, even when cooperation and solidarity were deeply felt—and this was often the case—they were always subject to the vagaries and arbitrariness of the international affiliations and priorities espoused by the designers of the narratives. For example, time and time again, solidarity campaigns were called off when they did not suit the line of the Comintern.[2]

Labor internationalism in the 1990s is unfolding in rather different circumstances and must exploit new opportunities and confront new challenges posed by the changed economic and political environment generated by globalization. The grand narratives of the Left are today rather threadbare, and their manipulative and antidemocratic features (often seen in the mixed record of "proletarian internationalism") have rightly been criticized by Third World unionists. However, although geographical contiguity can still be a powerful promoter of interworker cooperation and solidarity (the Mexican-U.S. border is resurfacing in the 1990s as an important site of labor internationalism), it is clear that the globalization of capital transforms the lives of workers scattered over vast distances. The workers of the maquiladoras, for example, are not really connected to workers on the other side of the border; rather they are integrated in productive processes that connect them to plants that may be hundreds if not thousands of miles away (Moody, 1993).

Labor Internationalism in the 1990s:
Mexico, United States, and Canada

The lead in building new transnational labor links in the early 1990s was taken by workers in Ford plants in the United States and Canada after thugs of the trade union federation affiliated to Mexico's governing PRI murdered rank-and-file activist Cleto Nigmo in January 1990. In response, rank and filers formed the North American Ford Workers Solidarity Network (MEXUSCAN), which brought together the Canadian Auto Workers (CAW) and sections of the U.S. auto worker union, the United Auto Workers (UAW), many of which (like Local 879 in Minneapolis) are bastions of the oppositionist New Directions movement. The first anniversary of Nigmo's death was commemorated around various plants in the United States by workers wearing black armbands, while in Mexico 750 workers and family members held a memorial service, many wearing on their uniform black ribbons supplied by the Canadians. The Ford activists spearheaded educational work about NAFTA during the period leading up to the treaty's signing in late 1993, confronted Ford officials at several gatherings (including a Ford stockholders meeting), and were instrumental in organizing innovative Fair Trade Coalitions in several states. At the end of October 1994, nearly five years after the murder, police arrested and charged the former general secretary of the Ford-Cuautitlan local of the CTM with Nigmo's killing (Peacenet, 1994b).

At a broader level Ford activists have participated in several international meetings (in Oaxtepec in November 1991, Detroit in 1992, and Ciudad Juárez in February 1993) of North, Central, and South American auto worker unionists sponsored by the Amsterdam-based Transnationals Information Exchange (TIE). Union delegates have agreed to share information about automobile company plans, labor laws, new technology and work processes, labor contracts, and other issues (Moody and McGinn, 1992:50–51; Keys, 1993).

The U.S.-based United Electrical Workers (UE), a small and self-consciously militant national union, signed a Strategic Organizing Alliance in 1992 with one of Mexico's leading independent labor federations, the Authentic Workers Front (FAT). As part of the alliance, the UE and FAT have agreed to work together "on projects involving workers at the Mexican plants operated by TNCs which employ UE members in the United States" (UE, 1992). In a linked project, known as the "Adopt an Organizer" campaign, UE finances campaigns by the FAT to organize electronics plants on the Mexican side of the border (Witt, 1992; McGinn and Moody, 1993:24; *La Jornada,* 23 February 1993:13). This is part of a more ambitious proposal the UE has put forward to establish "a beachhead of democratic unionism in strategic sectors of the [Mexican] economy: maquiladora and other U.S. and Canadian-related employers" (UE-FAT, August 1992). The initial target has been electrical- and machine-goods factories where the FAT is committed to unionization. Organizers hired for the project would also

> schedule delegations to participating sites in the United States and Canada, to assist in building up worker-to-worker contact and solidarity. Likewise, delegations of workers from the United States and Canada would visit the organizing drives in Mexico, thus developing a core of committed activists around the issue, much the same way labor tours to Central America developed an activist core around that struggle. . . . Given the level of repression against democratic trade unionists in Mexico, an important part of the adopt-an-organizer campaign must involve organizing rapid-response solidarity actions to support workers and organizers who are victims of firings, threats, violence etc. (UE-FAT, August 1992:2).

The Amalgamated Clothing and Textile Workers Union (ACTWU), whose members are mostly garment workers making men's clothes and auto trim, has a strong commitment to transborder union cooperation, especially with South African unions, and has been extremely active in the new trinational labor networking arena (Garver, 1989:69). The ACTWU has shared information about specific companies with several Mexican labor organizations, including some independent groups, and has sponsored cross-border exchanges by union members and activists.

The ACTWU's attention to cross-border work has undoubtedly been assisted by the fact that it has a large Spanish-speaking membership both within the mainland United States and in Puerto Rico and Canada. It also has several thousand Mexican resident members who cross the border each day to work in clothing plants on the U.S. side of the border. The union is particularly threatened by runaway shops (border assembly plants) and has been active in lobbying on behalf of Guatemalan workers in the textile industry. It has also been an enthusiastic sponsor of worker-rights petitions under the Generalized System of Preferences (GSP) trade program and is a major supporter of the U.S.-Guatemala Labor Education Project (GLEP) based in the ACTWU' s Chicago offices (Phillips–Van Heusen, 1992; US-GLEP, 1992; Coates, 1992).[3]

A New Era of Labor Internationalism?

These and many dozens of other cross-border labor exchanges have given rise to optimistic predictions about the revival of international worker solidarity. Certainly, the accelerating internationalization of production and its accompanying movement of capital from high- to low-wage economies heighten internationalism in many ways (Southall, 1988). More particularly, growing intrafirm trade has facilitated the development of cross-national links between workers employed by the same transnationals, as in the case of the Ford auto workers solidarity network. But is this evidence of the continued viability of that old axiom of Marxist theory according to which capitalism's major economic logic—the economic unification of the world—will provide the "objective" material base for working-class unity in that it homogenizes social and economic conditions on a global scale? Or is this one of countless myths (albeit potent ones) and euphoric predictions generated by the labor movement at a time of worldwide defeats for unions?

Certainly, the internationalization of production does lead to a degree of similarity of "work and life experiences for workers in core and periphery" (McNally, 1990:188–190). But talk of "objective grounds" should not blind us to the fact that globalization does not produce homogenization in any automatic fashion. It remains the case for Mexico that in spite of the growth of foreign investment and the development of export manufacturing, there is a striking lack of homogenization in productive processes. Large parts of Mexico's labor force work in industries with low-tech production and limited post-Fordism (de la Garza, 1992a, 1992b). The argument that internationalization of capital is finally laying the material framework for an end to national fragmentation of workers and their organizations is also excessively economistic. Changes in the organization of production do not determine everything in any mechanical way. Historical memory, cultural traditions, and the segmentation and division of workers by gender, race, and religion do count (Olle and Schoeller, 1987).

But there are other forces allegedly (and more convincingly) driving the creation of new forms of transnational labor solidarity. One such force is the end of the Cold War. Previous attempts at promoting labor internationalism have, it is generally accepted, fallen victim to the appeals of nationalism and chauvinism or have been constrained by the ideological and political rivalries that divided the post-1945 world when trade union international bodies were tied to the two rival power blocs and exploited Third World unions, frequently subordinating them to the logic of superpower conflicts (Langley, 1972; Lens, 1972; Sims, 1992).

The end of the Cold War, therefore, has removed several impediments to effective labor internationalism. Labor internationalism is no longer necessarily based on a simple notion of history evolving free of contradictions or on "one totalising antagonism (proletarians-capitalists; Third World/First World; nationalism/imperialism)" (Mires, n.d., cited in Waterman, 1977:11). However, we should not take this argument too far. Quite a number of rival and competing ideological and political agendas are operating in the Mexican, U.S., and Canadian scenes, and sectarian politics has certainly not disappeared for good.

The flight of capital to low-wage economies has also meant that the cost of the massive state intervention necessary to sustain consent in the labor process (the welfare state, for example) has come under challenge. Capital flight is driving reductions in nonwage remuneration and welfare entitlements in the high-wage economies to enable them to compete with low-wage societies. This makes the link between deterioration in working conditions (concession bargaining, lower benefits from state intervention) and the internationalization of production much more apparent. This issue has been particularly effective in exposing the social costs of free trade in Canada and the United States.

The links between labor regimes and global patterns of state–civil society relations are also becoming clearer. The Mexican model of economic growth, for example, is sustained by the repressive and authoritarian features of the state's relations with organized labor. In other words, the globalization of capital creates circumstances in which labor conflicts, though initially restricted to economic and labor bargaining issues, can be expanded to incorporate a questioning of the larger social order, including questions of democracy, human rights, and environmental protection.

Finally, it has been argued that new technology is facilitating a new form of labor internationalism. The growing use of e-mail and electronic conferencing in labor networking is a case in point. Do these developments signify the development of horizontal and more democratic labor communication in place of the vertical and bureaucratized channels so far in place (Waterman, 1992)? Perhaps so—but is there credible evidence that these new forms of electronic communication are changing the actual practices of unions and unionists? Have information flows just become faster and more effective, or has their character changed? Has communications technology qualitatively improved the bargaining power of unions and unionists at plant level or facilitated the possible creation of world company councils incorporating representatives of all sections of a multinational? How far is the new technology dependent on the emergence of new kinds of communication specialists or mediators (Peter Waterman's "information weavers")? Has the new technology even replicated the relations of neocolonialism (Waterman, 1992:29–30)?

Constraints on Labor Internationalism

Focus on TNCs

Much of the focus of commentators and unionists has understandably been on labor actions and networking that operate within the framework of TNCs (transnational corporations); the Ford automobile empire and the General Electric and Honeywell electrical plants in the border region currently targeted by the UE-FAT pact are just two examples. There is therefore a tendency (which some have labeled syndicalist) to privilege work in the transnational sector because this is precisely the terrain in which the development of TNCs is allegedly laying the material base for the unification of a world proletariat and form of wage labor.

This focus on TNCs is also based on the (correct) assumption that an ever larger proportion of trade within the Mexico–United States–Canada bloc is now intrafirm in character—which makes it attractive to concentrate on establishing "beachheads" in strategic sectors of the Mexican economy where U.S. and Canadian-related employers operate (once again the UE-FAT Strategic Organizing Alliance is a good example). However, we should not forget that Mexican, U.S., and Canadian workers operate outside of TNCs too, and that many of them, the growing majority, are not even unionized.

Another obvious problem is that TNCs are opposed to international union cooperation in existing plants. Such companies are not sitting targets and are quick to respond to challenges from labor initiatives. Thus, eroding the power of capital by nibbling away at it is unrealistic, as Hawarth and Ramsey pointed out. Borrowing a metaphor from R. H. Tawney, these authors noted that capital is a tiger, not an onion—"it is not peeled without resistance and replies with ferocity when attacked" (Hawarth and Ramsey, 1988:310). In setting up its new auto plant in the northwestern Mexican city of Hermosillo, Ford rejected the idea of sending U.S. technicians and workers to train Mexicans because they might

> transmit to the technicians traditional work rules, customs, wage levels and attitudes towards management. A retired maintenance superintendent remarked that U.S. skilled tradesmen are "not going to come down here and foster a program like we have here where you have two trades, where they come from a place that has 17 to 20 different trades. . . . All they'll do is tell these guys, 'Hey, you're doing that for a dollar an hour. We get twenty dollars an hour'" (Shaiken and Herzenberg, 1987:67).

Furthermore, if the experience with the maquiladoras is indicative, Mexico's comparative advantage in cheap labor, which is highly attractive to foreign firms relocating in Mexico, will be an added reason for TNC hostility; the vigorous responses of employers to the UE-FAT efforts to unionize Honeywell and General Electric plants in Chihuahua and Ciudad Juárez in late 1993, including firing thirty activists, are clear proof of this point. On this occasion the Teamsters and the UE tried to fight their case by using the "parallel" labor accords of the NAFTA (filing complaints with the National Administration Office, NAO); they were unsuccessful. However, U.S. unions and a FAT-affiliated metal workers union (STIMAHCS) did succeed in forcing GE to hold a secret ballot to elect union representation. The ballot on 24 August 1994 produced a defeat for FAT. Nevertheless, to secure its victory, GE was obliged to offer its Ciudad Juárez workers many of the benefits originally demanded by FAT (Peacenet, 1994a).

Nationalist Consciousness

But perhaps the most serious obstacle to effective labor internationalism is the fact that, as Roger Southall noted, "working class formation and consciousness tends to be nationally nurtured and structured in a world of vigorously competing states" (Southall, 1988:25). This structural asymmetry enhances multinational capital's ability to exploit trade-offs within multiplant empires to transfer work from one factory to another and therefore benefit particular plants and create obstacles to solidarity. This problem has been frequently encountered in Europe (the recent examples of Massey Ferguson and Timex are very eloquent), and there are numerous examples appearing in Canada and the United States. Also, as Hawarth and Ramsey argued, "the existence of contacts and intelligence says nothing about its power to cause managements to change decisions" (Hawarth and Ramsey, 1984:63). One might also ask whether there can be a real as opposed to rhetorical sense of identity, solidarity, or "belonging" outside the local level where shared experience, common interests, and proximity intersect. This identity is often further intensified by the social and cultural networks created by communities beyond the factory floor but that are local in nature. Hawarth and Ramsey concluded that at the most fundamental level, "there is a non-coincidence of labor strategies and TNC/international capitalist strategies" (Hawarth and Ramsey, 1984:73).

Weak Independent Unions

The environment for transborder links is further complicated because the last decade has been a period of weakness for the independent unions in Mexico that are the most likely protagonists in transborder labor initiatives. Dramatic signs of this decline are the removal of the telephone workers union and the Mexican Electrical Workers Union (SME) from the ranks of the standard-bearers of trade union independence and challenges to Mexican corporatism. A recent defeat of an independent union, or rather a rank-and-file fraction of a formerly independent union, occurred in Puebla in 1992 when Volkswagen decided unilaterally to terminate a labor contract and support the official union leadership against a majority of dissidents within the union during an intraunion struggle. The incident led not only to the defeat of the insurgent unionists but also to a radical revision of the Volkswagen contract that, among other things, weakened the power of the union delegates and strengthened the authority of the union's executive (Méndez and Quiroz, 1992). More generally, various indicators suggest that the combativeness of the Mexican union movement has declined over the past decade as measured by an 80 percent fall in the number of strikes between January 1982 and December 1991 (Quiroz and Méndez 1992:95).

The shrinking of the independent labor sector in Mexico has reduced the number of union interlocutors able and willing to collaborate in trinational actions critical of the enthusiastic embrace of free trade logic by the Mexican state and by the mainstream labor movement. A few unions—the Mexican Telephone Workers Union (STRM) and the SME (a union with an independent history, although somewhat weakened in recent years)—have combined support for NAFTA with calls for a labor rights charter and the creation of a North American Worker Bloc to improve communications and dialogue. The STRM has also formed a "permanent coalition" with the Telecommunications Workers Union of Canada and the Communications Workers of America (*Latin American Labor News*, 1992:7). Nevertheless, the principal Mexican partners interested in promoting internationalist projects have been the dwindling number of unions and union federations that retain a commitment to some form of socialist vision. Sectors of the democratic teachers movement in Mexico, for example, have established links with Canadian and U.S. education unions.

The principal and by far the most active Mexican partner in labor internationalist campaigns is FAT, one of the oldest of the independent union federations in Mexico. Founded in 1960, originally with a Christian Democratic focus (some of its founders were priests), the organization has undergone a radical transformation over the last decade. It now proclaims itself a "united, pluralist, democratic and independent workers organization" whose historical objective is "the transformation of society and the capitalist system into a self-managed form of socialism." FAT sees itself as both a union federation and a sociopolitical organization with nongovernmental organization status that receives financial support from international solidarity groups and engages in work around the goal of "designing new strategies for growth and the creation of new social institutions that lie outside of official structures" (García Urrutia, nd). Its membership, therefore, embraces workers in manufacturing workplaces and worker-owned cooperatives and among peasants and groups of poor urban residents. The nature of its membership base and the broad goals it articulates put FAT into rather a different camp from its U.S. and Canadian interlocutors. If anything in Mexico resembles social movement unionism, it is probably FAT.

FAT's membership, however, is small: The highest estimate provided by FAT itself is 50,000; other sources speak of only 40,000 members. Its membership is scattered over a number of areas, in public-sector unions such as employees of the Fisheries Ministry (SUTSP), worker cooperatives (formed when bankrupt companies were handed over to workers in lieu of termination payments), peasant organizations (of ejidatarios in the Jiménez district of Chihuahua, for example), the textile and garment industries, and auto parts and elevator manufacturing. In general, it has members in small- and middle-sized enterprises but no real strength in large plants. As part of its agreement with the UE, FAT has begun work building labor organizations in the maquiladora industry in northern Mexico and on the U.S.-Mexican border (Méndez and Quiroz, 1991; Loreto C., 1992:211–214). The organization also provides advice and assistance, sometimes in a clandestine fashion, to organizations affiliated with the official labor movement. Nevertheless, however impressive and audacious

FAT's actions may be, its small size and limited resources impose a definite limit on its ability to service the demands for Mexican "partners" being made by U.S. and Canadian unionists (Carr, 1993).

Transborder links are also made difficult by the reluctance of national federations like the AFL-CIO to break with their long-standing tradition of dealing only with the official movement in Mexico, the CTM. This is all the more so since independent unions, federations, and intraunion groups in Mexico inevitably take on a dissident status, thus strengthening another traditional argument used by union bureaucracies everywhere—that dealing with "dissidents" overseas may establish precedents that have disturbing implications for the domestic scene. Traditional union policies in many countries, after all, formally prohibit horizontal discussions between units in the same union. This is the case in the UAW, for example, where the leading role in trinational networking played by members of the oppositionist New Directions current has met with resistance from the union's national leadership (Laney, 1993). In Mexico, automobile companies like Ford were very careful when they set up their new plants in northern Mexico in the late 1970s and 1980s to prevent horizontal links between the "new" workers and workers from the older plants in southern Mexico with their longer history of combative union action, independent unionism, and defense of work practices that did not mesh with the post-Fordist agenda (Shaiken and Herzenberg, 1987:61, 67). Nevertheless, the CTM does harbor unions with a tradition of independence and militancy. The best-known example is the CTM federation in the border region of Tamaulipas with its long history of combative unionism and unusual success in penetrating the maquiladora plants of border towns like Matamoros (Quintero Ramírez, 1992).

Protectionism

John Hovis, president of the United Electrical Workers union, said he plans to build strong, independent Mexican unions by defending workers whose rights have been violated by U.S. firms operating in Mexico. "Strong Mexican unions stop job flight," Hovis said (*NAFTA Monitor*, 1994).

There is certainly no shortage of examples of chauvinism and overt protectionism in the U.S. labor movement. Note the incident in 1985 when, at a Pittsburgh labor parade centered around the slogan "Put America Back to Work: Buy American-made Products", a float "portrayed a brawny American steelworker smashing a Japanese-made car and its buck-toothed passengers" (Garver, 1989:61). Significantly, even leaders of UAW Local 879 in Minneapolis who have played an impressive role in promoting links with democratic automotive unionists in Mexico acknowledge that "their 2100 members have a stake in helping the Mexican auto-workers who earn $9 a day because these wages threaten the job security of Ford workers in St. Paul and elsewhere in America," and they argue that "if we can raise their current wages and benefits, it will make it less and less desirable for American companies to move there (Carlson, 1991:1)."

These discursive sorties raise one of the most difficult questions facing students and advocates of labor internationalism. Are First World and Third World workers "comrades or competitors" (Southall, 1988:37)? Will unions in First World nations always see international labor issues exclusively in terms of foreign bogey men, runaway industries depleting the labor force, intimidating workers to concession bargain more fiercely (under threat of more runaways), and demanding protectionist measures from their states—with sometimes racist and chauvinist rhetoric? And will labor movements in Third World nations always welcome economic integration and greater capital mobility because these bring or credibly promise to bring more jobs (Diamond, 1993)?

The role of protectionism in generating internationalist consciousness and action is complex. Historians would be the first to emphasize that self-interest has always been an important element in internationalist work; recall the earliest international alliances among European workers designed to prevent scabs being imported to break strikes and unions in the 1830s and 1840s. Historically there has always been a link between long periods of economic growth or stagnation and the level of intensity of labor internationalism. Thus labor internationalism has generally been stronger during economic stagnation (during the interwar period and since the mid-1960s) when unions have been under pressure. International trade union initiatives, it has been argued, "must . . . be interpreted as an attempt to defend an established national level of reproduction from any threat to it throughout any period when the trade unions are relatively weak. In this sense union internationalization can be described as being a trade union form of 'national protectionism'" (Olle and Schoeller, 1987:34). The history of the emergence of the World Corporation Councils (WCCs, coordinating bodies of unions in a particular TNC) also shows the importance of this quasi-protectionist element. This idea caught on in Europe (but not in the United States) as the importance of overseas production by European companies increased in the 1960s and when WCCs were viewed as effective ways of challenging and counteracting the export of jobs. The conclusion to be drawn is that the interests of workers in developed and underdeveloped countries, when viewed from an economic perspective, are invariably in a state of some tension. It would be dishonest to deny the existence of serious conflicts of interests, and labor internationalism can be easily rationalized as a "condition for national trade union survival" (Levinson, 1972, cited in Olle and Schoeller, 1987:39).

Conclusion

It is certainly the case that some of the internationalist initiatives undertaken by both rank and filers and union organizations have concealed what are essentially narrow, nationalist, protectionist, and even chauvinist concerns. But there is also evidence for the emergence of a geographically and sectorally very uneven effort at building a new form of citizen politics in the labor arena.

In several important ways the new labor internationalism has broken new ground. Something resembling "social movement unionism" has been pioneered in a few cases. The Maquiladora Project of the American Friends Service Committee (AFSC) and its Comité Fronterizo de Obreras, mindful of the problems and dangers of trying to organize women maquiladora workers at their workplaces, has concentrated its orientation systems in meetings scheduled at women workers' homes in border neighborhoods (La Botz, 1994:7–8). In the case of the Minnesota-based Fair Trade Coalition, labor internationalist actions built closer relationships between groups involved in workplace disputes and their community allies. Likewise, the Green Giant campaign has clearly moved beyond narrow defense of jobs in its demand that the Anglo-American multinational company fulfill its commitment to build infrastructure after it moved production from Watsonville, California, to Irapuato, Mexico. These are examples of how activists can build closer relationships between labor groups involved in workplace disputes and community allies—the kind of bridge building that is attempting to create a new "movement of movements," a democratic convergence or a "new social bloc," to use the phrasing of Jeremy Brecher and Tim Costello, who have traced and celebrated this development (Brecher and Costello, 1990a; 1990b; 1990c). This is, of course, not an entirely new practice. A historically self-reflective labor internationalism would acknowledge such important precedents as the close ties between the emergence of the CIO in the 1930s and union alliances with other social groups or community interests; the 1934 involvement of farmers in the Teamsters strike in Minneapolis; the involvement of Detroit black communities in the unionization of Ford in the late 1930s; and the ways in which the 1936–1937 sit-down strike at Flint "mobilized the entire working-class community" (Moody, 1990:220).

The verdict so far on the "democratization" of trinational labor exchanges is mixed, however. Although the same names (of leaders and prominent activists) seem to figure with amazing regularity in accounts of trinational meetings, it is also true that a great deal of energy has been expended in promoting cross-border visits by rank-and-file members of unions such as the ACTWU and UE. The worst excesses of protectionism and chauvinism have been avoided.

But a triumphalist conclusion would be a dangerous way to end this discussion of the new labor internationalism. There are still many dangers ahead. In particular, we need to avoid falling back into unreflective defenses of traditional positions. Crises and new challenges can provide creative opportunities for historical subjects in conflict. For example, a case can be made that workers (and more generally the "subordinate classes" in Mexico) might gain several crucial advantages in a more integrated North American region—with greater access to a more democratic environment, more democratic institutions within which to negotiate representation, and a state that is less committed to repressing "autonomous organizational efforts" and maintaining "artificially low wages" (Otero, 1993:15–16). The choice is not between keeping the undemocratic and statist neocorporatism of the present Mexican system and capitulating to a readjustment based on unfettered opening of markets combined with continuing blocks on worker self-expression. Free trade could offer spaces for challenging and overhauling arbitrary state actions provided, of course, that it was accompanied by radical modifications of Mexico's federal labor law to remove the state's powers to curb unions by denying them recognition, declaring strikes nonexistent, and decreeing closed shops—battles that have still not been won. Similarly, U.S. and Canadian unions and workers have much to learn from the history of the Mexican workers' movement. Mexico must not be simply constructed as "the problem," "the weak link in the chain," or a "Trojan Horse for multinational capital." The "advanced" character of Mexican labor legislation and the breadth of the social wage entitlements Mexican workers have won (poor enforcement and frequent violation notwithstanding) are not yet sufficiently acknowledged in the United States and Canada (Barkin, 1993–1994:3, 10, 11). More serious, an examination of the internationalist actions undertaken in the last few years reveals that initiatives have been launched almost exclusively from the north. NAFTA and its aftermath have unquestionably greatly increased Canadian and U.S. worker and union understandings of Mexico's labor-state pact. But compared with the more symmetrical exchanges of the late 1930s and early 1940s, there is a long way to go before U.S. and Canadian unions and workers begin to learn from their Mexican counterparts and Mexicans start to understand and contribute to the solution of the problems facing the embattled labor movements north of the Rio Grande.

Notes

1. The two unions are working to "create similar contracts in terms of housing, health care and other services important to migrant workers." The unions want to use provision H2A of the 1986 Immigration Act that "requires legal guest workers from Mexico to have a sponsor. FLOC would like to be this sponsor for SNTOAC's members when they come to the Midwest." The two unions are also working out a wage parity model "in which the two unions work towards wage levels that are comparable in relation to the cost of living in each country" (Moody and McGinn, 1992:49–50).

2. Note, however, this exchange between President Francisco Madero and three U.S. labor activists—Mother Jones, Jo Cannon (Western Federation of Miners), and Frank Hayes (United Mine Workers)—in September 1911. When asked by Madero what motivated U.S. interest in Mexican miners, the visitors replied that they were "compelled to either fight or raise the standard of living of the Mexican miner that lowered our wage scale, or accept lower wages, and we preferred the first to the last" (Foner, 1988:110).

3. A worker rights petition directed at Guatemalan exports to the United States was filed by the US-GLEP and nine other organizations in 1992. In June 1994 the U.S. government rejected the petition. However, according to unionists in Guatemala, the pressure of advocacy groups like the US-GLEP and the threat of loss of trade benefits have produced important gains for workers in a few maquiladora plants.

Bibliography

Andrews, Gregg. 1991. *Shoulder to Shoulder: The American Federation of Labor, The United States, and the Mexican Revolution, 1910–1924.* Berkeley: University of California Press.

Autoworker (The Local 879 UAW). 1991. 14(1), March.

Barkin, David. 1993–1994. "Building Trinational Labor Solidarity in an Era of Free Trade." *Latin American Labor News,* no. 9, pp. 3, 10, 11.

Bird, S., D. Georgakis, and D. Shaffer. 1985. *Solidarity Forever: An Oral History of the IWW.* Chicago: Lake View Press.

Bognanno, Mario, and Kathryn J. Ready, eds. 1993. *The North American Free Trade Agreement: Labor, Industry, and Government Perspectives.* Westport, Conn.: Praeger.

Brecher, Jeremy, and Tim Costello. 1990a. "Labor-Community Coalitions and the Restructuring of Power." Pp. 325–344 in Brecher and Costello, 1990c.

———. 1990b. "American Labor: The Promise of Decline." Pp. 195–297 in Brecher and Costello, 1990c.

Brecher, Jeremy, and Tim Costello, eds. 1990c. *Building Bridges: The Emerging Grassroots Coalition of Labor and Community.* New York: Monthly Review Press.

Carlson, Scott. 1991. "Ford Workers Honor Victim." Igc:carnet.mexnews, January 10.

Carr, Barry. 1992. *Marxism and Communism in Twentieth-Century Mexico.* Lincoln and London: University of Nebraska Press.

———. 1993. Interview with Bertha Luján, Mexico City, February.

Christopulos, Diana. 1980. "American Radicals and the Mexican Revolution, 1900–1925." Ph.D. thesis, State Unversity of New York at Binghamton.

Cleaver, Harry. 1994. "The Chiapas Uprising and the Future of Class Struggle in the New World Order." *Riff-Raff* (Padova, Italy), March, pp. 133–145.

Coates, Stephen. 1992. "Free Trade, Guatemala, and Us: A Christian Response to the Global Shopfloor." *Blueprint Reprint,* 46, 2 (October):1–7.

de la Garza, Enrique. 1992a. "El tratado de libre comercio y sus consecuencias en la contratación colectiva," *El Cotidiano,* no. 45 (Jan-Feb):3–12.

———. 1992b. "La polarización del aparato productivo en México." *El Cotidiano,* no. 46 (March-April):3–9.

Diamond, Stephen. 1993. "American Labor and North American Economic Integration: Toward a Cosntructive Critique." Pp. 251–259 in Ricardo Grinspun and Maxwell Cameron, eds., *The Political Economy of North American Free Trade.* Basingstoke: Macmillan.

Foner, Philip S. 1988. *The U.S. Labor Movement and Latin America, Vol. 1 1846–1919.* South Hadley, Mass.: Bergin & Garvey Publishers.

Friedrich, Paul. 1970. *Agrarian Revolt in a Mexican Village.* Englewood Cliffs, N.J.: Prentice-Hall.

García, Mario T. 1990. "Border Proletarians; Mexican-Americans and the International Union of Mine, Mill, and Smelter Workers, 1939–1946." Pp. 83–104 in Robert Ashe & Charles Stephenson, eds., *Labor Divided: Race and Ethnicity in United States Labor Struggles, 1836–1960*. Albany: State University of New York Press.

García Urrutia, Manuel. nd. *El Frente Auténtico del Trabajo*. Mimeo.

Garver, Paul. 1989. "Beyond the Cold War: New Directions for Labor Internationalism." *Labor Research Review*, 13 (Spring):161–171.

Hawarth, Nigel, and Harvie Ramsey. 1984. "Grasping the Nettle: Problems in the Theory of International Labor Solidarity." Pp. 59–85 in Peter Waterman, ed., *For a New Labor Internationalism*. The Hague: International Labor Education, Research and Information Foundation (ILERI).

———. 1988. "Workers of the World Untied: International Capital and Some Dilemmas in Industrial Democracy." Pp. 306–331 in Southall, 1988.

Hernández Padilla, Salvador. 1984. *El magonismo: Historia de una pasión libertaria 1900–1922*. Mexico City: Ediciones Era.

Keys, Eric. 1993. "Auto Workers Meet in Juárez to Discuss Solidarity." Peacenet: carnet.mexnews, 5 March.

La Botz, Dan. 1994. "Making Links Across the Border." *Labor Notes*, August, Pp. 7–10.

Laney, Tom. 1993. Personal e-mail communication from Tom Laney to the author, February.

Langley, David. 1972. "The Colonization of the International Trade Union Movement." Pp. 296–309 in Burton Hall, ed., *Autocracy and Insurgency in Organized Labor*. New Brunswick, N.J.: Transaction Books.

Lens, Sidney. 1972. "Labor Lieutenants and the Cold War." Pp. 310–323 in Burton Hall, ed., *Autocracy and Insurgency in Organized Labor*. New Brunswick, N.J.: Transaction Books.

Levenstein, Harvey. 1971. *Labor Organizations in the United States and Mexico: A History of Their Relations*. Westport, Conn.: Greenwood.

Levinson, C. 1972. *International Trade Unionism*. London: Allan and Unwin. Cited in Olle and Schoeller, 1987.

Loreto C., David. 1992. "Los trabajadores de la Secretaría de Pesca frente al Tratado de Libre Comercio." Pp. 211–214 in *Memoria de zacatecas*. Mexico City: Red Mexicana de Acción Contra el Libre Comercio (RMALC), February.

McGinn, Mary, and Kim Moody. 1993. "Labor Goes Global," *The Progressive*, March, pp. 24–27.

McNally, David. 1990. "Beyond Nationalism, Beyond Protectionism: Labor and the Canada-U.S. Free-Trade Agreement." *Review of Radical Political Economics*, 22(1): 179–194.

Méndez, Luis, and José Othón Quiroz. 1991. "El FAT: Autogestión obrera y modernidad." *El Cotidiano*, no. 40 (March-April):37–43.

———. 1992. "Respuesta obrera y acuerdos concertados." *El Cotidiano*, no. 49 (July-August):155–168.

Mires, Fernando. "La crisis del internacionalismo." *Servicio mensual de información y documentación* (No. 113). Quito: ALAI. Cited in Waterman, 1991.

Moody, Kim. 1990. "Building a Labor Movement for the 1990s: Cooperation and Concesions or Confrontation and Coalition." In Brecher and Costello, 1990c.

———. 1993. Presentation at Tijuana labor conference, February.

Moody, Kim, and Mary McGinn. 1992. *Unions and Free Trade*. Detroit: Labor Notes.

Mumme, Stephen P. 1993. "Environmentalists, NAFTA, and North American Environmental Management." *Journal of Environment and Development.* 2(1):215.

NAFTA Monitor. 1994. *NAFTA Monitor,* in Labr. global, 22 March.

Nelson, Bruce. 1990. *Workers on the Waterfront: Seamen, Longshoremen, and Unionism in the 1930s.* Urbana: University of Illinois Press.

Olle, Werner, and Wolfgang Schoeller. 1987. "World Market Competition and Restrictions upon International Trade Union Policies." Pp. 26–47 in Rosalynd E. Boyd, Robin Cohen, and Peter C.W. Gutkind, eds., *International Labour and the Third World.* Aldershot: Avebury.

Otero, Gerardo. 1993. "The State Transformed: New Political Relations in Mexico." Paper presented at the Annual Meeting of the American Sociological Association, Miami Beach, Fla., August.

Parlee, Lorena M. 1984. "The Impact of U.S. Railroad Unions on Organized Labor and Government Policy in Mexico, 1880–1910." *Hispanic American Historical Review,* 64(3):443–475.

Peacenet. 1994a. *Labornotes-sindicatos* (August 25).

———. 1994b. Carnet.mexnews. "Mexican Ford Union Leader Arrested." 5 November.

Peterson, Gigi. 1993–1994. "U.S.-Mexican Cross-Border Solidarity: Labor Precedents from the 1930s. "*Latin American Labor News,* no. 9, p. 9.

Phillips–Van Heusen. 1992. *Phillips-Van Heusen Campaign Update #5,* 15 December, pp. 1–4.

Quintero Ramírez, Cirila. 1992. "Región y poder sindical: El caso de Agapito González Cavazos." Unpublished paper, Colegio de la Frontera Norte–Matamoros. Pp. 1–25.

Quiroz, José Othón, and Luis Méndez. 1992. "El conflicto de la Volkswagen: Crónica de una muerte inesperada." *El Cotidiano,* no. 51 (November-December):81–91.

Richmond, Al. 1972. *A Long View from the Left: Memoirs of an American Revolutionary.* New York: Delta Books.

Rosswurm, Steve, ed. 1992. *The CIO's Left-Led Unions.* New Brunswick, N.J.: Rutgers University Press.

Scott, Jack. 1978. *Yankee Unions, Go Home! How the U.S. Unions Helped the U.S. Build an Empire in Latin America.* Vancouver: New Star Books.

Shaiken, Harley, and Stephen Herzenberg. 1987. *Automation and Global Production: Automobile Engine Production in Mexico, the United States, and Canada.* La Jolla, Calif.: Center for US-Mexican Studies, University of California, San Diego.

Sims, Beth. 1992. *Workers of the World Undermined: American Labor's Role in U.S. Foreign Policy.* Boston: South End Press.

Southall, Roger, ed. 1988. *Trade Unions and the New Industrialisation of the Third World.* London and Ottawa: Zed Books and University of Ottawa Press.

Spalding, Hobart. 1992–1993. "The Two Latin American Foreign Policies of the U.S. Labor Movement: The AFL-CIO Top Brass vs. Rank and File." *Science and Society,* 56(4):421–439.

Thorup, Cathryn. 1991. "The Politics of Free Trade and the Dynamics of Cross-Border Coalitions in U.S.-Mexico Relations." *Columbia Journal of World Business,* 26(11): 12–26.

———. 1992. "Redefining Governance in North America: The Impact of Cross-Border Networks and Coalitions on Mexican Immigration into the United States." Paper presented at the XII International Congress of the Latin American Studies Association, September, Los Angeles, Calif.

UE (United Electric Workers). 1992. *Resolution Passed at the UE National Convention 9/92.* Mimeo.

UE-FAT (UE and Frente Auténtico del Trabajo). 1992. *Proposal for Action: U.S.-Mexico-Canada Labor Solidarity Network Submitted by United Electrical Workers (UE) of U.S. and Frente Auténtico del Trabajo of Mexico.* No place of publication, 1 August.

US-GLEP (U.S.-Guatemala Labor Education Project). 1992. *A Campaign to Support the Basic Rights of Workers in Guatemala.* 18 June.

Velazquez, Baldemar, with Elise Blackwell. 1993. "Meeting the Transnational Corporate Challenge," *Beyond Borders,* 1(1):8–9, 23–25.

Waterman, Peter. 1991. "Understanding Socialist and Proletarian Internationalism: The Impossible Past and Possible Future of Emancipation on a World Scale." The Hague: Institute of Social Studies, Working Papers Series no. 97, March.

———. 1992. "International Labour Communication by Computer: The Fifth International?" The Hague: Institute of Social Studies, Working Papers Series no. 129, July.

Weber, Devra Ann. 1978. "El proceso de organización de los trabajadores agrícolas mexicanos en el Valle Imperial y en Los Angeles, 1928–1934." Pp. 158–206 in Juan Gómez-Quiñones and Luis Leobardo Arroyo, eds., *Orígenes del movimiento obrero chicano.* Mexico City: Ediciones Era.

Witt, Matt. 1992. "Labor and NAFTA." *NAWWN Free Trade Labor Events,* no. 5 (August):58.

Zogbaum, Heidi. 1991. *B. Traven: A Vision of Mexico.* Wilmington, Del.: Scholarly Resources.

12

Mexico's Economic and Political Futures

Gerardo Otero

Through detailed analysis of root causes and key social agents, this book's contributors have traced the main economic and political challenges and prospects facing Mexico during the 1990s and beyond. The critical issues discussed include the implications of continental economic integration and how this will affect various aspects of Mexican economy, society, and polity. A number of possible future scenarios have come forth. In this chapter I elaborate upon them after outlining research agendas emerging from these discussions.

Issues for a Research Agenda

As most contributors have argued, political democracy and an equitable income distribution are still largely unfulfilled goals in the Mexican agenda. The wave of economic restructuring along neoliberal lines poses immense difficulties for attaining equitable income distribution to the extent that neoliberal reform continues with its trend toward exclusionary practices that result in increased social polarization. The question still remains as to whether such an economic model can be made compatible with a transition toward political democracy.

The end of import-substitution industrialization has been coupled with growing trends toward continentalization of the economy. In the Enterprise Initiative for the Americas, former U.S. President George Bush proposed to build a free trade area in the entire American continent. As an initial step, the governments of Canada, Mexico, and the United States became trade and investment partners in the North American Free Trade Agreement, inaugurated on 1 January 1994. As a prelude to such changes in Mexico and North America, a number of critical variables were mobilized by Mexican entrepreneurs and the representatives of TNCs.

Francisco Valdés Ugalde has provided an account of how the private sector influenced major changes in the functioning of the Mexican state. From a situation of division and even conflict between political and economic ruling groups, there is now convergence. This involved the dismantling of "revolutionary nationalism" and its replacement by a "technical rationality" that places private-oriented ideologies at center stage. There has been a major withdrawal of the state from the economy, leaving both local and foreign private interests as the undisputed key economic actors. Furthermore, the transformation of corporatism in state-labor relations has not led to the creation of other vehicles by which workers may intervene in economic and political matters, as Judith Teichman has argued. Even if new forms of corporatism will emerge, it is likely that workers will remain in a clearly subordinate situation with respect to the private sector unless labor can offer a program alternative to economic nationalism and to neoliberalism.

With such clear predominance of private business in the process of economic restructuring and continentalization, workers in the United States and Canada were understandably worried during the debate over NAFTA that many companies would shift their production south in search of cheaper labor. The question in this regard is whether new jobs in Mexico will be created at the expense of old jobs in the northern countries. In other words, the question is whether NAFTA will involve a zero-sum game in which only companies established in Mexico will win. According to optimistic expectations, expanding trade will also mean expanding jobs for the whole area, although more so in Mexico. To the extent that the size of the economic pie grows, an expanding welfare for the people of the three North American countries will be possible. Otherwise it will be a question of who loses and who wins. It will take democratic participation in economic decisionmaking to avoid the win-lose prospect and enhance the possibility of achieving growth with equity for all.

Other questions regard the direction of the trends to equalize wage levels: Will equalization be downward to Mexican levels or upward to U.S. levels? Similar questions may be posited in regard to environmental standards: Will companies move to Mexico hoping to find fewer and cheaper regulations? If Mexican laws become tighter, more similar to those in the United States and Canada, will the state have the capacity or the willingness to enforce them?

Now that the Mexican legislation regarding land tenure has been modified to allow the privatization of ejidos, one possible outcome is that large masses of former peasants will migrate to the cities, a trend that will build downward pressures for already rock-bottom wages. Such "liberation" of labor power from the countryside, as Marilyn Gates has put it, will offset much of the beneficial effect that increased capital investments could have on Mexican workers' real wages. Will this mean that old-type maquiladoras are more likely to prevail instead of a move to a form of integration into the world economy that relies on skilled labor and technology transfer, as in the optimistic scenarios of Gary

Gereffi? The latter scenarios would probably require a much more aggressive state policy, including an industrial policy, as both Gereffi and Enrique Dussel Peters have argued, in order to promote a greater integration of maquiladoras and manufacturing exporting firms with the rest of the local economy.

During the early 1990s, as much as 75 percent of foreign investment going into Mexico went to the stock market in the form of portfolio capital. This is widely considered to be a volatile and speculative type of investment. Its swift flight during 1994 largely accounts for the depth of the economic crisis that followed the peso devaluation in December of that year. The composition of investment capital would have to be modified substantially, as Gustavo del Castillo V. and Enrique Dussel Peters have argued, so that most new foreign investment would be directed toward productive activities that create employment and expand Mexico's exporting capabilities and international competitiveness. Otherwise, the masses of workers "liberated" from agriculture will not only remain largely unemployed but will also constitute a heavy downward pressure on wages in Mexico as well as in the United States and Canada.

The Uruguay Round of GATT was finalized in December 1993, and now that NAFTA is in place, it remains to be seen whether or how fast other Latin American countries will be integrated into continental trade. As things stand in the mid-1990s, the danger for certain countries and regions of the Third World is to become marginalized from trends toward globalization. Losing the link to the world economy is currently the least desirable outcome, given the fact that 50 percent of world trade happens within the three main trade areas of Europe, North America, and East Asia. In contrast, intra–developing country trade blocs are dismal: "Out of more than a dozen regional trading arrangements among developing nations, none has intra-regional trade greater than 15 percent of total exports" (*The Economist*, 1992:69).

Another issue that needs to be resolved by future research and policy regards the social charter of the new regional trade associations. The European Union does have a social charter in its agenda, and labor power is allowed to flow freely among its member states. Given the tremendous disparities between living standards and wages in the North American case, free mobility of labor is currently ruled out under NAFTA, except for highly skilled workers.

One danger entailed in this situation is that national governments in the less developed countries will be tempted to keep wages down through stiff political control. This has happened in Mexico for more than a decade. To the extent that governments attempt to maintain the low-wage "comparative advantage" of their countries, neither economic nor political democratic goals will advance significantly. Instead, nation-states will function merely to prolong the viability of transnational corporations by cheapening their wage costs rather than by increasing their productivity or the quality of their products. This would amount to extending the defensive strategy on behalf of U.S. capitalism, which is certainly a losing proposition in confronting the Japanese and the

German-European challenges, based as they are on an offensive strategy that hinges on high quality, increased productivity, and technological innovation. The latter strategy has been compatible with simultaneously expanding the profitability of firms while raising the standards of living of the general population.

Thus, avoiding the formation of trade blocs is critical, even from the point of view of subordinate groups and classes: The formation of a continental trading bloc, closed to the outside world, could easily fall back into authoritarian forms of state in order to control wage demands. The latter would be an inevitable result of indefinitely pursuing a defensive economic strategy on the part of TNCs in global competition.

The character of nation-states is changing, and their efficacy to propose and advance a project of development has substantially diminished. They have become part of a larger organizational network in which suprastate international organizations have a large influence on decisionmaking at the national level. Needless to say, such suprastate organizations are in turn dominated by the governments of advanced industrial countries, especially by that of the United States.

Nevertheless, the importance of national processes cannot be dismissed in favor of an emphasis on the global economy only. It was thus critical to assess in this book the specificities of political institutions in Mexico. Although electoral politics became more of a contested terrain during the 1980s, this has not been tantamount to a democratic transition: Elections by themselves do not guarantee the broad representation of a multiplicity of citizens groups or their participation in policy decisionmaking. As Lynn Stephen has argued, even though women make up the majority of actors within social movements, they are largely excluded from decisionmaking processes. Furthermore, Mexico has not known clean and transparent elections as yet. Therefore, Mexico still finds itself in a democratic pretransition process. At best, the trends point in the direction of a democracy of elites rather than to a societal democracy as defined by Ilán Semo. One critical factor that could steer political development in a more democratic direction continues to be social movements.

In this regard, although the political lessons outlined by Barry Carr and Neil Harvey might initially appear to be contradictory, they are actually complementary. Both perspectives reflect the decreasing power of social movements to achieve their goals by merely addressing their struggles at the federal level of national government. Carr's analysis of various cases illustrates the need to develop cross-border grassroots organizations in order to affect policy at the suprastate level as well. Conversely, Neil Harvey calls for the need for peasant movements to lower the target toward the regional, state, and municipal levels of government, where entrenched *caciques* are hard to bypass, even by the federal officials. Only thus can Mexican presidentialist authoritarianism be pushed into a democratic transition at other levels of society.

In fact, all of these levels of struggle are relevant and necessary, not only for subordinate groups and classes in advancing their interests but also from a methodological perspective for understanding current development. Therefore, all those levels should be on the agendas for both democratic struggle and development research. This is why my introductory chapter proposed a "bottom-up linkages" approach, one that starts at the level of concrete social movements and economic agents and works its way up to account for the various levels of determination. Just as an approach that focuses primarily on global processes loses grasp of concrete national- and regional-level realities, a country-centered approach that blinds itself from the influence of the new global trends is out of place.

Future Scenarios

From a bottom-up linkages perspective, it becomes clear that labor and civic organizations in the United States and Canada also have an interest in a democratic transition in Mexico and may also influence the course of its politics. To the extent that the economic destinies of the three North American peoples are now closely bound together, those organizations have a clear stake in the consolidation of democracy and the respect for human rights in Mexico. Only through the strengthening of these aspects of the Mexican political system can there be any guarantee that workers and other subordinate groups from the three countries will not be merely pitted against each other, to the benefit of an already wealthy and small minority. Beyond mere electoralism, strengthening civic organizations and democratic institutions in Mexico may be the key to sustaining a high standard of living for U.S. and Canadian workers and to raising it in Mexico for the general population. This is perhaps the most critical link between economic restructuring and democratization on a continental basis.

I take into account both global and national-level processes in the following attempt to suggest the key parameters under which future economic and political scenarios might evolve in Mexico. This effort is inspired by an earlier attempt by Wayne Cornelius, Judith Gentleman, and Peter Smith (1989) that focused on political outcomes at the start of the Salinas years. They derived four alternative political scenarios (immobilism or political closure, modernization of authoritarianism, partial democratization, or full democratization from below) by exploring the interaction of two political variables: modernization of the regime and consolidation of the opposition:

> Regime "modernization," in this context, refers to *salinista* plans for reforming the PRI and the instruments of state control. Opposition "consolidation" refers to the process of institutionalization of the opposition, especially the *cardenista* opposition,

as an effective and durable electoral force. For the sake of simplicity we score each
variable on a dichotomous Yes/No basis, and the result is a fourfold set of combinations (Cornelius et al., 1989:37).

The legacy of the Salinas years (1988–1994) is mixed. One might say that
there were elements of both modernization of authoritarianism and partial democratization. As to the former, PRONASOL was the prime attempt to renew,
and in a way replace, the old corporatist structures of the PRI, based on the
CNC, the CTM, and the FNOC, with a new form of corporatism. Elements of
partial democratization, which Cornelius et al. likened to the Indian Congress
Party model, became present: Several gubernatorial posts have gone to the opposition in various states, an event that was unknown before 1989; until then
and since 1929 all state governors had been PRI members. Apart from the cases
of Baja California and Chihuahua, where the PAN (National Action Party) candidate was recognized as the winner from the outset, the authoritarian fact remained in all other cases, however: The president made the decision, beyond
the law, to remove the governors of his own party after widespread protest.
Furthermore, only in one case did he appoint an opposition replacement.

The third and fourth scenarios of Cornelius et al. are closer to materializing.
Although modernization of authoritarianism was attempted by the Salinas
government through PRONASOL and partial electoral reforms, it seems likely
that civil society will no longer be willing to accept anything less than significant democratization. Whether this will be "partial" or "full democratization
from below" is still open to question.

In order to account properly for recent developments and the main concerns
of this book, it is necessary to develop a new set of variables to then develop future scenarios. Unlike the exercise by Cornelius et al., the following attempt to
sketch Mexico's futures is based not only on political variables but also on the
type of economic development model that is pursued (Table 12.1). Also in contrast with the previous attempt, the question of "consolidation of the opposition" is no longer asked; it happened during the Salinas de Gortari era and it
is thus taken here as a given.

The political variable, which depends mostly on subnational- and national-
level factors, is now defined in two steps by which three columns are obtained.
First, is there a political transition, yes or no? Of three major outcomes, the "No"
answer provides the first alternative: a continuation of authoritarianism (no political opening). If the first answer is "Yes," then the main question for the second
step becomes whether political opening will be initiated by the state itself (modernization of authoritarianism with partial democratization) or whether it will
be gained or imposed by civil society (democratization from below).

With regard to the economic variable, which is increasingly determined by
global processes, the question is whether a wholesale neoliberal model will be
pursued, in continuation of the trend of the past decade, or if a new form of

TABLE 12.1
Mexico's Future Scenarios

Economic Model	Political Regime		
	No Political Opening	*Modernization of Authoritarianism*	*Democracy from Below*
Market-led	*Savage capitalism:* neoliberal policies with repressive hardening of social control; technocrats and military are key in ruling alliance but lacking legitimacy	*Social liberalism:* PRI-PAN alliance; neoliberalism continues; popular unrest in south and southeastern states continues	*Liberal democracy:* PAN wins presidency in 2000; neoliberal policies continue; TNCs and finance capital within ruling alliance
State-led	*Statist nationalism:* unviable	*Populist statism:* unviable	*Nationalist democracy:* unviable
Social economy	*Social reformism:* greater state role in social programs; key alliance of technocrats, social reformers, official labor unions, and international firms; but lack of accountability makes social unrest unavoidable	*Social economy:* PRI-PRD alliance; land reform is restored in south and southeastern states; industrial sectors for export are reserved for for national entrepreneurs in long-term plan	*Social democracy:* PRD or new centrist party controls the executive; clear social charter and industrial policies are central in new development with environmental sustainability

state interventionism might be obtained. The first row in Table 12.1 depicts the continuation of neoliberalism; this outcome is labeled "market-led" economy. As far as state interventionism is concerned, two possible outcomes are suggested: state-led economy, as during the time of ISI; or social economy, as in northern European states. The "state-led" variant would be merely a return to the old model of ISI, in which the state virtually substitutes for the market in key sectors of the economy, both directly through parastate firms and through subsidies to guide production into certain branches. This model would tend to go back to a closed economy and would thus be incompatible with the globalizing trends of the world economy.

In contrast, the "social economy" variant assigns a central place to market forces, but the state takes an important role in establishing protective corrections to the market, particularly in the form of a social charter. The state also takes an important role in designing an industrial policy in alliance with the private sector (and possibly with the labor unions as well, depending on the political outcome), so that they jointly define a long-term plan to target certain world-market niches. This economic alternative would be compatible with the current trend toward North American integration and the globalization of the world economy, introducing selective protection in strategic sectors of the national economy, but it would require a modification of trends in U.S. capitalism in favor of the social-economy model. This outcome begins to highlight the increasingly interdependent social and political interests of the various and fragmented civil societies of the North American nation-states.

In what follows, a brief characterization is provided for each possible or desirable outcome, after which the feasibility of each is discussed. Because they are antagonistic to global trends, all those scenarios involving a state-led economic model are deemed historically unfeasible and are thus not discussed. The forces in favor of globalization are just too strong to tolerate a return to any form of economic nationalism in the foreseeable future. They are presented in Table 12.1 merely to highlight the differences with other, more feasible scenarios.

Savage Capitalism

The first cell would be a mere continuation of the Salinas policies in the Zedillo administration (1994–2000), with no significant political opening or economic policy changes. In terms of the social group controlling the state, this scenario would involve an alliance between government technocrats and the military, for it would take increased repression to maintain political stability. Given the strong reactions that this variant has produced not only in Mexican civil society but also in the international community, it is unlikely that this scenario is historically sustainable for very long. Therefore, some change must take place, even though this trend was materializing as of mid-1995.

Social Reformism

One possibility for the political ruling group to remain in power without a major transformation in the regime is to introduce a greater role for the state in social programs. This would be achieved with a stronger presence of social reformers within the PRI. The key political alliance in this scenario would be technocrats and social reformers within the PRI and the government in coalition with official labor unions, entrepreneurs, TNCs, and international finance capital. From the point of view of large sectors of civil society, the problem with this outcome would be the continued lack of government accountability in general and the lack of adequate representation of citizens' interests in an unmodified authoritarian regime. Therefore, social restlessness and discontent would probably continue until a greater opening ensued. Because the opposition forces have been sufficiently strengthened, it is hard to see how this scenario could be obtained without the continuation of significant conflict. For instance, the rebellion in Chiapas could become extended to other states unless there is some further political opening.

Social Liberalism

This is the alternative that the Salinas administration vowed to implement after 1988, but it always remained on the back burner; economic reform took precedence over political reform, and social goals remained largely unfulfilled. The political discourse of PRI presidential candidate Luis Donaldo Colosio acknowledged this status before his assassination on 23 March 1994. If this kind of program were to be adopted by the Zedillo administration, it would likely involve an alliance with the right-of-center PAN, backed by the technocratic elements of the PRI. The PAN would gain increased access to power in the state and municipal governments but often thanks to previous negotiations with the PRI-state, not necessarily through clear electorate choice. The PRI would retain a firm hold on national-level politics and the federal structure of government, and there would be continuity in the neoliberal economic policies. A key condition for this outcome to become feasible is that the increased access of the PAN to political power actually offsets popular discontent. This would be a likely outcome in the northern and western regions of Mexico as well as in the state of Yucatán, which show an inclination to favor PAN candidates (although in Chihuahua and Baja California, both with PAN governors, the PRI won by a landslide in 1994). However, to the extent that popular discontent prevails, particularly in the south and the southeast, it could well be translated into increased support for a left-of-center alternative such as the PRD or for a new political formation with a centrist platform. The PRI and the PAN by themselves are unlikely to be able to address the social problems of the poorest regions of Mexico satisfactorily, since they would be inclined simply to throw money into patchwork-type social programs rather than to undertake structural social reform.

Social Economy

In contrast to social liberalism, this scenario would involve an alliance between the PRI's reformers and the PRD as well as some change of attitude and policies in the United States beyond neoliberalism. The PRD would gain some gubernatorial posts and a larger proportion of seats in Congress. The possibility for the state to engage in land reform would be restored partially, at least to end the most threatening social injustices in southern states such as Chiapas,

Guerrero, and Oaxaca and regions from Michoacán, Puebla, and Veracruz. The export orientation of development would be maintained, but important sectors of the economy would be preserved in which domestic capitalists could thrive according to an industrial-growth, long-term plan. This plan would be elaborated in an alliance among "nationalist entrepreneurs," the state, and some sectors of the labor movement, but there would also be an important place for TNCs and international finance capital. Some modification of the NAFTA rules would be necessary for such an industrial policy to be allowed. Given the dismal results (whether real or fabricated) of the PRD in 1994, there is no reason to believe that this scenario has much feasibility. To the contrary, the main focus of the PRI-state in the 1994 elections was on weakening the PRD by associating it with radicalism and the Chiapas revolt.

Liberal Democracy

In this scenario the right-of-center PAN would win the national elections by the year 2000, thus inaugurating the first federal administration with a non-PRI party. Economic policies would continue along neoliberal lines. Much of the PRI cabinet would be preserved, particularly the economic cabinet. Because of the backlash against the PRI from the economic crisis that erupted in December 1994, several gubernatorial and municipal-level posts went to the PAN during 1995, and this could be the prelude to making liberal democracy the most likely scenario for the year 2000. From the point of view of TNCs and transnational finance capital as well as from that of medium and large domestic entrepreneurs, this would be the most desirable outcome, as it might ensure greater political stability while keeping neoliberal economic policies intact. The greatest political problem to contend with would be located in the southern and southeastern states, where social polarization and marginalization ran deeper during the lost decade of the 1980s and have become aggravated during the 1990s. Such pressure would make it viable for the PRD or some other centrist political formation to become strengthened as an eventually viable opposition, at least in some poor states. A reformed and more populist PRI could also become an important contender in those regions of Mexico with the worst social inequalities.

Social Democracy

In this scenario some alliance around the PRD or a new centrist party would hold the main posts in the national government, including the presidency and at least a coalition majority in Congress. Gubernatorial posts would be distributed among the three main parties, PRI, PAN, and PRD, and all posts would be filled not as the result of negotiations among the parties but of voters' choice.

This government would still pursue an export-oriented industrialization, but there would be a clear social charter and an industrial policy designed in conjunction with the organizations of the entrepreneurial class and a strengthened and democratized labor union movement. The overall logic prevailing in this scenario would relfect a central concern: that all social groups and classes benefit from economic growth. That is, there would be concerted efforts to achieve an equitable distribution of income so that firms' profits would be based partly on the expanded consumption of the working masses. With regard to the maquiladora sector, policies would be developed to ensure that Mexico would move fast along the path leading from the old model of export processing to the stages of integration that involve higher technological contents and higher skills in the labor force. Training programs to upgrade the labor force would also be instituted, and environmental sustainability targeted. Although TNCs and international finance capital would clearly have an important place in this outcome, it would be indispensable that Canadian and U.S. civil societies steer development away from neoliberalism in their countries and toward social democracy with a social-economy approach. From the point of view of all subordinate groups and classes in North America, this would clearly be the most desirable outcome.

Conclusion: Viability and Critical Factors

The first two scenarios are the least feasible or desirable, especially "savage capitalism." The latter would involve heavy-handed repression that would be too costly for the ruling alliance, as Cornelius et al. pointed out in 1989:

> Increasing repression would be very costly for the regime's legitimacy . . . both at home and abroad. Indiscriminate use of coercion would divide the ruling political elite even more deeply than neoliberal economic policies have done. The country would become increasingly ungovernable, with the proliferation of bitter, unmediated conflicts. Private investment would be frightened away by the prospect of destabilization. For all of these reasons, it seems likely that any *endurecimiento* [hardening] of the regime would stop well short of overt repression (Cornelius et al., 1989:40).

Furthermore, the three scenarios without political opening would be the least compatible with raising standards of living in Mexico to the extent that the wages of Mexican workers could be maintained artificially low by recourse to repression. If NAFTA were to continue in either of these scenarios, the prime form of integration would be through the continued growth of the maquiladora sector, achieved via low wages and unskilled labor. The implication is that U.S. and Canadian workers would be pitted against Mexican workers and overall living standards in North America would tend to decline. This would be primarily the case for the savage-capitalism scenario.

In different ways, each of the middle scenarios involves a modernization of authoritarianism and partial democratization, with the PRI sharing some power with other major parties while maintaining overall political control. Therefore, neither case may be conceived of without the currently ruling PRI. Zedillo's administration could develop a regional combination of "social liberalism" and "social economy." Social liberalism could prevail in the capitalistically more developed northern and western states, and a social-economy approach might be tried in southern and southeastern states. Such a combination assumes, however, that the past trend to apply homogeneous neoliberal policy across a heterogeneous social structure will be abandoned. Instead, regional specificities would be acknowledged and corresponding policies applied. Such an approach may be the politically most enlightened for the regime, but the local ruling classes in the most socially polarized states of the south and southeast would strongly oppose it. And even if predominantly for ideological reasons, TNCs and international finance capital might also oppose a reformist approach to social problems. This scenario would depend partly on the type of policies promoted by the United States, which would not be very promising while the Republican Party is in control of the U.S. Congress or presidency.

Each of the last three scenarios presumes different relations of class forces in Mexican society. Liberal democracy would be premised on an increased cultural hegemony of middle-class values. Conversely, nationalist democracy (depicted as unviable in Table 12.1) would presuppose a much greater and autonomous strength of the working class and other subordinate groups and classes. Finally, the social-democratic scenario assumes a complex society in which the government represents the multiplicity of social interests with no clear domination by any sector. This would be a truly pluralistic society—with a societal democracy, in Semo's terms—that may lie far ahead in Mexico's future.

Nevertheless, the social-democratic scenario would have the greatest capabilities for long-term stability and growth. Similarly, it would be the most compatible with the possibility that North American integration results in higher standards of living for the majority of the population in the three NAFTA countries rather than in a downward pressure in the U.S. and Canadian standards of living toward Mexican levels. One critical variable that could help this scenario develop would be the adoption in the United States of a type of capitalism more similar to that of the northern European and Japanese variants. If this happened, workers and social-democratic entrepreneurs would have a greater influence in U.S. policymaking. A strong solidarity presence of NGOs and other organizations of civil societies around the world would also be critical in order for Mexico to achieve and maintain a democratic political regime with a social-economy orientation.

Bibliography

Cornelius, Wayne A., Judith Gentleman, and Peter H. Smith. 1989. "Overview: The Dynamics of Political Change in Mexico." Pp. 1–51 in Wayne A. Cornelius, Judith Gentleman, and Peter H. Smith, eds., *Mexico's Alternative Political Futures*. La Jolla, Calif.: Center for U.S.-Mexican Studies, University of California, San Diego.

Economist, The. 1992. "Building Blocks or Stumbling Blocks?" 31 October, p. 69.

Acronyms

AAGR	average annual growth rate
ACIEZ	Alianza Campesina Independiente Emiliano Zapata (Emiliano Zapata Independent Peasant Alliance)
ACTWU	Amalgamated Clothing and Textile Workers Union
AFL	American Federation of Labor
AFL-CIO	American Federation of Labor–Congress of Industrial Unions
AFSC	American Friends Service Committee
AGROASEMEX	Aseguradora Agrícola Mexicana (Mexican Agricultural Insurance Company)
ALTEX	Programa para las Empresas de Alta Exportación (Program for High-Export Firms)
AMCB	Asociación Mexicana de Casas de Bolsa (Mexican Association of Stock Market Brokers)
AMIS	Asociación Mexicana de Instituciones de Seguros (Mexican Association of Insurance Institutions)
ANAGSA	Aseguradora Nacional Agrícola y Ganadera (National Agency for Agricultural and Livestock Insurance)
ANCIEZ	Alianza Nacional Campesina Independiente Emiliano Zapata (Emiliano Zapata National Independent Peasant Alliance)
ARIC	Asociación Rural de Interés Colectivo (Rural Association of Collective Interest)
AS&R	American Smelting and Refining
BANRURAL	Banco Nacional de Crédito Rural (National Rural Credit Bank)
CAM	Consejo Agrarista Mexicano (Mexican Agrarianist Council)
CAMCO	Cámara Americana de Comercio (American Chamber of Commerce)
CANACINTRA	Cámara Nacional de la Industria de Transformación (National Chamber of the Transformation Industry)
CANACO-MEX	Cámara Nacional de Comercio de la Ciudad de México (National Chamber of Commerce of Mexico City)

CAW	Canadian Auto Workers
CBI	Caribbean Basin Initiative
CCE	Consejo Coordinador Empresarial (Entrepreneurial Coordinating Council)
CCI	Central Campesina Independiente (Independent Peasant Council)
CCRI	Comité Clandestino Revolucionario Indígena (Clandestine Revolutionary Indigenous Council)
CDLI	Comité de Defensa de la Libertad Indígena (indigenous Freedom Defense Committee)
CEMC	Convención Estatal de Mujeres Chiapanecas (Chiapas Women's Convention)
CEOIC	Consejo Estatal de Organizaciones Indígenas y Campesinas (Council of Indigenous and Peasant Organizations)
CEPAL	Comisión Económica para América Latina y el Caribe (Economic Commission for Latin America and the Caribbean)
CEPCO	Coordinadora Estatal de Productores de Café Oaxaca (State Network of Coffee Producers at Oaxaca)
CIDHAL	Colectivo Internacional para el Desarrollo Humano en América Latina (Collective of Human Development in Latin America)
CIO	Congress of Industrial Organizations
CIOAC	Central Independiente de Obreros Agrícolas y Campesinos (Independent Confederation of Agricultural Workers and Peasants)
CMHN	Censejo Mexicano de Hombres de Negocios (Mexican Businessmen's Council)
CNA	Consejo Nacional Agropecuario (National Agricultural Council)
CNC	Confederación Nacional Campesina (National Peasant Confederation)
CND	Convención Nacional Democrática (National Democratic Convention)
CNG	Confederación Nacional Ganadera (National Livestock Confederation)
CNI	Convención Nacional Indigena (National Indigenous Convention)
CNM	Convención Nacional de Mujeres (National Women's Convention)
CNOP	Confederación Nacional de Organizaciones Populares (National Confederation of Popular Organizations)

Partido Nacional Revolucionario (National Revolutionary Party)

Partido Popular Socialista (Popular Socialist Party)

Partido de la Revolución Democrática (Party of the Democratic Revolution)

Partido Revolucionario Institucional (Institutional Revolutionary Party)

Partido de la Revolución Mexicana (Party of the Mexican Revolution)

Programa de Apoyos Directos al Campo (Program for Direct Supports to the Countryside)

Programa Nacional de Solidaridad (National Solidarity Program)

Programa para la Promoción Integral de las Exportaciones (Integral Program for the Promotion of Exports)

Partido Revolucionario de los Trabajadores (Revolutionary Workers Party)

Pacto de Solidaridad Económica (Pact for Economic Solidarity)

Partido Socialista Unificado de México (Unified Socialist Party of Mexico)

Registro Agrario Nacional (National Agrarian Registry)

Red Mexicana de Acción Contra el Libre Comercio (Mexican Free Trade Action Network)

Secretaría de Agricultura, Ganadería, y Desarrollo Rural (Secretariat of Agriculture, Livestock, and Rural Development)

Secretaría de Agricultura y Recursos Hidráulicos (Secretariat of Agriculture and Water Resources)

Secretaría de Comercio y Fomento Industrial (Secretariat of Commerce and Industrial Promotion)

Secretaría de Desarollo Social (Secretariat of Social Development)

Sindicato Mexicano de Electricistas (Mexican Electrical Workers Union)

Sindicato Nacional de Trabajadores de la Educación (National Union of Educational Workers)

Sindicato Nacional de Trabajadores, Obreros Agrícolas y Campesinos (Union of Agricultural Workers and Peasants)

Secretaría de la Reforma Agraria (Agrarian Reform Ministry)

CNPA	Coordinadora Nacional "Plan de Ayala" ("Plan of Ayala" National Coordinator)
CNPC	Confederación Nacional de Cámaras del Pequeño Comercio (National Confederation of Chambers of Small Commerce)
CNPI	Consejo Nacional de Pueblos Indígenas (National Council of Indigenous Peoples)
CNPP	Confederación Nacional de la Pequeña Propiedad (National Confederation of Small Property Owners)
CNTE	Coordinadora Nacional de Trabajadores de la Educación (National Coordinating Committee of Educational Workers)
COCEI	Coalición Obrero, Campesino y Estudiantil del Istmo (Worker, Peasant, and Student Coalition of Isthmus)
CONAMUP	Coordinadora Nacional del Movimiento Urbano Popular (National Coordinating Committee of the Urban Popular Movement)
CONASUPO	Compañia Nacional de Abastos para la Subsistencia Popular (National Company for Popular Subsistence Provision)
CONCAMIN	Confederación Nacional de Cámaras Industriales (National Confederation of Chambers of Industry)
CONCANACO	Confederación Nacional de Cámaras de Comercio (National Confederation of Chambers of Commerce)
COPARMEX	Confederación Patronal de la República Mexicana (Employers' Confederation of the Republic of Mexico)
COR	Confederación de Obreros Revolucionarios (Workers Revolutionary Confederation)
CORFO	Corporación Forestal de Chiapas (Chiapas Forestry Corporation)
CPSU	Communist Party of the Soviet Union
CPUSA	Communist Party of the United States of America
CRI	Colectivo Revolucionario Integral (Integral Revolutionary)
CROC	Confederación Revolucionaria de Obreros y Campesinos (Revolutionary Confederation of Workers and Peasants)
CROM	Confederación Regional Obrera Mexicana (Regional Confederation of Mexican Workers)
CT	Congreso del Trabajo (Labor Congress)
CTAL	Confederación de Trabajadores de América Latina (Confederation of Latin American Workers)
CTM	Confederación de Trabajores de México (Confederation of Mexican Workers)

DAWN	Development Alternatives for Women in the New Dawn
DDF	Departamento del Distrito Federal (Department of the Federal District)
DFI	direct foreign investment
EAP	economically active population
EC	European Community
EOI	export-oriented industrialization
EPZ	export-processing zone
EZLN	Ejército Zapatista de Liberación Nacional (Zapatista National Liberation Army)
FAT	Frente Auténtico de los Trabajadores (Authentic Workers Front)
FDI	foreign direct investment
FDLDS	Frente para la Defensa de la Legalidad y los Derechos Sindicales (Front for the Defense of Legality and Union Rights)
FDN	Frente Democrático Nacional (National Democratic Front)
FESEBIS	Federación de Sindicatos de Empresas de Bienes y Servicios (Federation of Unions of Enterprises of Goods and Services)
FI	foreign investment
FIDE	Frente Intersecretarial para la Defensa del Empleo (Intersecretarial Front for the Defense of Employment)
FLOC	Farm Labor Organizing Committee (Ohio)
FNOC	Federación Nacional de Organizaciones y Ciudadanos (National Federation of Organizations and Citizens)
FSTSE	Federación de Sindicatos de Trabatadores al Servicio del Estado (Federation of Public Employees)
FTA	U.S.-Canada Free Trade Agreement
GATS	General Agreement on Trade in Services
GATT	General Agreement on Tariffs and Trade
GDP	gross domestic product
GNP	gross national product
GSP	Generalized System of Preferences
HTS	Harmonized Tariff Schedule
IMECAFE	Instituto Mexicano del Café (Mexican Coffee Institute)
IMF	International Monetary Fund
INEGI	Instituto Nacional de Estadística, Geografía e Informática
INFONAVIT	Instituto del Fondo Nacional para la Vivienda de los Trabajadores (Institute of the National Fund for Workers Housing)

INI	Instituto Nacional In Institute)	PNR
ISI	import-substitution	PPS
IWW	Industrial Workers o	PRD
LFA	Ley de Fomento Agr Livestock Promoti	PRI
LICONSA	Leche Industrializad (CONASUPO Ind	PRM
LOPPE	Ley de Organizacion (Federal Law of Pc Processes)	PROCAMF
MEXUSCAN	North American For	PRONASO
MITI	Ministry of Internati	
MTWU	Maritime Transport	PROPIEX
MWIU	Marine Workers Indu	
NAFTA	North American Free	
NAO	National Administrat	PRT
NGO	nongovernmental org	
NIC	newly industrialized	PSE
OCEZ	Organización Campe Zapata Peasant Or	
OECD	Organization for Eco Development	PSUM
PAC	Programa de Aliento Stimulation and G	RAN REMALC
PAN	Partido Acción Nacio	SAGDR
PARM	Partido Auténtico de Party of the Mexic	
PCM	Partido Comunista M Party)	SARH
PDM	Partido Demócrata M Party)	SECOFI
PECE	Pacto para la Estabili (Economic Growth	SEDESO
PGR	Procuraduría General Office)	SME
PITEX	Programa de Importa de Artículos de Ex Imports to Produc	SNTE
PLM	Partido Liberal Mexic	SNTOAC
PMS	Partido Mexicano Soc	
PMT	Partido Mexicano de Party)	SRA

STRM	Sindicato de Telefonistas de la República Mexicana (Mexican Telephone Workers Union)
STRPRM	Sindicato de Trabajadores del Petroleo de la República Mexicana (Petroleum Workers Union)
SUTSP	Sindicato Unico de Trabajadores de la Secretaría de Pesca (Ministry of Fisheries Unified Union)
TIE	Transnationals Information Exchange
TNC	transnational corporation
TRIM	trade-related investment measure
UAW	United Auto Workers
UE	United Electrical Workers
UELC	Unión Ejidal de Lucha Campesina ("Peasant Struggle" Ejido Union)
UEQTL	Unidos en Nuestra Fuerza ("United in our Strength" Ejido Union)
UETL	Unión Ejidal "Tierra y Libertad" ("Land and Liberty" Ejido Union)
UNAM	Universidad Nacional Autónoma de México (National Free University of Mexico)
US-GLEP	U.S.-Guatemala Labor Education Project
UU	Unión de Uniones (Union of Ejido Unions and Peasant Organizations)
WCC	World Corporation Council
WTO	World Trade Organization

About the Editor and Contributors

Barry Carr is reader in Latin American history at La Trobe University, Melbourne, Australia. He is the author of articles on Mexican labor and agrarian history and on the evolution of the Mexican Left. His most recent books are *Marxism and Communism in Twentieth-Century Mexico* (University of Nebraska Press, 1992) and (with Steve Ellner) *The Latin American Left: From the Fall of Allende to Perestroika* (Westview, 1993). He is currently researching a history of Cuban sugar workers in the period 1914–1935 and is preparing a manuscript on the development of new forms of labor internationalism in the era of NAFTA.

Gustavo del Castillo V. is associate professor in the Department of Economics at the Colegio de la Frontera Norte, Tijuana. His research over the last twenty years has concentrated on North American integration issues, primarily trade policy. Among his many publications is a book coauthored with Gustavo Vega, *The Politics of Free Trade in North America: A Mexican Perspective*, to be published in Ottawa by the Centre for Trade Policy and Law, Carleton University.

Enrique Dussel Peters is assistant professor in the División de Estudios de Posgrado, Facultad de Economía, at the Universidad Nacional Autónoma de México, Mexico City and is a Ph.D. candidate in economics at the University of Notre Dame. He has published articles in several journals, including *Investigación Económica*, *Prokla* (West Berlin), and *Review of Radical Political Economics*, and has contributed to edited collections. His recent research has focused on Mexico's macroeconomic strategy since 1988, particularly the structural change of Mexico's manufacturing sector.

Marilyn Gates is associate professor of anthropology in the Department of Sociology and Anthropology at Simon Fraser University, Vancouver, Canada. She is the author of *In Default: Peasants, the Debt Crisis, and the Agricultural Challenge in Mexico* (Westview, 1993). Her recent research concerns environmental policy and practice in Mexico, with particular emphasis on land-use management in biosphere reserves.

Gary Gereffi is associate professor of sociology at Duke University Durham, North Carolina. He is the author of *The Pharmaceutical Industry and Dependency in the Third World* (1983) and coeditor of *Manufacturing Miracles* (1990), both published by Princeton University Press. He also coedited *Commodity*

Chains and Global Capitalism (Praeger, 1994). His recent research has focused on rethinking development theory by comparing the experiences of Asian and Latin American countries.

Neil Harvey is assistant professor in the Department of Government at New Mexico State University, Las Cruces. He is author of *Rebellion in Chiapas: Rural Reforms, Campesino Radicalism and the Limits to Salinismo*, no. 5 in the Transformation of Rural Mexico series (Center for U.S.-Mexican Studies, University of California, San Diego, 1994). He is also editor of *Mexico: Dilemmas of transition* (Institute of Latin American Studies and British Academic Press, 1993). Since 1984 he has carried out research on peasant movements and politics in Mexico. His current research concerns issues of identity, citizenship, and political change in Mexico and Latin America.

Gerardo Otero is associate professor of Latin American studies and sociology at Simon Fraser University in Vancouver, Canada. His work has been published in several edited collections and scholarly journals, including *Canadian Review of Sociology and Anthropology, Sociological Forum*, and *Revista Mexicana de Sociología*. His recent research is on the globalization of capitalism, the biotechnology revolution as it affects Latin American agriculture, and the transformation of the Mexican state and the agrarian social structures under neoliberalism.

Ilán Semo is associate professor of history at Universidad Iberoamericana in México City. He is the author of *El Ocaso de los Mitos* (Editorial Alianza, 1983) and *Tierra de Nadie* (Siglo XXI, 1989) and many articles and book chapters in edited collections. His primary research focus is on the history of Cardenismo and postpopulism in Mexico.

Lynn Stephen is associate professor of anthropology at Northeastern University, Boston, Massachusetts. She is the author of *Zapotec Women* (University of Texas Press, 1991); *Hear My Testimony: María Teresa Tula, Human Rights Activist of El Salvador* (South End Press, 1994); and *Power from Below: Women's Grassroots Organizing in Latin America* (University of Texas Press, forthcoming 1996). Her current research focuses on two projects in Mexico: the impact of ejido reform on gender and family relations and the movement for indigenous autonomy.

Judith Teichman is associate professor of political science at the University of Toronto. She has published articles on the Argentinian entrepreneurial class and politics and on Mexican politics in the oil industry. She is the past editor of the *Canadian Journal of Latin American and Caribbean Studies* and has authored *Policymaking in Mexico* (Allan Unwin, 1988), and *Privatization and Political Transition in Mexico* (University of Pittsburgh Press, 1996).

Francisco Valdés Ugalde is associate research professor in the Instituto de Investigaciones Sociales at the Universidad Nacional Autónoma de México, Mexico City. He has published many articles on entrepreneurs and the private sector in Mexico; his work has appeared in *Cuadernos Políticos, Estudios Sociológicos, Lateinamerika,* and *Revista Mexicana de Sociología* and in several edited books in both English and Spanish. He has been a visiting faculty member at the University of Connecticut and Brown University and a research fellow at the Center for U.S.-Mexican Studies at the University of California, San Diego.

About the Book

Having unilaterally opened its borders to international competition and foreign investment in the mid-1980s, Mexico has become one of the world's leading proponents of economic liberalization. Nevertheless, as the recent uprising of native peoples in Chiapas has made clear, economic reforms are not universally welcomed.

This book addresses the challenges brought about by the restructuring of the Mexican economy at a time when multiple organizations of civil society are demanding a democratic political transition in a system that has been dominated by one party for nearly seventy years. The contributors identify the key social and political actors—both domestic and international—involved in promoting or resisting the new economic model and examine the role of the state in the restructuring process. They explore such questions as: In what ways is the state itself being reconstituted to accommodate the demand for change? How have Canada and the United States responded to the increased internationalization of their economies? What are the challenges and prospects for transnational grassroots networks and labor solidarity?

Answers are provided by scholars from anthropology, economics, history, political science, and sociology, all of whom promote interdisciplinary approaches to the issues. Each chapter traces the structural transformations within the central social relationships in Mexican society during the last decade or so and anticipates future consequences of today's changes.

Index